# Embracing the Social and the Creative

## *New Scenarios for Teacher Education*

Edited by Miriam Ben-Peretz,
with Sara Kleeman, Rivka Reichenberg, and
Sarah Shimoni

Published in partnership with
the MOFET Institute

ROWMAN & LITTLEFIELD EDUCATION
A division of
ROWMAN & LITTLEFIELD PUBLISHERS, INC.
Lanham • New York • Toronto • Plymouth, UK

Published in partnership with the MOFET Institute

Published by Rowman & Littlefield Education
A division of Rowman & Littlefield Publishers, Inc.
A wholly owned subsidiary of The Rowman & Littlefield Publishing Group, Inc.
4501 Forbes Boulevard, Suite 200, Lanham, Maryland 20706
www.rowman.com

10 Thornbury Road, Plymouth PL6 7PP, United Kingdom



British Library Cataloguing in Publication Information Available

**Library of Congress Cataloging-in-Publication Data**
Embracing the social and the creative : new scenarios for teacher education / edited by Miriam Ben-Peretz, Sara Kleeman, Rivka Reichenberg, and Sarah Shimoni.
pages cm
Includes index.
ISBN 978-1-4758-0292-4 (cloth : alk. paper) -- ISBN 978-1-4758-0293-1 (pbk. : alk. paper) -- ISBN 978-1-4758-0294-8 (electronic)
1. Teachers--Training of--Cross-cultural studies. 2. Teachers--In-service training--Cross-cultural studies. 3. Teacher educators--Training of. 4. Teachers--Training of--Social aspects. I. Ben-Peretz, Miriam.
LB1707.E62 2013
371.1--dc23
2012042350

™ The paper used in this publication meets the minimum requirements of American National Standard for Information Sciences Permanence of Paper for Printed Library Materials, ANSI/NISO Z39.48-1992.

Printed in the United States of America

# Contents

# Foreword

## Bat-Sheva Eylon

The twenty-first century has seen rapid changes in knowledge and in the personal, social, and political contexts of education. Many international reports and initiatives have called to reconsider the goals of education in order to prepare learners to cope effectively with the emerging changes. The acquisition of transferable knowledge and competencies, such as critical thinking, problem-solving, creativity, and collaboration, are underscored as central goals for enabling effective lifelong learning. Moreover, there is growing recognition of the need to give environmental and social justice goals of education top priority—"to create caring and just classrooms by making equity and respect explicit parts of the curriculum" (Cochran-Smith, 2008). Helping students integrate the knowledge they encounter in formal and informal educational settings and in particular, knowledge acquired through a variety of digital media, is yet another important goal in the information age.

The advocated cognitive, social, and affective goals for students and the fact that an increasing number of teachers educate in multicultural environments imply that teachers' responsibilities are extended and that there are increasing societal demands from them. In addition, the call to promote "deep learning" of students requires many teachers to adapt new teaching practices, often departing significantly from their former ones (Pellegrino & Hilton, 2012). To keep up with the growing demands, teachers should continually acquire new knowledge and competencies. In recognizing these needs, part and parcel of all of the initiatives for setting new goals for students is the requirement of providing teachers with appropriate resources and support.

What are the implications for teacher education? This timely book attempts to examine contemporary issues in teacher education in light of the new challenges of education in the twenty-first century. The book presents historical analyses and case studies of contemporary reforms in different countries as well as projections into the future of teacher education. The unique and important contribution of the book lies in its focus on the teacher educators' perspective.

Although there is a growing consensus that teachers are the most important factor in determining the quality of education, there is less agreement on the implications for teacher education and in particular regarding the role of teacher educators. For example, Crook and McCulloch (in this book) describe the identity crisis that is being experienced by teacher educators in universities and colleges in England because of the current national policy trends toward practical "on-the-job" teacher education based in schools. This policy, also found in other countries, restricts the role of the university and college teacher educators and degrades their status in their institutions and in the educational system as a whole. This book suggests that this trend is unjustified. The increasing demands of the teaching profession imply that the professional demands from teacher educators will increase as well, and therefore their status and professionalism should be fortified. In the following paragraphs we support this claim by discussing briefly the role of teacher educators in career-long professional development programs for teachers and in supporting teachers to introduce fundamental changes in the learning-teaching process.

*Career-long professional development frameworks for teachers*: The growing diversity in the composition of teachers, their routes into teaching, and their mobility between workplaces imply that it is important to apply career-long approaches to teacher education and to form closer collaborative partnerships among schools, universities, and local authorities (see Brown, this book). Teachers' needs should already be addressed during their preservice program or within the context of their induction stage, as well as in a variety of continuing professional development (CPD) frameworks. These can be realized in different forms, such as school-based programs, teacher learning communities, targeted programs for introducing certain innovations, and coordinated activities for introducing reforms.

Although the organizational schemes in these various frameworks may vary considerably, in all of them teacher educators play important leadership roles. They are involved in designing, setting up, and sustaining these frameworks. They support teachers in translating policy into practice and in promoting the necessary connections among the school, the curriculum, and professional development. In partnerships among schools, academia, and educational authorities, teacher educators are the ones who can provide the professional backbone for the activities and enhance the coherence between partners.

In light of the great diversity among teachers, an increasingly important requirement of teacher educators is to respond differentially to the needs of individual teachers. In particular, it is important to enhance the connections between different segments of teachers' professional experiences. Such connections are especially important when teachers are just starting out (i.e., ensuring continuity between preservice and CPD experiences) or when they are in their first stages of introducing innovations that require fundamental changes in teachers' practice. Teacher educators have a dual role: they act as agents of change who scaffold teachers when they attempt to introduce innovations into their classrooms, and they are the ones who can best ensure professional and cultural continuity in teachers' learning.

*Fundamental changes in the learning-teaching process*: To introduce fundamental changes in the learning-teaching process teachers have to examine their existing ideas and behaviors in light of new ones and make decisions whether and how to change them. More specifically, teachers need opportunities to experience four knowledge integration processes (Linn & Eylon, 2011): eliciting their prior ideas, learning about relevant new ones, developing criteria to distinguish among alternatives, and carrying out reflections that will lead to sorting out and reorganizing those ideas. Teacher educators have an important role in developing the relevant resources for providing teachers with these opportunities as well as supporting them in the change processes that often take years.

Research on professional development programs for teachers shows that fundamental processes of change are enhanced when teachers engage in collaborative long-term inquiries of their practice and of their students' learning. In particular, evidence-based customization of instruction is a recommended way of introducing fundamental changes into teachers' teaching and has been shown to impact student learning. In customization programs teachers develop and/or customize learning materials, teach them, and bring artifacts (records of practice) for collaborative reflection on their work and on their students' learning. In many programs teachers document their records with written commentaries in a portfolio. Research shows that the collaborative reflection around such artifacts serves as a catalyst for attaining high levels of sociocultural interaction between the teachers and can enhance the process of knowledge integration. The emphasis on evidence from classes helps teachers become more learner-centered in their teaching, a central goal of education. Guidance and support of collaborative long-term inquiry of the teachers is yet another important role of teacher educators (Harrison, Hofstein, Eylon, & Simon, 2008).

In order to carry out the various roles described above, teacher educators have to be well versed in theory, ongoing research, and teacher practice. They need a deep understanding of the disciplines that they teach and the relevant pedagogical content knowledge as well as competency in mentoring teachers in ways that will enable them to build ownership and autonomy. Like teachers, teacher educators also need frameworks and programs to promote their professional development and lifelong learning. They need opportunities to engage in research on learning and teaching and on the professional development of teachers. In addition, since the diversity in the community of teacher educators is also likely to grow, experienced teacher educators will need to support newcomers and provide an ongoing influx of contemporary advances in research and practice. Teacher educators based in academic institutions can play an important role in responding to this need.

The implication is that in contrast to some current policy trends, in order to achieve the new visions of education for the twenty-first century a strong status and professional development opportunities for teacher educators should be a central goal of academic institutions and the educational system as a whole.

## REFERENCES

Cochran-Smith, M. (2008, March). *Toward a theory of teacher education for social justice.* Paper presented at the Annual Meeting of the American Educational Research Association, New York.

Harrison, C., Hofstein, A., Eylon, B., & Simon, S. (2008). Evidence-based professional development of teachers in two countries. *International Journal of Research in Science Education, 30*(5), 577–91.

Linn, M. C., & Eylon, B. S. (2011). *Science Learning and Instruction: Taking Advantage of Technology to Promote Knowledge Integration.* New York: Routledge/Taylor & Francis Group.

Pellegrino, J., & Hilton, M. L. (Eds.). (2012). *Education for Life and Work: Developing Transferable Knowledge and Skills in the 21st Century.* National Research Council report. Washington, DC: National Academies Press.

# Preface

This book focuses on the special status and roles of teacher education in a globalized, uncertain, and anxiety-ridden world. It is argued that the single most important factor in the quality of education is linked to the professional education of teachers. Teacher education programs bear the responsibility for preparing student teachers for the complexities of teaching in our rapidly changing world. The success and quality of teacher education programs depends to a large measure on the effectiveness of teacher educators.

Teacher educators might be viewed as fulfilling a dual role in the culture of schools. On the one hand, they associate themselves with cultural and professional continuity. On the other hand, teacher educators are ambassadors of change and innovations. They are the agency for adapting schools and education modes to current social and political trends, and needs, in a globalized world. This book portrays both roles and their impact on the evolving profession of teacher educators. The profession of teacher educators is viewed in this book as dynamic, evolving in relation to societal demands, and changes in the practice and policy of schools.

A wide array of issues is portrayed from international perspectives, including both conceptual and empirical chapters, based on present-day research of major scholars in education in different countries.

Several critical issues are raised and discussed, among them: demographic changes, equity, racism, and environmental sustainability. Viewing teacher education as drama provides lenses and insights for the construction of teacher education. Historical analyses contribute to the understanding of the relationship between societal changes and teacher education.

The book is divided into two parts. Part I is entitled "Teacher Education in the Service of Change." This part presents cases of the role of teacher education in reform movements in different cultures, and the impact of social changes across time on teacher education.

In the first chapter of this part, "General Issues in Teacher Education," Lilian G. Katz focuses on the dilemmas inherent in the preparation of newcomers to the teaching profession that all teacher educators are confronted with, and notes the developmental stages of teacher preparation. Special emphasis is put on the preparation of early-childhood educators and the specific characteristics of the field of early childhood education.

The second chapter, "History, Policy, and the Professional Lives of Teacher Educators in England," written by David Crook and Gary McCulloch, is a historical analysis that provides insights into the involvement of national policy in the design of teacher education processes. This historical survey of teacher education in England demonstrates how policy trends affect the role of teacher educators, how professional identity is constructed and strengthened, and how national policy affects teacher educators' professional lives.

Yuval Dror, in his chapter, "Three Decades of Teacher Education in Israel and Their Impact on Professional Development of Teacher Educators," discusses different elements that have affected teacher education programs and teacher educators' professional development, and the organizational structure of teacher education colleges. This chapter shows that teacher educators' development is affected by processes external to the education system, such as social and political divides.

The chapter by Sally Brown, "Teacher Educators in the Midst of Scottish Educational Reform," presents a local perspective on the role of teacher educators in school reform. Brown discusses the impact of Scotland's CfE (Curriculum for Excellence) school reform on teacher education, namely, career-long approaches to teacher education; closer collaborative partnerships among schools, universities, and local authorities; and a firmer focus on mentoring support as well as research.

In their chapter, "Teacher Educators as Agents of Change: A Hong Kong Perspective," Teresa Tsui-san Ng, John Chi-Kin Lee and Chun Kwok Lau present John's and Teresa's stories of professional development in a different culture. Their stories reflect the conflicts encountered by teacher educators who often need to restructure their priorities while trying to reach the right balance between theory, policy, and practice.

Part II, "A Look into the Future: Societal Issues in Teacher Education," focuses on several critical societal issues such as racism, feminism, and environmental sustainability.

New roles for teacher educators are part of the development of their profession. The chapter by Miriam Ben-Peretz and Efrat Toov Ward, "Teacher Education as Drama: Possible Roles for Teacher Educators," suggests using the metaphor of teacher education as drama. Several concepts related to the world of drama and theater are presented and discussed, providing the basis for a variety of roles for teacher educators, for instance, as "playwrights," developing programs of teacher education that are congruent with the changing contexts of schooling.

In their chapter, "Feminine Culture and Teacher Education," Michal Zellermayer and Esther Hertzog suggest adopting Eisler's feminist ideas for teacher educators, and to act as participants in the cultural transformation from domination to partnership—not only in gender relations, but in the creation of a more effective, humane, and sustainable economy and society.

A crucial component of the work of teacher educators concerns their commitment to social justice and equity. The chapter written by Anna E. Richert and Colette Rabin, "Preparing Teachers for Teaching Dilemmas Raised by Race and Racism: One Case Example of Teacher Education for Social Justice," tells the story of ethical dilemmas that occur when student teachers are confronted with racist comments made by students in their classrooms. The analysis of these dilemma cases leads the authors to the conclusion that teacher educators concerned with social justice have to do more to prepare their students to deal with issues of race and racism.

The chapter written by Sara Pe'er, Bela Yavetz, and Daphne Goldman, "Environmental Education for Sustainability as Values Education: The Challenge for Teacher Educators," discusses the place of teacher education in value-based education in general, as well as specifically regarding sustainability. The chapter is based on the perception of the role of education in educating an environmentally literate citizenship. The writers regard the issue of sustainability as a critical component in value-based education in the third millennium. Empowering teacher educators as change makers in this area is one of the challenges teacher education faces.

The book ends with a chapter by Debbie Samuels-Peretz, "Teacher Education for the Twenty-First Century: Are We Preparing Teachers for Obsolete Schools?" After discussing the advantages as well as the negative implications of the technological advances of the twenty-first century, Samuels presents the challenges facing education preparing students for the life in the complex and uncertain future. The main focus of this chapter concerns appropriate modes of teacher education. Different approaches are analyzed and discussed, providing readers with a wide array of frameworks and possible ways of structuring teacher education. As Samuels concludes: "Perhaps teacher educators need to think like inventors and reconceptualize teacher education for the twenty-first century."

Editors:
Miriam Ben-Peretz
With
Sara Kleeman

Rivka Reichenberg
Sarah Shimoni

Michal Golan, head of the MOFET Institute

# Acknowledgments

With feelings of gratitude we thank the people whose assistance was vital for this book.

Special thanks go to Tom Koerner, vice president and editorial director of Rowman & Littlefield, and to Michal Golan, head of the MOFET Institute, for their encouragement, advice and help.

We wish to express our sincere gratitude to Bat-Sheva Eylon for writing the foreword to this book.

We thank Carlie Wall, assistant editor, Rowman & Littlefield, Education Division, Laura Grzybowski, associate editor, Rowman & Littlefield, and Yehudit Shteiman, head and chief editor of the MOFET Publishing House, for their support and assistance in the preparation of this book.

For his support enabling the writing of this book we thank Noah Greenfeld, head of the Division of Teacher Education at the Ministry of Education in Israel.

The contribution of Madene Shachar to the preparation of the manuscript of this book, her assistance in the editing and proofreading, as well as her constant care for the references, have been invaluable.

We thank Jean Vermel for editing several chapters of this book.

Many thanks to Efrat Toov Ward and Tali Aderet-German for their dedicated assistance in the final stages of preparing the manuscript of this book.

# *I*

# Teacher Education in the Service of Change

*Chapter One*

# General Issues in Teacher Education

Lilian G. Katz

Like many other countries, in the United States the education of teachers is a topic of constant public and professional discussion and dispute today. In many of our countries there is the widespread belief that whatever is lacking in the society is the fault of the schools, and schools are not as effective as they should be in large part because of the teachers who are said to need more and better and perhaps different training. Furthermore, there is reason to believe that in most countries, graduates of teacher education programs characterize their experiences of training as less than satisfying and of doubtful practical value. In other words, no one seems to be satisfied with the way teachers are trained. This level of dissatisfaction may also be true of the education of all other professions as well.

In most countries, several different groups have a stake in the education of teachers. These include national, regional, and local government authorities; higher education and teacher training institutions; the professors and instructors responsible for training teachers; their students; and to some extent, the teachers themselves, as well as the communities served by teachers and, of course, ultimately the children as well.

Educators in every field and every subject must address at least four basic questions: (1) What should be learned? (2) When should it be learned? (3) How is it best learned? and (4) How can we tell how well we have answered the first three questions? The latter question addresses issues of assessment and evaluation. Not all of these questions can be addressed fully here. The main focus of this chapter will be on answers to the first question about what should be learned.

## GENERAL ISSUES IN TEACHER EDUCATION

In response to the first question about what should be learned, there are many problems that all teacher-training programs have in common. The education of teachers for all age levels, and most likely of teachers of all subjects, must address many similar problems. The answers to this first question should include (a) the *knowledge and understandings* that are deemed necessary for teachers and that are usually referred to as *content*, (b) pedagogical *skills*, (c) pedagogical *dispositions*, and (d) the variety of *feelings* that are considered essential for the prospective teacher to have (and not to have) and to learn. In the case of elementary and secondary teachers, full knowledge and understanding of the content to be taught is needed. However, in the case of preschool teachers, mastery of content knowledge to be taught is not a major concern.

For example, formal instruction in mathematics, sciences, and so on, is not usually part of the preschool curriculum and therefore does not require teachers to have extensive preparation and training in those fields.

Answers to the four categories of what should be learned listed above are explored here in terms of a set of dilemmas most likely facing all teachers of all subjects and all professions, at least to some extent (Katz & Raths, 1992). In other words, all teacher educators are confronted by dilemmas inherent in the preparation of newcomers to the teaching profession. The six dilemmas that are outlined below most likely apply to the preparation of teachers of all ages and all subjects.

However, there are also some complex problems exceptionally important in the education of teachers of our youngest children that are distinct from those involved in the preparation of teachers of older children.

## DILEMMAS OF TEACHER EDUCATION

All teachers of every subject, for learners of every age level, are faced with at least six major dilemmas. In this discussion the term dilemma is defined as a predicament that has two main features (Room, 1985). It involves a choice between at least two alternative courses of action that are equally problematic and most likely equally potentially beneficial (See Katz & Raths, 1985). The underlying principle, then, is that each of the two available choices in such predicaments require “a choice of error.”

It is customary in the English language to define situations in which there are two competing and mutually exclusive choices as the two “horns” of a dilemma. To make a choice of which one of the two alternative possible courses, that is, which of the two “horns” involved in the predicament is preferred, means that the potential advantages of the “horn” that is not chosen are sacrificed. Thus part of our task is to determine which of the two "horns" of the dilemmas outlined below will yield the "least worst" errors in each relevant predicament. A brief discussion of how to identify some potential bases upon which to select which error is preferable is also presented. Furthermore, even though each of these dilemmas is discussed separately, it is very likely that they are interrelated in many ways.

## Dilemma #1: Emphasis on Coverage versus Mastery

All teachers, of every subject and at every level of education, face conflicting pressures concerning the extent to which they should emphasize *coverage* of all the potentially relevant content and skills to be learned versus limit the amount of content and instead strive to ensure full mastery of the most important content and skills. In this sense, all teachers are pulled in opposite directions: the larger the scope of content and skills covered, the fewer of them the students are likely to master, and vice versa. Teachers of any subject cannot do equal justice to both coverage and mastery at the same time. In teacher training for the field of early education there is usually strong emphasis on studying child development, of which there is a very large body of content from which to choose (Galinsky, 2010). The difficult issue is whether the mastery of a carefully selected but small body of the main theories and facts about early learning and development is more effective for teacher training than covering the vast amount of relevant content in the field. Who is responsible for answering this question, and on what principles should the answers be based?

Another consideration inherent in this dilemma is that if the coverage "horn" of this dilemma is chosen and students are expected to learn a substantial body of content and skills rather than focusing on the mastery of a carefully selected smaller set of major content and valuable skills, then the dispositions to apply the knowledge and skills are unlikely to be acquired and strengthened. Students' energy is focused primarily on meeting content and skills acquisition requirements and passing the tests. Under these conditions they may not acquire or strengthen the dispositions to make appropriate and frequent use of them.

Dispositions are difficult to define, but they are generally thought of as "habits of mind" or tendencies to respond to certain provocations in certain ways. In the case of teaching, for example, important dispositions would include patience, accepting of children, observing and listening thoughtfully to the children, and exercising insight in making decisions about how to respond to particular teaching predicaments. One example that comes to mind is of a teacher of four-year-olds whose training had emphasized what was known as social learning theory, that is, children's development is dependent on rewards.

At mid-morning every day the teacher carried a tray of crackers around the classroom to offer the children. One girl in the class for more than four months had never spoken in class, though her verbal behavior was quite normal outside of the preschool setting. Every morning when the teacher approached that particular child she said to her "You can't have a cracker unless you use your words." And every morning the child turned away without speaking. When I suggested to the teacher that she might try saying to the girl next time in a clear and friendly way "I know you don't want to say anything today. That's okay. But if you change your mind, I'll be over there for you." The teacher used the suggestion and within a week the girl was talking normally in the classroom. The teacher's training apparently did not include the disposition to reflect on, or experiment with possible alternative pedagogical approaches for solving different behavioral issues.

When the instructor of teacher education courses chooses the coverage "horn" of the dilemma, she or he is unlikely to provide a good model of such important dispositions needed by teachers—especially by teachers of young children. Unfortunately dispositions are not likely to be learned from instruction. They are most likely to be learned from experience observing them in action and thus experiencing their value and effects.

As already suggested, teacher educators for all age groups are under constant pressure to expand the curriculum so as to cover more content and skills that an increasing body of relevant contemporary research indicates could be effective and valuable elements of their students' future pedagogical practices. In the United States and many other countries, there has been an increasing trend to expand the content coverage of teacher education programs so as to include sensitizing students to minority group cultures, ethnic and cultural diversity, second-language learning (See Gonzalez-Mena, 2001), gender stereotyping, the inclusion of children with special needs, relations with parents, computer-based instruction, and the rapidly growing body of research on the nature of early neurological development. Rarely, if ever, are proposals put forward to reduce the size and scope of the content and skills required of students, or to eliminate any component of a teacher education program.

How should a teacher educator respond to increasing pressures to cover more pedagogical knowledge and skills rather than to increase their focus on deeper mastery of a smaller body of such knowledge and a narrower but most important set of skills? If the pedagogical decision makers opt for greater coverage rather than greater mastery of a more limited body of knowledge and skills, then the training program is most likely to give students a superficial "smattering" rather than deep understanding of what they are to teach, what teaching is all about, and the issues at stake.

Under such conditions the students are unlikely to achieve sufficient mastery of a wide range of content and skills to permit their application later when they have completed their training and are subsequently in the "trenches" of real life in the schools. Furthermore, a teacher education program devoted to wide coverage may undermine the learners' dispositions to delve deeply into problems and to take their responsibility for their own continuous learning seriously. In the case of very strong pressure to cover a large body of knowledge and skills, desirable dispositions are unlikely to be addressed in most of the components of their training.

I suggest that it is important to keep in mind that having relevant knowledge and skills must be accompanied by the dispositions to use them. I suggest that teacher education should take opportunities to foster in students the dispositions to pursue problem solutions, to enquire, and as teachers to seek insights and suggestions from more experienced colleagues throughout their careers.

Given the short life of information, much content knowledge, and many skills learned under the pressure of time, I suggest that the preferred choice in this dilemma would seem to be to strive toward deep *mastery* of a relatively small range of the important content and skills that are deemed essential to good teaching practice in the relevant field. It seems reasonable to assume that compared to the *coverage* choice, the *mastery* option could give students greater feelings of competence and confidence in the content and skills they have learned, and therefore a greater sense of satisfaction with their professional preparation.

When the faculty of a teacher education program chooses the mastery "horn" of the dilemma, they are more likely to be able to emphasize support and encouragement in their relationships with students, and to therefore to become a strong source of support and feedback that could help students develop self-confidence in the long term.

## Dilemma #2: Evaluative versus Affective Emphasis

Part of a teacher's role, at every level of education in every profession and in every subject is to evaluate the progress of the learner. In teacher education, assessment and evaluation of the learners' progress is undertaken in order to ensure that weak, poorly motivated, or inept students are excluded from entering the profession. Another part of the dilemma that pulls the instructors in the opposite direction is pressure to address the students' needs for support and encouragement. However, an instructor's responsibility to conduct realistic evaluations and assessments of their students' progress requires of them a certain distance between themselves and their students, which, in turn could create a certain wariness in their relationships. On the other hand, when the faculty chooses to emphasize support and encouragement and to create feelings of closeness, they are likely to give only positive responses to students and to withhold any less-than-positive feedback, and in that way they are likely to weaken the quality of students' learning.

When teacher educators emphasize their evaluative role they are more likely to exclude those weak students who should not be encouraged to enter the teaching profession. In such cases, those students who do survive a stringent evaluation process may enter the profession with some pride, knowing that not just anybody can become a teacher. Hence, those teacher education programs that choose the evaluative rather than the affective side of the dilemma convey a message to their students about the seriousness and significance of the profession they are hoping to join.

## Dilemma #3: Emphasis on Students' Current versus Future Needs

Students who enter a teacher education program have typically completed some dozen years of success as elementary and secondary school students—in the narrow sense of that term. They adapted to meeting clear teacher expectations, to specific course requirements (e.g., the length of term papers), to studying for examinations, and to following explicit criteria by which to maintain good standing in the program. If college instructors responsible for teacher training follow such patterns, the students will feel comfortable in the program and reasonably satisfied with the experience of teacher training. However, the impact of the program, though adequate in the short term, is unlikely to be valuable in the long term.

This dilemma can be examined in terms of the "feed-forward effect" that is probably generic to all socialization. In teacher training programs, the "feed-forward effect" refers to the fact that to a large extent they consist of providing students with answers to questions they have not yet asked, and of preparing them for eventualities rather than actualities. Much of the content and skills presented in teacher training courses are likely to seem remote and inert to the students at the actual time of their training, but are expected to be relevant and useful at a later time, once they are on the job.

The underlying principle of the "feed-forward effect" is that while the actual experience of the student during training does not change, the evaluation and meaning of it may change retrospectively as time passes and subsequent experiences and understandings accrue. Thus a graduate may think later, a year or two into her career as a teacher, that a learning experience she had during training did not seem relevant or useful at the time, but now, *in retrospect*, "I am so glad I had it." Or, the feed-forward effect could be the reverse in that the student welcomed a particular training experience at the time it occurred, but once in actual practice later on reevaluates that experience retrospectively as irrelevant to the situations or contexts or the kinds of pupils she now faces.

The major implication of this hypothesized "feed-forward" effect—that applies to all socialization—is that decisions concerning what is in the teacher training students' best long-term interests cannot be based entirely upon their evaluations of their training experiences at the time they are undergoing them, because their evaluation may be quite different later on in retrospect. This dilemma raises the troubling question: On what basis should decisions about the content of teacher training be made? Given the possible differences between current and retrospective evaluations of the training experience by those who receive it, what other bases should be used to design a teacher education program? This question warrants extensive discussion among those responsible for designing teacher education programs.

In a study of the retrospective evaluations of graduates of a master's degree program in business, Neel and Warren (1978) reported variations related to their length of time as practitioners. Especially interesting were differences in the participants' retrospective evaluations of the value of their business training and professional education. Those who had less than five years' experience wished they had had more practicum or "on-site" training—actual experience in the field. Participants with five to ten years of experience said that they would have liked more training related to how to get along with coworkers, interpersonal skills, and so on. But those who had ten to fifteen years of work experience indicated that they wish they had had some courses in philosophy, ethical matters, and how to live a good life. Similar retrospective evaluations of teacher training could provide some insight into its value and its potential strengths and weaknesses, and perhaps recommend possible changes in content and processes.

## Dilemma #4: Eclectic versus Thematic Philosophical Approaches

Some teacher education programs are designed around a coherent theme that includes a particular philosophy and pedagogical approach. For example, in the field of early childhood education the Montessori Method, which has over a century of application, is perhaps the best known thematic approach to teaching and teacher training. In such cases, every class and all members of the faculty in the training program are largely committed to a common philosophical theme as well as fixed pedagogical practices. On the other hand, teacher training programs without an overarching theme or philosophy provide an eclectic approach so that students can become knowledgeable about a wide range of possible and even contradictory or conflicting approaches to teaching, especially in the early childhood field.

The two "horns" of this dilemma, then, are whether to organize the teacher training program around a main theme and model of teaching or curriculum, or whether to give the members of the faculty license to take an eclectic approach in which each professor may advocate his or her own preferred philosophy or pedagogical model, or leave it to the students to select their own preferences.

It seems reasonable to assume that during their teacher training when students are exposed to a single coherent theme or philosophy concerning educational practices, their training will have a greater and deeper impact on their subsequent professional practices. However, in an eclectic approach in which students are exposed to a wide variety of possible pedagogical practices, some of which contradict others, it may be that students can feel free to elect courses and practices that seem easiest or are more consistent with their own past and personal preferences and goals.

It has been reported informally that students being trained in an eclectic teacher education program perceive the faculty as a group of competing ideologues and develop closer relationships with the teachers in the schools where they do their practice teaching, and that together they reject the university or college professors as "out of touch" with the real world of schooling and teaching. Research concerning this possible dilemma could be very helpful in improving teacher training practices in various higher education institutions.

## Dilemma #5: Emphasis on Current Practices versus Innovative Practices

Along similar lines, teacher training programs can choose to focus on helping their students to acquire competence in the current standard practices of the local schools available to them and where they are likely to be employed when their training has been completed. On the other hand, another alternative could be for the program to give high priority to helping the students to master the most recently developed innovative teaching practices not yet adopted by the local schools. Given the finite amount of time available during a teacher training program, it is unlikely to be possible that all teaching methods—all the current customary ones, as well as the brand new ones—can be studied, observed, and learned. Teacher educators may be pulled in opposite directions: emphasis on current conventional teaching methods versus the new and innovative ones they are creating and developing. On what basis could their choices between these two "horns" of the dilemma be made? What would be best for their students as well as education practices—in the long run?

Of course, new teachers can become discouraged if they enter the current school scene and find the innovative practices they have learned in their training courses are rarely implemented or, in some cases, are rejected by local school practitioners. To equip novice teachers with innovative teaching methods may result in difficult adjustments and considerable stress during their initial teaching careers.

On the one hand, a good grounding in current standard local teaching practices prepares their graduates to take up their future positions with a minimum of adjustment problems. However, a main raison d'être for a professional training program in an institution of higher education is that it is expected to be a source of new knowledge and innovative practices based on research and development and, thereby, to raise the profession's effectiveness and standards and to make contributions to society. The new methods of education that are being developed in institutions of higher education probably should be learned by the students while they are undergoing training and, in addition, their understanding of the nature of this dilemma should be encouraged.

## Dilemma #6: Specific versus Global Criteria for Assessing Students in Training

A teacher education program might define its objectives in concrete and specific terms, thereby making it clear to all of its students how they will be assessed and precisely what is expected of them to acquire their teaching certificates, diplomas, and degrees.

The more specific the criteria of assessment used by their training institution, the more easily students will understand what is expected of them. Furthermore, it is most likely that students are accepted into teacher training programs in colleges and universities because of their successful socialization into the disposition to work for good grades and good examination scores. Such students are likely to feel most comfortable in a training program that uses specific criteria for assessing their performances.

While teaching undergraduates in a major American university that had very high admission standards for their students, I opened the course by presenting to them the usual outline of topics and required readings, and so on. In addition I recommended a list of essays and novels that I suggested could help deepen their understanding of environments, social and cultural conditions, and a range of family issues that they had not experienced themselves and that would give them deeper insight into some of the issues they are likely to encounter when they become teachers.

Following my presentation one of the students asked the question "Are you going to tell us which pages will be covered on the examinations?" When I explained that I did not yet know the answer to that she responded with the statement "How will we know what to read if you don't tell us what will be on the examination?" While the student's questions were adaptive to the patterns of conventional secondary and university education, were they predictive of suitability for a career as a teacher? The purpose of the recommended reading was to help students to develop the disposition to seek insight into the multiple factors responsible for many of the complexities of teaching.

On the other hand, the more global an approach to assessing the progress and success of students, and their personal qualities, the more likely they are to take into account the complex nature of teaching and the wide range of situations and predicaments they will face in their daily work as teachers. However, the latter choice between these two "horns" of the dilemma leaves the matter of their evaluation as students very vague to the students themselves as well as their trainers.

If the six dilemmas briefly outlined above apply to all teacher education programs, then teacher educators are faced with a series of choices of errors: there are no error-free alternatives related to the issues outlined. Thus the next step seems to be to determine which are the "least worst" errors in considering the long-term development of the members of the teaching profession. These are issues that affect all teacher education programs and would benefit from extensive research, especially of teachers' own retrospective views of their training.

## THE DEVELOPMENTAL STAGES OF TEACHERS

The concept of development and associated developmental stages has a long history in the field of psychology and education. The concept of professional developmental that is likely to occur in broadly defined stages has been widely used and translated into many languages and since its original publication (Katz, 1972). The concept is used here in its modern sense to mean that both the thought and behaviors that constitute a teacher's competence are most likely learned in some kinds of developmental sequences. They are sequences in which both the relevant understandings and the appropriate professional behaviors gradually improve to the extent that they are adaptive to the environment in which the individual lives and works. In other words, no one can enter into a profession—or even begin a social role, such as that of a teacher or a prime minister or a physician—as a veteran. It is reasonable to assume that in most cases, professional competence improves with practice and the experience that comes with it.

The assumption that there are developmental stages in professional competence does not deny that various kinds of support during the early years of professional practice can facilitate and even expedite professional development. The type of support that best serves teachers is likely to vary depending on the extent of the teacher's experience as well as the context in which he or she is working. Broad definitions of possible developmental stages in becoming a competent teacher are outlined below. Increasing use of "coaching" and "mentoring" in some countries seems to be helping beginning teachers and those working under new conditions to move successfully through the stages (Filippini, 1993; Ackerman, 2008)

## Stage 1: Survival

During this first stage of a teacher's career, which may last throughout the first full year of teaching, his or her main concern is how to *survive* the daily challenges of carrying responsibility for a whole group of children and their development and learning. This preoccupation with survival may be expressed to the self in terms such as "Can I get through the day in one piece? Without losing a child? Can I make it to the end of the week?" and so on.

During this survival period the teacher is most likely to need support, understanding, encouragement, reassurance, comfort, and guidance. She or he very likely will need direct help with specific skills, and insight into the complex causes of behavior—all of which are best provided in situ as the need for help arises.

## Stage 2: Consolidation

By about the end of the first year of teaching, the teacher has usually come to see herself or himself as capable of surviving the usual daily crises. She is now ready to consolidate the overall gains made during the first state of her professional development and to differentiate specific tasks and skills to be mastered next. During this Stage 2, teachers usually begin to focus on individual problem children and problem situations. This focus may take the form of looking for answers to such questions as: "How can I help a clinging child? How can I help a particular child who does not seem to be learning simple things? These kinds of questions are now differentiated from the general survival issues of keeping a whole class running smoothly.

During Stage 1, Survival, the neophyte acquires a baseline of information about what children are like, and what to expect of them, as well as of their parents. This stage also includes confidence in how to organize the day, the week, and progress through the main curriculum as required. But by Stage 2, the teacher is beginning to identify individual children whose behavior departs from the pattern of most of the children he or she knows. Thus the teacher identifies the more unusual or exceptional patterns of behavior that have to be addressed to ensure the steady progress of the whole class. During this second stage, on-site training and support continue to be potentially helpful. An on-site trainer can observe the teacher and child in situ and arrive at specific suggestions and tentative solutions and fairly quickly can recommend some strategies to try that might solve the problems at hand.

## Stage 3: Renewal

Often during the third, fourth, or perhaps fifth year of experience, the teacher begins to tire of doing the same old things over and over again. For example, in many countries the school year in the early years seems to consist of celebrating the same sequence of national and religious holidays, one after another. After four or five years of such repetition of the holiday-related activities, the teacher is likely to be asking more questions about new developments and perhaps new practices and materials being used in the field. She may be asking herself and others questions like "What are some new approaches to supporting children's language development?" or "What are some new materials, techniques, approaches, and ideas being developed nowadays?" Teachers in this developmental stage are particularly receptive to experiences in local, regional, and national conferences and workshops, and can benefit from membership in professional associations and participation in their meetings. They also benefit from opportunities to visit other classes and educational programs that are thought to be on the cutting edge of the field.

## Stage 4: Maturity

Teachers vary in how long it takes for them to reach something like a stage we might call *maturity*. At this stage the teacher has come to terms with himself or herself as a teacher and has reached a comfortable level of confidence in his or her own competence. The teacher now has enough perspective to begin to ask deeper and more abstract questions, such as "What are my historical and philosophical roots?" What are we learning these days about the nature of development and learning? How are educational decisions really made? Can schools change societies? She or he has very likely asked these questions before. But with experience now behind him/her, the questions represent a more meaningful search for insight, perspective, and realism and a desire to contribute to society.

Throughout maturity, teachers can continue to benefit from opportunities to participate in conferences and seminars and perhaps to work toward an advanced degree. Mature teachers usually welcome the chance to read widely and to interact with educators working in many problem areas at many different levels. The support that would be useful to teachers at this stage would be different from that needed in the preceding three developmental stages outlined above.

By way of example, as part of the regular daily routine, a kindergarten teacher called the children together to come and sit in front of her for story time during which she read selected stories to the whole class. On one such occasion, one of the boys said to her "I don't want to listen to a story today."

A teacher in the first stage would most likely have insisted that the child comply with the schedule, perhaps by taking him to the required location in the classroom physically. A teacher in the mature stage might say to the child something like "OK. That's fine. Just find something to do that won't disturb the rest of us while we're having story time." That teacher's suggestion was most likely based on her insight derived from knowing that particular child well, having confidence in his ability and his willingness to follow her suggestions, and her own confidence in her ability to inspire his compliance to her request. The insights that account for effective teaching are most likely related to experience over time as well as innate abilities of many kinds.

## SPECIFIC ISSUES IN THE EDUCATION OF EARLY CHILDHOOD TEACHERS

As indicated in a recent national publication (Neugebauer, 2011), the matter of teacher qualifications and training in the field of preschool education and care is a "hot issue" in many countries. There are many possible factors contributing to the constant squabbling about what training and qualifications are necessary for those who work with our youngest children. Certainly the salaries of those who work in preschools and childcare programs compared to those who teach in elementary and secondary schools, contributes, to some extent, to resistance to increasing the training and credentialing requirements for early childhood educators. Another important factor is that in classes of children under about five years of age, more than one adult must be present at all times. In this way, the cost of salaries multiplies rapidly, and decent salaries for two or three adults per class of twenty-five children could make preschool education unaffordable to many government and community agencies and families.

Furthermore, the question of what content should be mastered by preschool teachers is a difficult one. To a large extent the training of teachers for elementary and secondary education addresses the mastery of the content they are expected to teach and the appropriate pedagogical methods for doing so, depending upon the age group to be taught. However, in the case of preschool education, there is no clear agreement of what content they will be expected to teach the children. One of the characteristics of the field of early childhood education is constant contention about which pedagogical theories, teaching methods, content and skills should be included in the curriculum. For more than one hundred years, many teachers of young children around the world have been trained to use the Montessori approach. But that is only one of many competing approaches to preschool pedagogy. In the 1970s in the United States, ten different curriculum models were implemented in Head Start programs for three years and their comparative effectiveness was evaluated. The results were not clear and the importance of variations in the implementation of the models made the establishment of clear effects of different curriculum and philosophical models difficult to discern.

More recently preschool practitioners in many countries have been under strong pressure to prepare preschool children for their first year in elementary school. This has often been expressed in terms of the importance of the *alignment* of preschool pedagogical approaches to those of the next stage of education (Kamil, 2010). This new focus on *alignment* has in turn led to increasing pressure on teachers to include formal academic instruction in the preschool curriculum. Thus programs for the preparation of early childhood teachers in many countries are once again caught in the conflict between its traditional emphasis on spontaneous play and other informal activities versus strong pressure to prepare preschoolers for school and for the increasing frequency of test-taking, sometimes referred to as the increasing "schoolification" of preschool education (Oberhuemer, 2010).

## Academic and Intellectual Goals in Early Education

Teacher education programs for early childhood teachers could address this traditional conflict between informal and formal instruction by helping students to focus on the distinction between an academic and intellectual emphasis for the early childhood curriculum (Katz, 2010). I suggest that much of the discussion and debate about appropriate preschool curricula is based on a misleading dichotomy, that is, between emphasizing formal academic instruction versus spontaneous play and other free-flowing activities for the young ones (e.g., painting, cutting and pasting, etc.). While the case can be made that there is a place for some of both of these two types of activities, the element that is overlooked in this dichotomy is the nature of *intellectual* goals and activities highly appropriate for all ages (see Katz, 2010).

Intellectual goals and their related activities address the life of the mind in its fullest sense, including a range of aesthetic and moral sensibilities. The formal definition of the concept of *intellectual* emphasizes reasoning, hypothesizing, predicting, the quest for understanding cause-effect relationships, and so forth. When young children engage in investigations, now referred to as the Project Approach (Katz & Chard, 2000) they are employing their intellectual dispositions, and in addition, seeking help with basic academic skills (e.g., writing, measuring, etc.) *in the service of their intellectual pursuits*. The Project Approach involves children in conducting investigations of significant objects, activities, and events around them for which they have developed the research questions, in the course of which their intellectual capacities are provoked and strengthened. The education of teachers of young children should include emphasis on supporting young children's intellectual abilities and dispositions by incorporating the Project Approach in the curriculum for which they are prepared. [1]

## Role Diffusion of Teachers in Early Childhood Settings

Another characteristic of teaching young children is that the adults' role boundaries are diffuse and unclear, compared to the roles of teachers of older children and of specific content areas. In the case of very young children, there is very little about the child's functioning that is not of concern to the caregiver or teacher. Their responsibilities are wide ranging and include physical care (e.g., feeding and toileting) as well as helping children learn to use modern computer technology. With the increasing age of the learner, the role of the teacher becomes more clearly defined, especially in terms of the subject matter and academic skills to be taught and the expected effects on the children. Learning how to cope with unclear role boundaries in advance of actual experience, that is, during training, is difficult and probably is best achieved by available colleague support once employed in the first developmental stage of the teachers.

## Frequent and Close Contact with Parents

In principle, the younger the child being taught, the more frequent and intimate will be the contact between their parents and the children's teachers. Such intimate contact with parents is often accompanied by incidents of conflict and stress, attributable to both participants in the relationship. Learning how to cope effectively with tension or conflicts with parents probably cannot be learned in advance through lectures or even by reading about them. Some role-play activities may help to prepare students in training for possible ways of interacting with challenging parents. Perhaps well-designed case studies would also be an effective approach to helping students to learn some basics about working with parents. Furthermore, in the case of many children, the teacher can contribute to their growth, development, and learning by involving and informing the parents about their progress or lack of progress, and many of the best ways to do so can most likely be learned during the training period.

As indicated above, all early childhood settings provide at least two adults per classroom. It is not unusual for staff conflicts to arise concerning responsibilities and pedagogical strategies, Whether competent management of such occasions can be learned in advance during the training period is not clear and has not been studied. Many of these kinds of professional competencies could be learned during a practicum experience in which the students can observe closely how competent and mature teachers behave in various complex situations they are likely to face in the future.

## CONCLUSION

The training of teachers for all age groups and for teaching all subjects involves many dilemmas, stresses, and conflicts. Some of these stresses and conflicts are especially critical in the case of teaching our youngest children. Among the many research questions that can be generated from this discussion, one to begin with might be to identify a substantial group of competent and effective early childhood teachers, and to probe their *retrospective* views as to what experiences they attribute their competence and effectiveness to. Thus far, such potentially helpful research has not yet been reported.

## NOTE

1. Every issue of the free on-line journal, *Early Childhood Research & Practice*, includes a report of a project conducted by young children. See http://ecrp.uiuc.edu.

## REFERENCES


Ackerman, D. J. (2008). Coaching as part of a pilot quality rating scale initiative: Challenges to—and supports for—the change-making process. *Early Childhood Research and Practice, 10*(2). Retrieved April 28, 2012, from http://ecrp.uiuc.edu/v10n2/ackerman.html.

Filippini, T. (1993). The role of the pedagogista. In C. Edwards, L. Gandini, & G. Forman (Eds.). *The hundred languages of children: The Reggio Emilia approach to early childhood education* (pp. 113–118). Norwood, NJ: Ablex.

Galinsky, E. (2010). *Mind in the making.* New York, NY: HarperCollins Publishers.

Gonzalez-Mena, J. (2001). *Foundations: Early childhood education in a diverse society.* 2nd ed. Mountain View, CA: Mayfield Publishing Company.

Kamil, M. L. (2010). A comprehensive perspective on early childhood educator professional development. In S. B. Neuman & M. L. Kamil (Eds.), *Preparing teachers for the early childhood classroom: Proven models and key principles* (pp. 1–15). Baltimore, MD: Brookes.

Katz, L. G. (1972). The developmental stages of preschool teachers. *Elementary School Journal, 73*(1), 50–54.

Katz, L. G. (2010). STEM in the early years. *Collected papers from the SEED (STEM in Early Education and Development) conference.* Cedar Falls, IA: ECRP. http://ecrp.uiuc.edu/beyond/seed/katz.html.

Katz, L. G., & Raths, J. D. (1985). Dispositions as goals for teacher education. *Teaching and Teacher Education, 1*(4), 301–307.

Katz, L. G., & Raths, J. D. (1992). Six dilemmas of teacher education. *Journal of Teacher Education, 43*(5), 376–385.

Katz, L. G., & Chard, S. (2000). *Engaging children's minds: The project approach.* Greenwood, NJ: Ablex Publishing Corp.

Neel, C., & Warren, C. (1978). Business school curriculum design: Some issues of concern. National Forum. *Phi Kappa Phi Journal*, *63*(3), 7–10.

Neugebauer, R. (2011). Qualifications of preschool teachers: A hot issue in our field. *Exchange, 33*(202), 23–28.

Oberhuemer, P. (March 2010). *Balancing traditions and transitions: Early childhood education in Germany.* Unpublished paper presented at Early Childhood Curriculum, Policy and Pedagogy in the 21st Century: An International Debate. Anglia Ruskin University, England.

Room, A. (1985). *Dictionary of confusing words and meanings.* London: Routledge & Kegan Paul.

## *Chapter Two*

# History, Policy, and the Professional Lives of Teacher Educators in England

David Crook and Gary McCulloch

Teacher education has been the focus of a great deal of attention from politicians and policy makers in England over the past thirty years, and the recent White Paper, *The Importance of Teaching*, suggests that this level of scrutiny is unlikely to decline in the foreseeable future (Department for Education, 2010). The approach to teacher education that has become the official orthodoxy in recent times has favored an emphasis on method over theory, and an increasing preference for practical "on-the-job" apprenticeship models based in schools, rather than in universities or other institutions of higher education (see, for example, Standing Committee for the Education and Training of Teachers, 2011).

In this context, it seems timely to review the historical characteristics of teacher education in England over the past century in order to understand more fully the aims and aspirations that have motivated it during that time. It is useful to observe the changes in policy with respect to teacher education over the longer term, and to this end we inspect the key developments that have taken place particularly since the Second World War. However, as a means of understanding teacher education it is also important to shift our attention to the teacher educators themselves, highlighting what has been, until recently, a somewhat neglected history of the institutions of teacher education and the lives and careers of teacher educators (Crook, 2012. In this way, more broadly, it is possible to move beyond a preoccupation with professionalization, which has been the dominant approach to the history of teacher education hitherto, to a concern with professional lives.

## PROFESSIONALIZATION AND PROFESSIONAL LIVES

The history of teacher education in England has tended to focus on the rise and progress of teacher education, often envisaged as a struggle against ignorance and prejudice. This has been part of a broadly "liberal" approach to the history of education that was dominant in the first half of the twentieth century and that has continued to have resonance in some quarters since the 1960s. When applied to the history of an occupational group or sector, such a story of progress against the odds tends to translate into one of professionalization. This centers on the efforts of an occupational group to be publicly accepted as a "profession" through such means as securing self-regulation, qualifications, security of tenure, a code of behavior, sanctions and procedures for expulsion, and control over the application of knowledge and labor. For example, Harold Perkin (1969, 1973) argued that the work of the Association of University Teachers, established in 1919, had established the "professionalization of university teaching," with a growing demand over a sustained period for longer training, higher qualifications, and influence over terms, conditions, and standards of work.

In relation to schoolteachers, Asher Tropp and Peter Gosden (Tropp, 1957; Gosden, 1972) provided detailed accounts of the rise and progress of a teaching profession in the nineteenth and twentieth centuries. Such approaches reflected and endorsed the optimistic, liberal model of gradual social progress that remained prominent at that time.

This kind of perspective was particularly influential with regard to the history of teacher education. One characteristic study was that of R. W. Rich (1933), who charted the emergence and development of the training of teachers in England and Wales during the nineteenth century, from the monitorial system through the introduction of a training college system to the growth of training for teachers in the secondary schools. Marjorie Cruickshank (1970) produced a similar historical survey of the training of teachers in Scotland from the early nineteenth century to the period after 1945.

An account of the Association of Teachers in Colleges and Departments of Education as a professional association from 1943 until 1973 was provided by Joan D. Browne (1979, 1980), while the work of John B. Thomas (1979, 1982, 1986, 1988) on the role of universities in teacher education consolidated this kind of approach. In 1993 Christine Heward commented that "The history of teacher educators as a professionalizing occupation poses important questions for social historians seeking to explain the rise of professional society" (p. 11). Studying the example of teacher educators, she argued, was important not only because it provides an early example of a public profession, germane to the work of Harold Perkin, but also because its history can be read as one of competition between other professional groups, namely the clergy, civil servants and university dons.

This general preoccupation with the processes involved in professionalization tended to exclude issues relating to professionalism and professional lives. Professionalism concerns the everyday lives of professionals, including the exercise of their responsibilities and their daily interactions with colleagues and clients or consumers. Professional lives are the medium- and long-term development of individual careers, including an awareness of their daily experiences. The study of these issues has often entailed the development of different methods from those involved in traditional histories of professionalization. In relation to teachers and teaching, Kate Rousmaniere (1997) in the United States produced a detailed historical investigation of teachers' work in the 1920s and 1930s based on the oral testimonies of former teachers, while in Israel Miriam Ben-Peretz (1995) interviewed forty-three retired teachers to understand the nature of teacher identities and memories over time.

New work on teachers and teaching in the UK context has also begun to document the history of teacher professionalism and professional lives, engaging with the insights of researchers such as Andy Hargreaves, Ivor Goodson, Christopher Day and Pat Sikes (see, for example, Goodson & Hargreaves, 2001; Day, Fernandez, Hauge, & Moller, 2000). For example, Wendy Robinson's (2004) historical study of teachers' attempts to learn through practice deals with similar issues. These concerns were also embedded in a detailed analysis by Cunningham and Gardner (2004) on the historical development of the student teacher in the early decades of the twentieth century. The authors made use of contemporary written materials of different kinds, and also drew on the memories of retired former student teachers, interviewed for the study, to understand the experiences of student teachers from their own perspectives (see also McCulloch, 2011, pp. 90–91).

In the light of these recent research trends, therefore, there is both need and opportunity to begin to understand the history of teacher educators in terms of their professional lives and careers. It is important that such work be undertaken in a critical spirit, that is, that it should avoid the temptation to indulge in sentimentalized hagiography of the great teacher educators, perhaps as a reaction against the unsympathetic policies of the present day. It should also attempt to contextualize this history in relation to broader educational, social, policy, and political contexts within which teacher educators themselves lived and worked. With this in view, let us briefly review some of the key policy trends around teacher education, particularly in the years since the Second World War, before setting out a prospectus for further study of the history of teacher educators.

## TEACHER EDUCATION POLICY SINCE THE SECOND WORLD WAR

Although the notion of a teaching "profession" was occasionally used during the nineteenth century, this is something of a misnomer. Masters in the elite private schools were generally recruited directly from the ancient universities, as were those who taught in grammar schools for the emerging middle classes. Good teachers were born, not made, according to a still-used adage, and "training," in the shape of attendance at residential, mainly church-run colleges and pupil-teacher apprenticeships, was thought suitable only for those associated with schooling for the working classes. As late as 1941 the *Times Educational Supplement* reported that the "great" boarding schools actually boasted that their teachers were not trained, while training a secondary school teacher "would reduce his social status by associating him with the trained teacher of the lowly elementary school" (Thomas, 1990, p. 24). When, during the 1860s, the "Revised Code" necessitated financial cutbacks, it was suggested that elementary school teachers were "over educated," leading to the closure of some residential colleges. Such perceptions and prejudices became entrenched, but an appeal, set out in a minority report of the Cross Commission (1888) for "places of higher instruction" to become involved in teacher education was eventually acted upon by various British universities.

From the 1890s professorial chairs in education and university day training colleges were established, prefiguring the eventual development of full university departments of education by the mid-1920s, though "their presence was neither accepted nor acceptable in many quarters" (Patrick, 1986, p. 247). Joint examining boards strengthened the association between universities and teacher-training colleges during the interwar years, but there were tensions—still present in the twenty-first century—between university expectations that Education staff would engage in high-quality research and writing and the administrative aspects of the work, including teaching-practice observation visits to schools.

As the Second World War drew to a close, England was faced by a crisis of teacher supply that invites comparison with current difficulties in recruiting teachers to such shortage secondary school subjects as mathematics, science, and modern languages. The formulation of recommendations for teacher supply, recruitment, and training formed part of the brief assigned, during the spring of 1942, to an inquiry chaired by Dr. Arnold McNair, vice chancellor of the University of Liverpool (Crook, 1997). Over the next two years, while the McNair Committee was pondering the development of a long-term policy, it became evident that urgent improvisations would be necessary in order to staff schools adequately during the immediate postwar period. It was for this reason that an emergency training scheme, aimed principally at men and women serving in the armed forces with few, or no, academic qualifications, was launched (see Crook, 2006).

After 1945 the Labour government pursued a contradictory dual policy for initial teacher education. It lent its support to the McNair Report (Board of Education, 1944), which emphasized the inadequacy of the two-year courses in training colleges, underlined the desirability of a highly educated, as well as trained, teaching force, and sought to associate the profession more closely with the universities. Simultaneously, however, it promoted the one-year emergency training scheme. This scheme, which operated between 1945 and 1951, produced some 23,000 male and 12,000 female teachers, most of whom found employment in primary or secondary modern schools, as did those who emerged from established training college courses (Crook, 2006). Posts in the prestigious secondary grammar schools, meanwhile, remained the preserves of university graduates with a one-year postgraduate teaching qualification.

The postwar improvement in the level of schoolteachers' paper qualifications impacted upon university- and college-based teacher trainers, who increasingly pursued their own postgraduate and doctoral studies. New sociological understandings and theories about how children learn infused teacher training curricula from the 1960s, but the academicization was to become the subject of deep suspicion in some quarters. During the 1980s and 1990s the "new right" and several prominent media commentators accused "trendy" teacher trainers of shunning "proven" methods, such as teaching children to read using the phonic method and whole-class teaching (see the criticisms, for example, of Melanie Phillips, 1996, pp. 39–42). The reforms of the past twenty-five years have not completely suppressed these attacks. For example, in a 1996 House of Lords debate, a Conservative peer, Lord Pearson of Rannoch, described teacher educators as the "soldiers of political correctitude, the gender, race and class brigade" responsible for introducing the "cancer" of politicized teaching into schools (House of Lords Debates, 1996, col. 1740). Those professionally involved in teacher education have regularly sought to challenge allegations of this kind, sometimes by means of intellectual dialogue and sometimes through furious rebuttals. To date, however, neither of these approaches has proved especially successful.

Links between the colleges and the universities were strengthened in most regions of England and Wales as a result of the establishment of area training organizations, as recommended in chapter 4 of the McNair Report. Hopes that these bodies would "bring university standards into teacher education and a new dignity to the teaching profession" (Judge, 1984, p. 133), however, were only partially realized before they were disbanded in the 1970s. In the meantime, the length of training college courses was extended from two to three years in 1960, a move which highlighted another status difference within the teaching profession, between graduates and nongraduates.

In 1963 the Robbins Committee's report on the future of higher education supported the development of an all-graduate teaching profession (CHE, 1963). It was recommended that this should be facilitated by the launch of a new BEd degree to be offered mostly over three years, but also available as a four-year honors program for very able students. English and Welsh university and college BEd courses developed rapidly during the late 1960s. The trend then spread to Scotland and Northern Ireland. By the mid-1970s four-year courses had become the norm, rather than the exception.

The BEd qualification has had a difficult history. In its early years it struggled to gain public confidence and in 1972 the James Committee favored an altogether different model of undergraduate training that, if implemented, would have transformed the BEd into an in-service degree for teachers (DES, 1972). Most of the Report's far-reaching recommendations were shelved or ignored, but a number of higher education institutions opted independently to replace their BEd degrees with courses leading to BA (Ed) awards. Perhaps more significantly, the government accepted the James Committee's recommendation that the Council for National Academic Awards should be permitted to validate polytechnic and college bachelor and postgraduate teacher education courses. The resulting competition forced the universities to review their own work in this field, particularly in relation to the organization and quality of school teaching practice arrangements (Silver, 1990). A consequence of this was that, by the mid-1970s, there was a clear trend toward the establishment of partnerships between higher education institutions and schools.

More central control of teacher education was introduced during the early 1980s. A Council for the Accreditation of Teacher Education was appointed in 1984, with responsibility for determining whether courses were conforming to national criteria laid down by the secretary of state for education. Five years later, revised criteria introduced a competence-based model for the assessment of students. Still more radical approaches were advocated by "new right" commentators who believed that teacher education was in the grip of progressive-minded, left-wing academics (Lawlor, 1990). One such suggestion was that it might be possible to train teachers "on the job," with minimal or no involvement of higher education institutions, where, it was alleged, "spurious forms of academicism" (Kelly, 1993, p. 132) and "modish educational theory" (*Times* [London], 1990) were imparted.

In 1992 the then secretary of state for education, Kenneth Clarke, proposed that postgraduate student teachers should spend 80 percent of their time in schools. He also proposed that BEd courses should be restricted to three years, but with students spending more time in schools (*Times Educational Supplement*, 1992). An accommodation was subsequently reached whereby two-thirds of the postgraduate training year would be school-based. New regulations also introduced teacher education partnership agreements, reinforced school mentoring arrangements and provided for the transfer of funding from higher education institutions to partnership schools. The possibilities of wholly school-based training were also recognized. In March 1993 it was announced that, from the coming September, 250 teachers would be trained exclusively in schools as a School-Centered Initial Teacher Training, or SCITT, pilot. The pilot was immediately declared a success and the scheme was developed on a national basis from the following year.

Conservative prime minister John Major's government decided in 1993 to replace the Council for the Accreditation of Teacher Education with a government agency. The Teacher Training Agency, established under the terms of the 1994 Education Act, was transmuted into the Training and Development Agency in 2005 and, since April 2012, known simply as the Teaching Agency. Over the past eighteen years this body, in its various guises, has exercised a powerful control over the accreditation of course providers, the specification of program content and of the competences that trainees must demonstrate. Simultaneously, higher education course providers have been forced to compete for available student numbers, which are now in significant decline as allocations for training new teachers are increasingly handed directly to schools.

## TOWARD A SOCIAL HISTORY OF TEACHER EDUCATORS

Detailed consideration of the contribution made by teacher educators over the past century is long overdue. One exceptional study, by William Taylor, investigated the forms of social control and patterns of social change in the teacher training colleges and departments of education, placing an emphasis on the social relationships and values of the colleges. Taylor noted that, before the Second World War, there were only 181 men and 515 women working in the colleges, a figure that increased markedly to 4,027 men and 2,665 women by 1966 (Taylor, 1969). This account tends to reinforce the argument, set out by Heward, that the social history of teacher educators is a gendered story. The nineteenth-century origins of English teacher training had emphasized male clerical authority, but from 1910 to 1960,

> women were dominant, their authority legitimated by academic qualifications, the prevalence of sex-segregated institutions and the Board of Education regulations. From the late 1950s men entered the profession in large numbers and the legitimacy of women's authority in the profession was eroded. From the mid-1970s initial teacher education has been absorbed into large diverse institutions of higher education in which managerial authority, seen as overwhelmingly masculine, is legitimated. (Heward, 1993, pp. 11–12)

Behind such statistics as these lie a multitude of teacher educator life histories, with significant potential to inform our understandings of professional achievements, opportunities and barriers, personal qualities, ambitions, and sacrifices. In his various studies of day training colleges and university education departments, J. B. Thomas has offered some such insights (see Thomas, 1979, 1982, 1986, 1988, 1990). Heward's study, meanwhile, followed the earlier example of Browne in recovering hidden-from-history women teacher educators, paving the way for more detailed studies of the "culture of femininity" within women's training colleges and of individual female college principals, including Mary Allen and Alice Skillicorn, both of Homerton College, Cambridge; Florence Johnson from Bishop Otter College, Chichester; and Lillian de Lissa of Gipsy Hill College, London (see Elizabeth Edwards, 1993, 2001a, 2001b; Whitehead, 2010).

More work is undoubtedly needed if we are to understand the contributions and dominance of two generations of female teacher-training college principals in the interwar, wartime, and immediate postwar periods. Some key figures from this period remain relatively unexplored and some important questions arise about the separate cultures inhabited by teacher educators in university departments of education and their counterparts in training colleges, widely seen as isolated seminaries linked to the working-class elementary schools (Gardner & Cunningham, 1998).

The colleges were "knocking at the door of the higher education club with no obvious prospect of entry" (Gardner & Cunningham, 1998, p. 238). In spite of the rhetoric of a "university connection," for the first three-quarters of the twentieth century the college experience of this was largely confined to examination matters, with university education department staff endorsing assessment recommendations. In different ways, early twentieth-century teacher educators cut isolated figures in both the training colleges and university education departments. Although Gardner and Cunningham point to examples of dedicated professionalism among some early twentieth-century teacher educators, a 1941 *Times Educational Supplement* article was scathing:

> A large number of very second-rate people, who in some cases have been themselves products of the colleges and have never known any other kind of discipline, have thoroughly enjoyed exercising over young lives a power with which they should never have been entrusted.

There appear to have been very few prewar examples of teacher educators moving from a university to a college or vice versa. Helen Wodehouse was an important exception. The holder of a teachers' higher diploma, though never actually a schoolteacher herself, Wodehouse was principal of Bingley Training College from 1911 to 1919, when she became the first woman to hold a chair at Bristol University, outshining other applicants among whom were Isaac Kandel and Godfrey Thomson, both leading educationists of their day (Thomas, 1988; Warnock, 2004). Outwardly, university education departments projected a more attractive, liberal and academic tradition (Gardner and Cunningham, 1998). Thomas identifies some notable university day training college staff, including some key women, who helped to establish an elite profession of women teachers and significantly contributed to educational scholarship. Within universities, however, academics from other departments and faculties often queried the place of teacher education work in the academy. Departments and institutes of education were invariably the poor relation of the university, tending to be "small, inadequately staffed, badly housed and held in poor regard within the university and in the schools" (Taylor, 1969, p. 219).

Thus far, we have only scattered published examples of the roles played by these teacher educators over this long period of time, and even fewer cases that illuminate their everyday experiences and professional lives. However, these may help to provide a base for further, more intensive research in this area.

Two such cases, who both worked in Cambridge in the late nineteenth century, are Oscar Browning and Elizabeth Hughes. Browning was the founder and first principal of the Cambridge University Day Training College for Men, established in 1891; Hughes led the establishment of the Cambridge Training College for Women in 1885. Pam Hirsch and Mark McBeth (2004), who combined forces to discuss these two remarkable figures in unusual depth, suggest that by reconstructing their experiences we are able to understand their perspectives and hear their voices, the better to "recover not only what they did but also what they felt" (Hirsch & McBeth, 2004, p. xi).

Browning was particularly concerned with teaching and student-teacher relationships, favoring a Socratic method in his pedagogy (Hirsch & McBeth, 2004, p. 82), and also worked to extend the training of the college from elementary school teaching to include secondary school teaching. Hughes established close relations with her students, for example setting up a ritual of having cocoa in one of the students' rooms every Saturday evening (p. 137). As Hirsch and McBeth suggest, "In many ways both characters have been buried under the debris of neglected archives and a minute amount of scholarly attention" (p. 210).

The same might be said of the teacher educators at the Institute of Education, University of London—formerly the London Day Training College at its foundation in 1902—were it not for the work of Richard Aldrich in producing the Institute's centenary publication (Aldrich, 2002). Aldrich himself acknowledges that in such a work, covering the span of a hundred years, it was "impossible to do justice to the work and influence of the many outstanding staff (and students) who have been members of the LDTC and of the Institute" (p. 100). There is also a danger in such accounts of concentrating exclusively on the institutional heads, especially the directors and leading professors.

One individual staff member whom Aldrich does highlight is Susan Isaacs, who promoted the teaching of child development at the Institute in the 1930s. Isaacs was one of the foremost child psychologists of her generation, but she was not rewarded with a chair or a readership, and the Child Development Department which she led comprised one room, which served as a study, office, and tutorial space.

Another key teacher educator in the postwar period was Brian Simon, who was appointed to the Education Department at Leicester University College in 1950 and retired as a professor in 1980. In his published memoir, Simon later recalled that the department was unusually progressive in outlook, reflecting the approach of its director, J. W. Tibble (Simon, 1998). Simon himself was responsible for a course for students preparing to teach social studies in secondary schools or technical colleges, and later for the teacher training course as a whole (the Post Graduate Certificate of Education, or PGCE), and he also developed a course in the history of education for student teachers.

Donald Jones has contributed a more detailed review of the School of Education at Leicester that explains the wide range of staff involved in the department's life and work (Jones, 2001), while accounts of other university schools of Education provide interesting and useful information on teacher educators (see, for example, Gosden, 1991; Robertson, 1990).

In more recent times there is perhaps no English teacher educator more influential than Ted Wragg, who achieved a national prominence as a fierce defender of teachers and of children, a trenchant critic of education policies associated with both major political parties, the writer of a satirical column in the *Times Educational Supplement*, and as a contributor to radio and television programs, making him "the most famous man in education of his day" (Berliner, 2009). Upon his death, in 2005, former student teachers were among those who paid tribute to Wragg, remembering his advice that had helped them to sustain long careers, as well as his delightful eccentricities (see, for example, Gregory, 2005, p. 37).

These provide helpful starting points for a deeper understanding of the professional lives of teacher educators in England over the past century, but in essence they are limited to offering only tantalizing glimpses in themselves. The task of developing a social history of teacher educators that can both establish the relationships of their lives with the wider society and reconstruct the daily patterns of their work is an imposing one, and remains to be achieved.

## CONCLUSIONS

This chapter has examined the history of teacher education in England and seeks to understand how the role of teacher educators has been affected by the dual trends of professionalization and professionalism.

For much of the twentieth century, the trends of professionalization and professionalism both appeared significant and durable, but they were also sometimes in tension. Teacher educators built and strengthened their professional identity through scholarship and by means of learned society and subject association membership. During the final years of the twentieth century, however, the trends towards the professionalization and professionalism of higher education–based teacher educators were curtailed by national education policies as responsibilities for the formation of teachers were handed—or returned, in fact—to schools. Simultaneously, routes into teaching in England have become ever more diversified. Trainees registered for employment-based training pathways, accelerated, part-time and online training have required different kinds of support.

Already a heterogeneous "tribe,"[1] divided along research-active and teaching-only lines, as well as by gender and power (Maguire & Weiner, 1994), the diversity of teacher educators seems set to accelerate in the period ahead. The present government views head teachers, their senior colleagues and third-party consultants, sometimes from universities but also from the private sector, as the most suitable teacher educators for the twenty-first century, as policy increasingly appears to favor a return to the nineteenth-century apprenticeship model for teacher training. The role of the university and college tutor has become more restricted and endangered and, on the basis of recent research, the self-identities of present-day teacher educators are confused (Murray, Czerniawski, & Barber, 2011).

Academic teacher educators in England, as Christopher Day (1995) has argued, may be experiencing a crisis of identity, caught between a rock and a hard place, often viewed as out of touch with contemporary classroom practice but also seen as peripheral figures in higher education institutions. Amid all the changes and reforms affecting English teacher education in recent years, historians will identify continuities in this dilemma and in others, too. Historians can also offer perspectives from studying past professional lives and show that teacher educators have made a significant contribution to teacher education and to education in general. Further research is necessary to document the full range and depth of this contribution, and indeed to demonstrate to a new generation the importance not only of teaching, but of teacher education and teacher educators.

## NOTE

1. The title of a recent research project, "The Academic Tribe of Teacher Educators: student and Staff Constructions of the Identities of Pre-Service Teacher Educators," is influenced by the title of Tony Becher's important text, *Academic Tribes and Territories: Enquiry and the Cultures of Disciplines* (1989). For details, see www.ioe.ac.uk/study/departments/eype/5519.html (accessed 24 December 2011).

## REFERENCES

Aldrich, R. (2002). *The Institute of Education, 1902–2002: A centenary history*. London: Institute of Education.

Becher, T. (1989). *Academic tribes and territories: Enquiry and the cultures of disciplines*. Milton Keynes, UK: Open University Press.

Ben-Peretz, M. (1995). *Learning from experience: Memory and the teacher's account of teaching*. Albany: State University of New York Press.

Berliner, W. (2009). Wragg, Edward Conrad (1938–2005). In *Oxford Dictionary of National Biography*. Oxford: Oxford University Press. Retrieved December 24, 2011 from www.oxforddnb.com/view/article/96170.

Board of Education. (1944). *Teachers and youth leaders: Report of the committee appointed by the president of the board of education to consider the supply, recruitment and training of teachers and youth leaders* (McNair Report). London: HMSO.

Browne, J. D. (1979). *Teachers of teachers: A history of the Association of Teachers in Colleges and Departments of Education*. London: Hodder and Stoughton/National Association of Teachers in Further and Higher Education.

Browne, J. D. (1980). The transformation of the education of teachers in the nineteen sixties. In E. Fearn & B. Simon (Eds.), *Education in the Sixties* (59–79). Leicester, UK: History of Education Society.

Crook, D. (2012). Teacher education as a field of historical research: Retrospect and prospect. *History of Education, 41*(1), 57–72.

Crook, D. (1997). *The reconstruction of teacher education and training, 1941–54, with particular reference to the McNair committee*. Unpublished doctoral dissertation, University of Wales, Swansea.

Crook, D. (2006). Challenge, response and dilution: A revisionist view of the Emergency Training Scheme for Teachers, 1945–1951. *Cambridge Journal of Education, 27*(3), 379–389.

Cruickshank, M. (1970). *History of the training of teachers in Scotland*. Edinburgh: Scottish Council for Research in Education.

Cunningham, P., & Gardner, P. (2004). *Becoming teachers: Texts and testimonies 1907–1950*. London: Woburn Press.

Day, C. (1995). Qualitative research, professional development and the role of teacher educators: Fitness for purpose. *British Educational Research Journal, 21*(3), 357–369.

Day, C., Fernandez, A., Hauge, T. E., & Moller, J. (Eds.). (2000). *The life and work of teachers: International perspectives in changing time*. London: Falmer.

Department for Education. (2010). *The importance of teaching*. London: HMSO.

DES. (1972). *Teacher education and training: A report by a committee of inquiry appointed by the secretary of state for education and science, under the chairmanship of Lord James of Rusholme*. London: HMSO.

Edwards, E. (1993). The culture of femininity in women's teacher training colleges 1900–50. *History of Education, 22*(3), 277–288.

Edwards, E. (2001a). Women principals, 1900–1960: Gender and power. *History of Education, 29*(5), 405–414.

Edwards, E. (2001b). *Women in Teacher Training Colleges, 1900–1960: A culture of femininity*. London: Routledge.

Gardner, P., & Cunningham, P. (1998). Teacher trainers and educational change in Britain, 1876–1996: "A flawed and deficient history"? *Journal of Education for Teaching, 24*(3), 231–255.

Goodson, I., & Hargreaves, A. (Eds.). (1996). *Teachers' professional lives*. London: Falmer.

Goodson, I., & Sikes, P. (2001). *Life history research in educational settings: Learning from lives*. Maidenhead, UK: Open University Press.

Gosden, P. H. J. H. (1972). *The evolution of a profession: A study of the contribution of teachers' associations to the development of school teaching as a professional occupation*. Oxford, UK: Basil Blackwell.

Gosden, P. H. J. H. (1991). The growth and development of Leeds University School of Education, 1891–1991. In P. H. J. H. Gosden (Ed.), *The University of Leeds School of Education, 1891–1991* (1–73). Leeds, UK: Leeds University Press.

Gregory, A. (2005, November 15). Obituary letter: Ted Wragg. *Guardian*, p. 37.

Heward, C. (1993). Men and women and the rise of professional society: The intriguing history of teacher educators. *History of Education, 22*(1), 11–32.

Hirsch, P., & McBeth, M. (2004). *Teacher training at Cambridge: The initiatives of Oscar Browning and Elizabeth Hughes*. London: Woburn Press.

Jones, D. (2001). *School of Education, 1946–1996*. Leicester, UK: University of Leicester.

Judge, H. (1984). *A generation of schooling: English secondary schools since 1944*. Oxford: Oxford University Press.

Kelly, A. V. (1993). Education as a field of study in the university: Challenge, critique, dialogue, debate. *Journal of Education for Teaching, 19*(2), 125–139.

Lawlor, S. (1990). *Teachers mistaught*. London: Centre for Policy Studies.

Maguire, M., & Weiner, G. (1994). The place of women in teacher education: Discourses of power. *Educational Review, 46*(2), 121–139.

McCulloch, G. (2011). *The struggle for the history of education*. London: Routledge.

Ministry of Education. (1963). *Higher Education: Report of the committee appointed by the prime minister under the chairmanship of Lord Robbins 1961–63* (Robbins Report) (Cmnd 2154). London: HMSO.

Murray, J., Czerniawski, G., & Barber, P. (2011). Teacher educators' identities and work in England at the beginning of the second decade of the twenty-first century. *Journal of Education for Teaching, 37*(3), 261–277.

Patrick, H. (1986). From Cross to CATE: The universities and teacher education over the past century. *Oxford Review of Education, 12*(3), 243–261.

Perkin, H. (1969). *Key profession: The history of the Association of University Teachers*. London: Routledge and Kegan Paul.

Perkin, H. (1973). The professionalization of university teaching. In T. G. Cook (Ed.), *Education and the professions* (69–84). London: History of Education Society/Methuen.

Phillips, M. (1996). *All must have prizes*. London: Little, Brown.

Rich, R. W. (1933). *The training of teachers in England and Wales during the nineteenth century*. Cambridge, UK: Cambridge University Press.

Robertson, A. B. (1990). *A century of change: The study of education in the University of Manchester*. Manchester, UK: University of Manchester.

Robinson, W. (2004). *Power to teach: Learning through practice*. London: Woburn.

Rousmaniere, K. (1997). *City teachers: Teaching and school reform in historical perspective*. New York: Teachers College Press.

Silver, H. (1990). *The Council for National Academic Awards and British Higher Education, 1964–1989* (79–81). London: Falmer Press.

Simon, B. (1998). *A life in education*. London: Lawrence and Wishart.

Standing Committee for the Education and Training of Teachers. (2011). *In defence of teacher education*. London: Author.

Taylor, W. (1969). *Society and the education of teachers*. London: Faber and Faber.

Thomas, J. B. (1979). The curriculum of a day training college: The logbooks of J. W. Adamson. *Journal of Educational Administration and History, 11*(2), 29–34.

Thomas, J. B. (1982). J. A. Green, educational psychology and the *Journal of Experimental Pedagogy*. *History of Education Society Bulletin, 29*, 41–45.

Thomas, J. B. (1986). Amos Henderson and the Nottingham Day Training College. *Journal of Educational Administration and History, 18*(2), 21–33.

Thomas, J. B. (1988). University College, Bristol: Pioneering teacher training for women. *History of Education*, *17*(1), 55–70.

Thomas, J. B. (1990). Day training college to department of education. In J. B. Thomas (Ed.), *British universities and teacher education*: *A century of change* (19–38). London: Falmer.

Tropp, A. (1957). *The school teachers: The growth of the teaching profession in England and Wales from 1800 to the present day*. London: Heinemann.

Warnock, M. (2004). Wodehouse, Helen Marion (1880–1964). In *Oxford Dictionary of National Biography*. Oxford, UK: Oxford University Press. Retrieved December 2011 from www.oxforddnb.com/view/article/48473.

Whitehead, K. (2010). Contesting the 1944 McNair report: Lillian de Lissa's working life as a teacher educator. *History of Education, 29*(4), 507–524.

## *Chapter Three*

# Three Decades of Teacher Education in Israel and Their Impact on Professional Development of Teacher Educators

Yuval Dror

## PERIODIZATION AND METHODOLOGY

There are several reasons for choosing the past three decades of educating teachers in Israel as an aspect of periodization. The guiding model for the academization of training teachers for which colleges awarded the BEd degree was determined in 1981 by a committee of the Council for Higher Education (CHE) in Israel, headed by Prof. Joseph Dan (Dan, 1981). From 1981 and until the time of writing, nine more committees set up by Israel's Ministry of Education and the Council for Higher Education (CHE) have engaged in teacher education and academization, and they included college-based programs for a graduate degree in education (MEd) (Dror, 2008, p. 59). In 1983, the MOFET Institute was founded to research and develop programs for training teaching staff, and today, it is the supra-institutional framework for teacher educators encompassing all Israel's colleges of education. Major trends in Israeli society have also influenced the periodization and the education system, and they are described in this chapter.

Teacher educators, primarily in the colleges of education, constitute the core of Israel's teacher training system: the innermost circle of several concentric circles. Teacher education is a part of the education system that is overseen by the Ministry of Education and also by the academic educational system that comprises the teacher education colleges (under the Ministry of Education's administrative responsibility and the academic responsibility of the CHE and its Planning and Budgeting Committee [PBC]), and the schools of education in the universities. Encompassing all of these is the circle of wider Israeli society. This chapter first discusses the circle of Israeli society, then the educational circle, and finally the academic circle where teacher education is positioned and the impact of all these factors on teacher educators.

The research that provided the basis for this chapter is historical—a meta-analysis and a systematic review—based on the database of the MOFET Institute and its publications, which reflect most endeavors in Israel's teacher education colleges.[1] MOFET publications—*Dapim* (Journal for Studies and Research in Education), *Shvilei Mehkar* (Research Pathways), and the MOFET Newsletter—were meticulously surveyed as well as primary sources, such as position papers and informative documents, and secondary (research-based) sources, engaging with various aspects of teacher education. With assistance from the MOFET database and other databases, I located the syllabi of courses given in the colleges, reports by forums and think-tank teams, as well as relevant research studies, most of which were conducted in collaboration with the MOFET Research Authority. Also helpful were the websites of colleges and universities engaged in teacher education.

## SOCIAL AND POLITICAL DIVIDES IN ISRAEL AND THEIR REFLECTION IN THE TEACHER EDUCATION ARENA

From the 1980s on, fluctuations between peace and war have marked Israeli society, with an associated broadening of social and political divides. Over these three decades, and slightly beforehand, peace agreements were signed with Israel's neighboring nations: in 1979 with Egypt; 1993, the Oslo Accords with the PLO; 1994, with Jordan, and recurrent attempts for a peace treaty with the Palestinian Authority from 2007 onward. Conversely, wars, intifadas, and military operations constantly erupted: 1982, the First Lebanon War; 1987, the first intifada; 1991, the Gulf War; 2000–2005, the second intifada; 2006, the Second Lebanon War; 2009, the Cast Lead operation in the Gaza Strip. The shifting pendulum between peace and war swung wider, further deepening the ideological and political divides between left and right, secular and religious, trends that worsened with the assassination of Prime Minister Yitzhak Rabin in 1995 and Israel's unilateral evacuation from the Gaza Strip, in 2005. Yet despite their sensitivity and powerful presence in Israeli society, all these events and the resulting divisions and turmoil were not discernible in the curricula of teacher education institutions. They were marked only in various informal frameworks, as shown in Leah Shagrir's exhaustive analysis of curricula at three colleges of education: Levinsky College of Education, the Kibbutzim College of Education, and Talpiot College of Education from the 1970s to the 1990s (Shagrir, 2007, pp. 187–188).

Societal and political tensions were discernible—between immigration absorption as a social collectivist mission and the lessening of the welfare state perception—and were reflected in the privatization and decentralization of state and public institutions. In Israel's public discourse, the pluralist, multiculturalist perception (also known as postmodernism) intensified, with a preference for ethnic, religious, and educational distinction at the expense of the common core (Yogev, 2011, pp. 29–30). Those perspectives, compounded by the launch of political parties with an ethnic-social foundation (1981, Tami; 1984, Shas) together with a large-scale immigration from the FSU and Ethiopia in the 1980s and 1990s were clearly reflected in the colleges' curricula. An analysis of the curricula of Levinsky College of Education, the Kibbutzim College of Education, and Talpiot College of Education elicited that several courses dealing with ethnic groups, customs, habits and traditions, religions and beliefs, demographic traits, and social attitudes were offered at the colleges during the 1980s and 1990s, in scopes ranging from 5 percent to 15 percent of the entire program (Shagrir & Iram, 2005).

Various colleges, mostly located in Israel's peripheral regions, offered special courses and programs introducing students to distinctive, often disadvantaged, populations—the Arab, Bedouin, Druze, Ethiopian, and the ultra-orthodox Jewish citizens of Israel. The courses were aimed at helping students to understand those populations' identity and heritage.

Social-community education BEd programs in formal and nonformal education offered at Beit Berl College, Oranim Academic College of Education, and Efrata/Emunah Academic College of Education and Arts (and as an MA track in Bar-Ilan University) trained students to acknowledge multiculturalism in Israeli society and to apply that perspective in their work. The Ben-Peretz Committee (2001) engaged with teacher education institutions and acknowledged the need to upgrade existing institutions and to deploy colleges appropriately in terms of geography and ethnicity, including the seminaries for ultraorthodox Jews. MEd programs in educational leadership and administration that prepare future school principals according to a format crystallized by the Ministry of Education are applied in many colleges, some of which train the teaching staff and administrators for working in Arab state education and religious state education. Examining multiculturalism in the Israeli teacher education system by James Banks's typology shows that the system is still only in the initial stages of cultural identity: Stage 3, "cultural identity clarification," in which "individuals are able to clarify their personal attitudes and cultural identity and to develop clarified positive attitudes toward their cultural group" and, at Stage 4, "biculturalism" in which they "have a sense of cultural identity and the psychological characteristics to participate successfully in their own culture community as well as in another cultural community" (Banks, 2008, pp. 63–64).

## TRENDS AND TENSIONS IN THE EDUCATION SYSTEM AND THEIR REFLECTION IN THE TEACHER EDUCATION SYSTEM

Since the 1970s, Israel's education system has been in a state of tension between the collectivism embodied in the "integration reform" that followed the 1968 Knesset resolution for interethnic socio-educational merging, and the "autonomy reform" of schools, which is, to a great extent, individualistic and privatized, and accords with social pluralism. The junior high schools that were set up as part of this integration were aimed at easing the transition of children from weaker populations in elementary school to the higher classes in high school, where they take the *bagrut* (matriculation exams).

Two main strategies were applied in effecting this change in education policy: "(1) decentralization and the development of school autonomy and school-based management and (2) quasi-market competition and 'privatization'" (Nir & Inbar, 2004, p. 218). A boost for those strategies derived from achievement-oriented learning and the trend for exploiting students' individual potential, which became pivotal to educational endeavors. This also found expression in the burgeoning of "supplementary education" for personal enrichment, in growing efforts by the Ministry of Education and academic institutions to foster gifted and talented students, and in the Special Education Law of 1988, which underscored working with children with learning disabilities. At the same time, this law strengthened the policy for the educational inclusion of children with special needs in mainstream schools (Dror, 2011).

The educational policy for merger and inclusion of challenged individuals and populations is visible in the teacher education system, in the development of special education programs, and in the addition of courses on inclusion and learning disorders for teacher trainees in the regular tracks. Training for uniqueness, emphasizing individual potential and educational autonomy, was also reflected in several areas. During the period discussed, several colleges and universities introduced training tracks for different kinds of specialized schools. The David Yellin College offers the Experimental Open Education track, a track that educates for sustainability, as well as a training course for elementary education in the Waldorf anthroposophical approach. Kaye College launched "Shahaf" (the Hebrew acronym for Active Educational Collaboration), a program that trains for school teaching with an inter-track, interdisciplinary, and multicultural approach (Barak & Gidron, 2009).

The Institute for Democratic Education at the Kibbutzim College of Education trains teachers holding a BEd degree for working in democratic schools. Tel Aviv University's School of Education launched an MA program in educational policy, with a specialization in democratic education, chiefly targeting graduates of the Institute for Democratic Education and teachers at specialized schools, and a similar track operates at the Faculty of

Education of Haifa University, granting a graduate degree in alternative education within the Department of Learning, Teaching and Training.

At Beit Berl College and the Kibbutzim College of Education, whose ideological roots lie in the Labor movement and the Kibbutz movement respectively, there are special frameworks for training "'movement' graduates" (young people who were members of the "pioneering" youth movements). They are trained for teaching and living in the geographical and social peripheries of Israel, where they engage in unique nonformal and community education, partly as social education classes in the schools. Through training that is mostly conducted in the field, these two colleges help absorb youth-movement graduates, usually in their twenties and thirties, into the formal education system.

Another form of distinctive training is "inter-collegiality," partnerships between colleges and schools who operate Professional Development Schools (PDS) together. Here, the practical experience of teaching trainees and their educators at the college is concentrated in one or a few schools. This enables the teacher educators to hold numerous and more intensive meetings with the trainees, and encourages the formation of "learning communities" in the schools. In addition, the communities and their "coaching teachers" also benefit from the teaching and training resources of their fellow colleagues from the college. The experience gained by nine such colleges of the "collegial" relationships they maintain with schools in the field is featured in a book describing partnerships with schools dedicated to developing linguistic arts, dialogue-based teaching, interdisciplinary teaching, learning values, and other themes (Silberstein, Ben-Peretz, & Greinfeld, 2006).

## TEACHER EDUCATION IN ISRAEL: BETWEEN THE MINISTRY OF EDUCATION AND THE HIGHER EDUCATION SYSTEM

Academization brought the teacher education colleges into the higher education system but left them with a shortfall in terms of their academic freedom and autonomy as compared to the universities and the general colleges. From the start of the academization process, the colleges of education were qualified to award academic degrees. However, the 1978 Amendment to the Higher Education Law (legislated in 1958) had already excluded them from the clauses conferring autonomy in defining curricula, budgets, and more, since the education minister is entitled under certain conditions "to enact amendments concerning the freedom of action of the institution (for training education employees)" (Liebman, 2011, p. 85). For three decades, the colleges of education have tried without success to lift these restrictions. The Ministry of Education continues to supervise such basic academic aspects as admission requirements, approval of appointments, the promotion of faculty members, and prior approval of curricula. The CHE (Council of Higher Education) has supreme oversight over the curricula and degrees awarded at the colleges of education (Liebman, 2011; Hofman & Niederland, 2012; Hofman & Kfir, 2012). Colleges of education must submit their curricula to the Ministry of Education's Training Division and then to the CHE, in compliance with binding guidelines: from 1981 until the early 2000s, with guidelines for the BEd degree. From 2006, the "Ariav format," determined by a professional committee at the CHE headed by Prof. Tamar Ariav of Beit Berl College, decided on guidelines for educating teachers in all higher education institutions. The Ariav Committee was intended to close the gap between the colleges and universities in terms of teacher education.

Teacher education in the schools of education in the universities tends to have a low priority, as universities see themselves as research institutions. This worldwide phenomenon is addressed by Jaap Tuinman, a former dean of the education faculty at Simon Fraser University in Canada—in a contribution to a volume titled *Changing Times in Teacher Education: Restructuring or Reconceptualization*, which presents a comprehensive international perspective: "Another institutional barrier is the low status of teacher education within colleges of education. Ironically, while most academics in other colleges within the university see teacher preparation as the major calling for the faculty in the college of education, the education faculty often has bigger fish to fry.

"Status within the college of education tends to be inversely related with one's distance from the enterprise of teacher education. Many senior people within teacher education specialize in the study of teaching rather in the preparation of teachers" (Tuinman, 1995, p. 128). Until 2006, the universities were not required to obtain academic approval from the CHE for the teaching diplomas they awarded.

At the colleges of education, a maximum number of hours are called for (sixteen hours per week until age fifty) and very little research assistance is given. The teaching profession's low status in general, and more particularly in view of Israel's problematic position in international achievement tests, has drawn stringent and prolonged criticism of the whole education system. The BEd and MEd are unique degrees awarded to a profession with a poor image, and this projects onto the colleges of education in comparison to the universities and general colleges that confer different degrees.

The growing number of colleges of education in Israel caused competition for students, faculty and resources. The institutional ethos is still not sufficiently academic since the colleges of education were created from the teacher seminaries that were originally launched as the highest level of high schools; most of their teachers came from the field and only studied at universities.

The majority of the teaching faculty at the colleges of education are members of teacher organizations, for which the academic ethos is foreign (Liebman, 2011). Moreover, the analysis that Hofman and Niederland (2010) performed on the Ministry of Education and CHE documents from 1970 to 2006 found significant differences between perceptions of the teacher profile sought by the Ministry of Education (an educating teacher, whose practical experience is vital, and whose studies of education, pedagogy, enrichment, and disciplines are important) and those sought by the CHE (primarily an academic-disciplinary teacher, whose experience, education studies, and enrichment studies are secondary in importance).

Yogev (2000), who specializes in studying higher education in Israel, identified another sociological-class aspect: stratification between the "top-ranking" universities and colleges in general; the colleges of education in particular are "ranked lower." Various sorts of university assistance, collaborations, and integrations throughout the years were unsuccessful despite the recommendations that were not, in fact, implemented. Several committees dealt with various aspects of the colleges' academic status: the recommended structure for the colleges' academic management by academic councils and academic regulations; opening study tracks for the MEd graduate degree; reducing the number of academic colleges of education; and creating models for merging colleges of education with other academic institutions to boost their status as higher education institutions (Dror, 2008).

## THE ACADEMIZATION REFORM AND TEACHER EDUCATION ITSELF

Studying the significance of the field of teacher education in Israel, Kfir and Ariav (2004) summed up the academization reform as a "partial step" that originated in a position paper on the topic, submitted to the Ministry of Education's pedagogic secretariat (Chen & Gottlieb, 1989). Influenced by the worldwide waves of reform in this sphere, its title was "Toward a New Era in Israeli Teacher Education" which reflected an optimism that stemmed from the academization process in colleges and the need for innovation in training teachers in universities. This was cited in the report by an international committee for examining schools of education in universities undertaken for the CHE (Elkana, 1988). No real change has occurred in the universities, and while the colleges of education have gradually undergone academization, it is only partial. Though theoretical subjects have been added to the curriculum in the teacher education colleges, practical training has not been academized. The organizational structure of the colleges of education was not adapted to match that of an academic institution. In 2001, only 60 percent of the teacher education institutions were academic and 14 percent were undergoing the academization process.

The partial nature of the academization process found expression in all the aspects cited, including the fact that, in the early twenty-first century, close to 30 percent of the trainees were attending small ultra-orthodox and nonacademic institutions, and the same holds true for the teacher educators there (Kfir, Ariav, Fejgin, & Liebman, 1997; Kfir & Ariav, 2004).

Ariav mapped the "state of the art" in Israel and elsewhere, and listed four perspectives on the teaching crisis: the *sociological* perspective (changes in perceptions of schools, and the population turning to teaching); the *professional* (difficulties in defining teaching as a profession, and designing training for it); the *research-based* (expectations that the improved study program for teachers will yield better achievements from their students); and the *political-economical* (what are the outputs of teaching as compared with the costs of training, and what is the optimal cost-benefit ratio?).

Ariav analyzed three principal processes that have accompanied the teaching crisis over the past decade: (1) the lack of consensus over the appropriate division between initial training and the professional development of teachers in "the field"; (2) the ever-growing blurring between the traditional programs and short, alternative programs that prepare students for teaching after shortened or partial training; and (3) differential salary policies for teachers. The solutions that she presented are: broadening research into teacher education and intensifying it so as to make decisions on an informed basis; transferring the majority of training to diploma studies and a graduate degree in education (including the retraining of academics); positioning junctions for leaving the profession after ten or fifteen years; structuring professional development tracks without direct teaching for relatively veteran teachers; and a public battle for the profession's status.

Her proposals also directly addressed the teacher educators: they should enhance their involvement and leadership in the public-political discourse on questions of education in general and teacher education in particular, and also in the discourse and efforts to promote social justice and the creation of a democratic climate. The implication of these solutions illustrates the lack of involvement and leadership demonstrated by most teacher educators in the above-mentioned areas (Ariav, 2008, 2011; "Alternative Training Programs," 2010).

To one degree or another, the solutions that Ariav cites are found in the teacher education "field." Noach Greinfeld, head of the Division for Training Education Employees, found five types of alternative programs that are offered in Israel: retraining for teaching in two tracks: (1) retraining academics to become teachers and (2) training programs for special populations, such as native speakers of English or former high-tech employees interested in teaching subjects where teachers are lacking, such as mathematics and the sciences; (3) the programs for outstanding students that are offered in many colleges, targeting students whose grades are well above the average of their peers, these being three-year programs with options for individual choices; (4) programs centering around a specific educational worldview, such as democratic education, the "Education Pioneers," the youth-movement graduates program, and anthroposophist education or open education, which is social-community based by nature and trains both for formal and nonformal education; and (5) experimental training programs, such as "Shahaf" and "Nahar" (Hebrew acronyms for multitrack training programs), that are based on partnership between the college, the kindergarten and schools, and the municipalities, conducted with the collaboration of the Experiments and Initiatives Division at the Ministry of Education (Greinfeld, 2010).

## THE IMPACT ON TEACHER EDUCATORS

Over the past thirty years, the educational and institutional processes described thus far, and above all, the academization that the CHE and the Ministry of Education are pursuing, have impacted teacher educators at the colleges of education in four aspects: (1) promotion opportunities; (2) the teacher educators' division into types and subtypes; (3) the resulting severe problems in their professional identity; and (4) the transformation of many of them to researcher teacher educators whose research is mostly unique and qualitative.

## PROMOTION OPPORTUNITIES AND PERCENTAGES OF WORK LOADS OF TEACHER EDUCATORS AT COLLEGES

In the 1960s, the Teachers' Federation founded the "Seminary Teachers Organization," which, during the academization that began in the 1970s, was renamed the "Organization of College and Seminary Teachers." In May 1997, an agreement was signed by the Teachers' Federation and the Ministry of Education. It concerned the opportunities for promotion in the colleges of education and was strongly opposed to the academization steps of the Ministry of Education, the funding entity that was entitled to decide the colleges' fate.

The promotion opportunities proposed differed from those applied in other higher-education institutions: they enabled promotion for people with only a master's degree or more, did not include professorship, and defined restrictive quotas regarding them; tenured lecturers with a workload of no less than 75 percent could be considered for promotion (the vast majority of teacher educators have a smaller workload); the weight of scientific publications was lower than what is accepted in other colleges and universities; and the Teacher Training Division in the Ministry of Education and the Teachers' Federation were stipulated as partners and supervisors of the promotion processes, a situation that is unconscionable in an institution of higher education.

Following the signing of the agreement, which was transformed from an agreement over promotion opportunities into a wage agreement, a substantial protest was leveled by colleges of education, chiefly Beit Berl and Achva colleges, whose lecturers founded the "Organization of Faculty of Academic Colleges for Teacher Education." The organization's struggles against the Ministry of Education and the Teachers' Federation, who were signatories to the agreement, were unsuccessful. The reasons were the teacher educators' powerful desire, over the years, for academic promotion of any kind; the significant salary increases that were awarded; and most particularly the formation of a shortcut promotion track following resolutions by the CHE in 2003 and 2005 regarding the academic structure of the colleges of education. In this framework, the academic councils were now entitled to set up their own appointment committees for the ranks of lecturer and senior lecturer (though without salary increases), and in tandem, nationwide appointment committees of the CHE for the rank of professor at the colleges of education were structured (Hofman, 2012).

## DIVIDING TEACHER EDUCATORS INTO CATEGORIES AND SUBCATEGORIES

A number of doctoral dissertations, research reports, articles, and conference presentations reveal the division of teacher educators into categories and subcategories, as well as the problematic nature inherent in defining their professional identity. The relatively simple division is between teacher educators at universities ("institutions with a research orientation") and at colleges of education ("institutions with a teaching orientation") (Levy-Feldman, 2008; Eckstein, 2009, pp. 84–85).

In the research institutions, the teacher educators are further divided into lecturers from disciplinary faculties, involved indirectly in training, and lecturers from schools of education. The vast majority of these lecturers from the schools of education are part of the tenured faculty, but also include pedagogical mentors—from the various disciplines at the schools of education, in most cases, "external teachers."

At the colleges of education, the basic division is into disciplinary teachers who teach various areas of subject matter, teachers of education subjects, teachers of pedagogy for the teaching of specific disciplines, and comprehensive pedagogical mentors, mainly in the field of early childhood and in elementary schools (Ziv, Katz, Silberstein, & Tamir, 1995; Horin, 2004; Dvir, 2005; Ezer & Mevorach, 2009; Eckstein, 2009, p. 41). Shiloah (2004) studied an intermediate type—the "pedagogical disciplinary mentors"—who, as well as pedagogical courses, also teach subject matter in a college. Eckstein (2009, p. 85) researched lecturers in science at colleges of education, and found a lack of connection, bordering on alienation, between the pedagogical mentor and the disciplinary science lecturer.

Qualitative research that explored how teacher educators in the colleges position themselves in terms of the crisis in teacher education identified a more ramified division: "a management group," people with positions in coordinating, management, and research vis-à-vis "a teaching and training" group comprising lecturers and supervisors. The latter were divided into disciplinary lecturers, emphasizing the importance of knowledge, and pedagogical mentors, who asserted the importance of experience in teaching. Another group, with tertiary degrees, was identified as opposed to the group lacking that degree. At a religious college a difference was found between teachers of religious studies and teachers of secular subjects (Vardi-Rath, Horin, Greensfeld, & Kupferberg, 2010, pp. 99–102, 110).

Bzalel (2004) researched the "status of pedagogical mentors" at Kaye College and found that despite their self-esteem, they are aware that they are near the bottom of the hierarchy of positions at the college. The academization process has greater esteem for disciplinary knowledge and degrees (most pedagogical mentors do not possess a tertiary degree), and less for experience and practical training. In view of all these research studies, it appears that within the "teaching and training group," we can indicate two poles on a continuum: teacher educators who respect and advance scientific knowledge (in most cases, disciplinary lecturers with some from the sphere of education; holders of a tertiary degree; teachers of general subjects in religious colleges; and teacher-researchers) as compared with those for whom the educational and practical training aspects are more important (in most cases, the pedagogical mentors; teachers lacking a PhD; teachers of religious subjects in religious colleges; teachers not engaged in research).

## THE PROBLEMATIC NATURE OF TEACHER EDUCATORS' PROFESSIONAL IDENTITY

Very few research studies have been conducted into teacher educators in Israel and their distinctive professional identity. The meager attention paid to the topic between 1975 and 1990 evidences, among other things, the difficulty in defining their identity (Ben-Peretz, 1990, pp. 13–14). Examining the abstracts of the five international conferences held in Israel under the aegis of the MOFET Institute in 1993, 1996, 1999, 2002, and 2007 leads one to a similar conclusion. It was only at the fifth congress (*Fifth International Conference*, 2007) that time was allocated for the subject "Teacher Education as an Emerging Profession" with subtopics on training and professionalization, the accumulated knowledge of that community of learners, and "Research at the Service of the Profession."

The actual voices of teacher educators in Israel attest to their difficulties in defining their own professional identity (Ziv et al., 1995; Dvir, 2005). Elam (2004) partnered in research on pedagogical mentors at Kaye College, and reported their difficulties as regards their professional identity: "It is a profession that requires 'intuition,' 'experience,' 'the ability to identify needs from the field' . . . professional components that cannot be acquired through conventional studies" (Elam, 2004, p. 93).

Tomer (2000), who studied pedagogical mentoring in teacher education colleges, devoted a detailed chapter of her doctoral dissertation to the question of whether pedagogical mentoring is a job or a profession, and noted the lack of proper training and professionalization of all its aspects among the pedagogical mentors at the colleges, who, as a result, are liable to disappear and be replaced by coaching teachers (pp. 222–227). Tohar and colleagues (2003) investigated the personal stories of lecturers at Kaye College who do not hold mentoring or managerial roles, and reached conclusions that match the other colleges of education in general: "Among the lecturers, perceptions regarding their roles at the college are non-uniform. . . . The professional teachers at the colleges are involved in questions of *belonging*. . . . On the one hand, they have no disciplinary ascription group, yet on the other, they have no other groups they belong to. . . . A central group has dilemmas regarding their endeavors at the college. . . . An organization that has constantly undergone change processes over thirty years has difficulties in creating and defining norms that could provide a permanent backbone at times of change and transformation" (Tohar, Asaf, Kainan, & Shachar, 2003, pp. 19–22).

Kainan and Hoz (2007), also from Kaye College (the latter also from Ben-Gurion University), found other difficulties among teacher educators: they relate to teaching at a college (and in schools) as an occupation with a low social and professional status, lower wages, and lack of professional advancement, and they project this to their students, the trainee teachers. Eckstein (2009), who researched disciplinary lecturers in the exact sciences, identified five types among them: "the scientist," "the educator for values," "the expert in teaching," "the nurturer of learning," and "the submitter to constraints" (who differentiates between what's desirable and what's available), and also remarked on the "lack of the definition of teaching in the colleges as a distinctive profession requiring distinctive skills and training." Beyond having a command of a specific discipline, a person seeking admission to teaching at a college does not need a teaching certificate or teaching experience, not even for promotion (Eckstein, 2009, pp. 215, 237).

Elkad-Lehman and Greensfeld (2002) and Greensfeld and Elkad-Lehman (2002) also note the disparity between the disciplinary knowledge that teacher educators possess, and insufficient knowledge for the purpose of training teachers for the classroom in the same discipline.

## TEACHER EDUCATORS AS RESEARCHERS WHOSE RESEARCH IS MOSTLY UNIQUE AND QUALITATIVE

In recent years, due to the intensifying academization process spurred by the CHE and the Ministry of Education, and taking into account the additional steps for promotion, the identity of "researcher" has now been added to the professional identity of Israel's teacher educators (Kozminsky & Klavir, 2010, p. 16; Ezer & Mevorach, 2009, p. 40; Eckstein, 2009, pp. 45–46). The research emphasis in teacher educators' work began with the request for INSET courses that include keeping up-to-date and tracking research innovations, raised in the Etzioni Committee of the Ministry of Education (1979) and the Dan Committee of the CHE (1981). Ultimately, research activity by teacher educators at colleges of education was institutionalized with the assistance of the MOFET Institute, chiefly through the research unit and research committees that allocate support as incentives for undertaking research or are interested in researching in connection with their promotion (Kfir, Liebman, & Shamai, 1999; Shamai, Kfir, Liebman, & Kainan, 2000; Yogev & Yogev, 2005).

The "think-tank" team about advancing research in the colleges was active from 1998 to 1999 and examined endeavors in this sphere in sixteen out of the eighteen academic colleges as well as in four out of the seven colleges that were in the process of receiving academic recognition. The researchers identified three difficulties for carrying out research: insufficient budgets; lack of expert researchers; and dilemmas concerning the organization of the research activity. A number of prerequisites are essential: long-term planning, the initiative of the head of the college, an advanced academization process, and a sufficiently large college in terms of its research staff and potential resources (Shamai et al., 2000).

The research efforts conducted by teacher educators, examined in two comprehensive studies by Yogev and Yogev (2005) and Fejgin and Tzarfati (2006), engage chiefly with training for teaching, teacher trainees and their educators, professional development, and several themes in education. There are also disciplinary research studies in various fields. Yogev and Yogev (2005) defined the research methods of teachers in general, and of teacher educators in Israel specifically, as "action research," "practitioners' research," "participatory research," and "self-study" by teachers—mostly connected to teacher education, and qualitative and interpretative by nature. Kfir et al. (1999) also mentioned in-house evaluation of a college, its curricula, and endeavors as some of the chief characteristics of research in colleges.

Four research genres connected to the distinctive role of teacher educators at colleges of education are:

- *Forums and "think tanks" of position holders from colleges that produce position papers featuring research.* For example, the forums of education coordinators for early-childhood, elementary, and special education, and coordinators for studies of the sciences, computerized communication, and retraining academics who drafted position papers that were sent to the Implementation Committee of the Ariav Format (Summary of Forums' Activity, 2007). The forums and the research-based position papers that they produced match the varied division of roles at colleges of education: coordinators of age-level tracks; coordinators for studies of certain disciplines; coordinators of instruction-learning methods (study trips, computerized communication, and computer applications); senior executives at the colleges (deans of students, library directors, heads of research units and committees); holders of positions typical of colleges (training coordinators, mentoring course coordinators, coordinators of professional development programs, coordinators of courses for coaching teachers, coordinators of programs for outstanding students) (Glasner, 2006).
- *Research into teacher educators that was carried out by teacher educators.* The doctoral dissertations cited above (Tomer, 2000; Horin, 2004; Shiloah, 2004; Dvir, 2005; Levy-Feldman, 2008) as well as books published by the MOFET Institute about science lecturers (Eckstein, 2009) and lecturers in science and literature (Greensfeld & Elkad-Lehman, 2008) as well as others were all conducted by teacher educators. These studies focused on illustrating the varied and complex roles of teacher educators, particularly those at colleges, but in universities as well.
- *Narrative literary research on teacher educators.* Personal stories of teacher educators, researched by their teacher educator colleagues, have become a widely used research tool (for example, Tohar et al., 2003; Ezer, Millet, & Patkin, 2005; Kainan, Asaf, Hoz, Elam, Bzalel, & Back, 2004; Greensfeld & Elkad-Lehman, 2008). These narrative-literary research-studies deepen engagement with the unique role of the various types of teacher educators and their professional development tracks.
- *Studies published by colleges, and authored by their heads and teams.* Examples of this are the book by Norman (Nisan) Schanin from David Yellin College on *The Academic Development of Teacher Education in Israel: Chapters in the History of David Yellin Teachers College.* (Schanin, 1996); *Tell Me about It: Aspects of Narrative Analysis*, a book edited by Merav Asaf, Erga Heller, Vered Tohar, and Anat Kainan (2000); the book by Anat Kainan et al. (2004) *Pedagogical Tutoring: Social and*

*Cultural Aspects*; the book by Hanna Ezer and Miriam Mevorach (2009), *The Changing Face of Teacher Education: The Story of Change in a Teacher Education College*; the book edited by Esther Yogev and Ruth Zuzovsky of the Kibbutzim College of Education, *Magnifying the Glass: Pedagogical Training under Inspection* (2011), which summarizes the work of their think-tank team that dealt with pedagogic and pedagogic training and supervision.

Three other research genres, relating to ways of organizing research, also typify colleges of education; these "collective" genres derive from their objective difficulties in performing research in conditions inferior to those customary at the universities.

- *Joint research by teacher educators in a single college.* Several such models were found: the closed centralized model in which the majority of research at a college is conducted by a core team of researchers (in most cases, members of the research unit), the centralized model that involves teacher educators and other researchers, and the multi-core model—with several research teams within the same college (Shamai et al., 2000, pp. 157–158; Kozminsky, 2009).
- *An inter-college network of research colleagues.* This kind of network has been in place at the MOFET Institute since 2004, and in 2007 there were five research teams engaged in different aspects of teacher education at colleges, such as: initial training and professional development of teachers; the profile of teachers as reflected in teacher education: a historical perspective; teacher education colleges positioning themselves in an era of change; examining evaluation and training for evaluation in colleges; a comparison between the perception of training for teaching at colleges of education and in universities, from the viewpoint of the clients (supervisors, principals, and coordinators) (Klavir, 2007, pp. 42–73; Kozminsky et al., 2007).
- *Interest groups in qualitative research.* These groups are composed mostly of teacher educators from colleges and are coordinated by the MOFET Institute. Their output attests to their variety: "action research," "narrative research," "the story of a school," "ethnographic research," "text and discourse research," in general, and in "online courses" in particular (Guberman & Spector-Mersel, 2011).

Two genres stem from the colleges' relationships with the educational field surrounding them—in schools, in nearby towns—and in college-based initiatives with the Ministry of Education's participation.

- *School-college partnership research.* This type of research includes setting up professional development schools (PDS) together with the college, and numerous partnerships between schools and colleges where teacher trainees gain experience have yielded many research studies undertaken by teacher educators, in which they summarized and analyzed a range of collaborative models. These studies are based on the world research literature but develop and fine-tune it by relying on the Israeli teacher educators' experience. Their research method is "grounded theory," integrated with other theories. For example, the role of "coordinator" of collaboration at the college and at the schools was defined and institutionalized, and the role of pedagogical mentor was fine-tuned; a range of college-wide collaborations was structured and researched as well as a collaboration between a college and a nearby town; "School-based curriculum development" (SBCD) programs were integrated in some collaborations; some collaborations established a process of reform and change in schools (Silberstein, Ben-Peretz, & Greinfeld, 2006).
- *Research on college-based trials of alternative teacher education, with collaboration from the Ministry of Education's Experiments and Initiatives Division.* These are the experimental-democratic programs at the Kibbutzim College of Education (Yuval, 2007); "Shahaf"—an active educational collaboration between all the educational actors at Kaye College (Barak & Gidron, 2009); "Nahar"—at Levinsky College (Margolin, 2010); as well as an experiment by the Training Division itself in working with outstanding students (Klavir, Cohen, Abadi, & Greinfeld, 2009). What is common to all these experiments at the colleges is that they are conducted and researched by the teacher educators themselves as "action research" of various types; they are based on differing formats of collaborations between the college and the field; and above all, they display an "ecological approach," with wide-ranging attention to everything that trainee teachers learn.

The two final genres expand beyond the colleges and the field, and touch on academic research in general.

- *Research into instruction-learning methods and training, in general, and in the context of teacher education specifically.* It is only natural that research by teacher educators in the colleges of education engages with these methods, as reflected, for example, in the anthology of articles written and edited by teacher educators (Margolin & Zellermayer, 2005; Barak & Gidron, 2009). Another example is the anthology *Magnifying the Glass* (Yogev & Zuzovsky, 2011) in which one section is devoted to "Training Models Based on Educational Worldviews," and another to "Unique Practices in Training" (these include "reflection," a "reading

travel-diary," "developing personal responsibility for learning," "personal stories," and "self-learning").
- *Publications on research approaches and genres of qualitative research.* The book *Crossroads in Educational Research: Researchers' Deliberations* (Lidor, Fresko, Ben-Peretz, & Silberstein, 2005) is an example of a collection of research approaches presented by teacher educators at colleges (and a minority from universities) with the aim of "shedding light on the 'black box' of the process of planning research-studies and their implementation . . . [at] central intersections of the research . . . choosing the research topic and the questions it will examine . . . [and] choosing the research method." (Lidor et al., p. 7). Edited by two teacher educators and two university-based experts in the field, the work is divided into research approaches to questions of "instruction and learning," and "training teachers and professional development of teachers."

Also published by the Klil Books series at the MOFET Institute are books written and researched by teacher educators on defined research genres: *Narrative Research* (Tuval-Mashiach & Spector-Mersel, 2010) in which eleven of the twenty-one authors are teacher educators at colleges; *Action Research* (Levy, 2006) where the editor and ten college faculty members are among the twenty-one authors, and *Ways of Writing Qualitative Research* (Shlasky & Alpert, 2007). Teacher educators at colleges serve also as editors, and played central roles in a series of research books published by Ben-Gurion University. The book *Tell Me about It: Aspects of Narrative Analysis* (Asaf et al., 2000) was written and edited by a group of eight women from one college of education, the majority of them teacher educators; *Text and Discourse Analysis: A RASHOMON of Research Methods* (Kupferberg, 2000) was edited by a professor at a college of education, and seven of the nine authors are teacher educators at colleges of education, five of whom are faculty members of Levinsky College of Education.

Teacher educators have been affected by change regarding steps toward promotion and the percentages of their work loads, the substantial differentiation that is found within their tasks, the problematic nature of their professional identity, and the transformation of many of them into researching teacher educators whose unique and qualitative research genres are in the field of teaching-learning and training but also in academic research in general. The nature of teacher education in Israel has developed over time, namely in view of the academization process of teacher education.

## NOTE

1. The author wishes to thank the staff of the intercollegiate database and the publishing house of MOFET Institute for their substantial help in collating material for this chapter.

# REFERENCES


Alternative training programs (2010). *MOFET Bulletin, 41,* 31–33. [In Hebrew: Tochniot ha-toar hasheni (M.Ed.) Bamichlalot ha'akademiot lechinuch—bimat diyun].

Ariav, T. (2008). Training for teaching: A snapshot of the situation worldwide and in Israel, with a view to the future. In D. Kfir & T. Ariav (Eds.), *The crisis in teacher education: Reasons, problems and possible solutions* (pp. 19–55). Jerusalem & Tel Aviv: Van Leer & Hakibbutz Hameuhad. [In Hebrew: Hahachshara lehora'a: Tmunat hamatzav baolam uba'aretz vemabat la'atid. In Mashber hahora'a: likrat hachsharat morim metukenet].

Ariav, T. (2011). The crisis in teaching: Origins, processes, and solutions. In D. Kfir (Ed.) *A fateful search: Israeli society in search of good teachers* (pp. 7–21). Tel Aviv: MOFET Institute. [In Hebrew: Mashber hahora'a: Mekorot, tahalichim vepitronot. In Chipus gorali—hachevra beIsrael mechapeset morim tovim].

Asaf, M., Heller, E., Tohar, V., & Kainan, A. (Eds.) (2000). *Tell me about it: Aspects of narrative analysis*. Beersheva: Ben-Gurion University of the Negev Press. [In Hebrew: Ma hasipur shelcha? Modelim lenituach nerativim].

Banks, J. A. (2008). Diversity and citizenship education in global times. In J. Arthur, I. Davies, & C. Hahn (Eds.), *The Sage handbook of education for citizenship and democracy.* Los Angeles: Sage.

Barak, J., & Gidron, A. (2009). *Active collaborative education: A story of teacher education.* Tel Aviv, Beersheva and Jerusalem: MOFET Institute, Kaye Academic College of Education, The Ministry of Education—The Teacher Training Department and the Experiments and Initiatives Division. [In Hebrew: SHAHAF—Shituf Chinuchi Pail: Sipur shel hachsharat morim.].

Ben-Peretz, M. (1990). Research into training teachers in Israel: Topics, methods, and findings. *Dapim, 10*, 9–24. [In Hebrew: Mechkarim behachsharat morim beIsraek: Nos'im, shitot vemimtza'im].

Ben-Peretz, M. (Chairperson) (2001). *Training teachers in Israel for the turns of time: Report of the Committee for the Examination of Teacher Training in Israel.* Jerusalem: Ministry of Education. [In Hebrew: Hachsharat hamorim beIsrael betmurot hazman: din vecheshbon hava'ada lebdikat hachsharat hamorim beIsral.].

Bzalel, Y. (2004). Important unconsidered: The status of pedagogic supervisors in colleges. In A. Kainan, M. Asaf, R. Hoz, N. Elam, Y. Bzalel, & S. Back, *Pedagogical tutoring: Social and cultural aspects* (pp. 47–58). Beersheva: Ben-Gurion University of the Negev Press. [In Hebrew: Chashuvot lo nechshavot: maamad hamadrichot hapedagogiot bamichlala. In Mi at hamadricha hapedagogit? Hebetim tarbuti'im vechevrati'im].

Chen, M., & Gottlieb, E. (1989). Towards a new era in training teachers in Israel. In Y. Danilov (Ed.) *Planning education policy in Israel: Position papers and resolutions of the Standing Committee of the Pedagogic Secretariat* (pp. 47–70). Jerusalem: Ministry of Education and Culture, the Pedagogic Secretariat. [In Hebrew: Likrat idan chadash behachsharat morim beIsrael. In Tichnun mediniut hachinuch beIsrael: Niyarot emda vehachlatot vaadat hakeva shel hamazkirut hapedagogit].

Dan, J. (Chairperson) (1981). *A guiding model for the curriculum for the B.Ed. degree*. Jerusalem: Council for Higher Education, the Standing Committee for Academic Tracks in Institutions for training Teaching Employees. [In Hebrew: Degem manche letochnit limudim latoar "Boger Hora'a"].

Dror, Y. (2008). The policy of training teachers and educators in Israel: What can be learned from the past and present committees and position papers regarding the future? In D. Kfir & T. Ariav (Eds.), *The crisis in teacher education: Reasons, problems, and possible solutions* (pp. 56–90). Jerusalem & Tel Aviv: Van Leer & Hakibbutz Hameuchad. [In Hebrew: Mediniut hachsharat ovdey hahora'a vehachinuch beIsrael: Ma nitan lilmod mehava'adot veniyarot haemda beavar ubahove beyachas la'atid? In Mashber hahora'a: Likrat hachsharat morim metukenet].

Dror, Y. (2011). From a private-sectorial system at the time of the Yishuv to supervised privatization and its reinforcement after the establishment of the state. *Dor LeDor [Studies in the History of Jewish Education], 39,* 119–170. [In Hebrew: Mima'arechet pratit migzarit betkufat haishuv lehafrata mevukeret veha'amakata bemedinat Israel].

Dvir, N. (2005). *Pedagogical mentors: Identities, knowledge and pratices in the teaching of teachers.* Dissertation submitted for the Doctor of Philosophy degree. Jerusalem: The Hebrew University. [In Hebrew: Madrichot pedagogyot: zehuyot, praktikot veyeda behavnayat profesiyat hahora'a].

Eckstein, L. (2009). *Science lecturers in teacher education colleges: Pieces in a puzzle.* Tel Aviv: MOFET Institute. [In Hebrew: Martzim lemada'im bamichlalot lechinuch: psifas shel tipusim].

Elam, N. (2004). Discussion. In A. Kainan, M. Asaf, R. Hoz, N. Elam, Y. Bzalel, & S. Back (Eds.), *Pedagogical tutoring: Social and cultural aspects* (pp. 91–101). Beersheva: Ben-Gurion University of the Negev Press. [In Hebrew: Mi at hamadricha hapedagogit? Hebetim tarbuti'im vechevrati'im].

Elkad-Lehman, I., & Greensfeld, H. (2002). I think "Science," you think "Literature": Let's talk about it. *Theory into Practice in Curriculum Planning, 17,* 59–74. [In Hebrew: Choshvim mada, choshvim sifrut: Bou nesocheach al ze].

Elkana, Y. (Chairperson) (1988). *A report of the international visiting committee to review The Schools of Education.* Jerusalem: The Planning and Grants Committee of the Council for Higher Education.

Etzioni, M. (Chairperson) (1979). *Report of the State Committee for the Examination of the Status of the Teacher and the Teaching Profession.* Special Bulletin of the General-Manager, III (1980). Jerusalem: Ministry of Education and Culture. [In Hebrew: Din vecheshbon hava'ada hamamlachtit lebdikat ma'amad hamore umiktzoa hahora'a.].

Ezer, H., & Mevorach, M. (2009). *The changing face of teacher education: The story of change in a teacher education college.* Beersheva: Ben-Gurion University of the Negev Press. [In Hebrew: Pane'a hamishtanim shel hachsharat hamorim: sipura shel michlala lechinuch].

Ezer, H., Millet, S., & Patkin, D. (2005). Revealing the multicultural aspects of curricula in two teacher-training institutions. In R. Lidor, B. Fresko, M. Ben-Peretz, & M. Silberstein (Eds.), *Crossroads in educational research: Researchers' deliberations* (pp. 150–180). Tel Aviv: MOFET Institute. [In Hebrew: Chasifat hahebet harav tarbuti betochniot halimudim beshney mosadot lehachsharat morim].

Fejgin, N., & Tzarfati, I. (2006). What do teacher educators research at teacher training colleges in Israel? *Shvilei Mehkar, 13,* 82–85. [In Hebrew: Ma chokrim morey hamorim bamichlalot lehachsharat morim beIsrael?].

*Fifth International Conference: Teacher education at a crossroads—conference abstracts.* (2007, June). Tel Aviv & Beersheva: MOFET Institute and Kaye Academic College of Education. [In Hebrew: Hakenes habeinleumi hachamishi: hachsharat morim al parashat drachim, sefer hataktzirim]

Glasner, R. (2006). Forums. *MOFET Bulletin, 24,* 31–32. [In Hebrew: Forumim].

Greensfeld, H., & Elkad-Lehman, I. (2002). Science and Literature: Two disciplines with disparate ways of thinking? *Megamot, 42*(1), 58–82. [In Hebrew: Mada'im vesafrut: shtey distziplinot shonot mibchinat darkey hachashiva-haomnam?].

Greensfeld, H., & Elkad-Lehman, I. (2008). *On walking down paths and reaching the crossroads: Life stories about teachers' professional development and conceptual changes.* Tel Aviv: MOFET Institute. [In Hebrew: Bashvilim, badrachim, batsmatim: sipurim al tahalichey hitpatchut miktzo'it ve'al shinuy tfisati].

Greinfeld, N. (2010). Various tracks for entering the teaching profession. *MOFET Institute Bulletin, 41,* 8–11. [In Hebrew: Maslulim shonim leknisa lemiktzo'a hahora'a].

Guberman, A. & Spector-Mersel, G. (Eds.) (2011). The interest group in qualitiative research. *Shvilei Mehkar, 17,* 9–163. [In Hebrew: Kvutzat ha'inyan bemechkar eichutani].

Hofman, A. (2012). The Teachers' Union Association and the teacher educators: The history of a professional struggle. In R. Klavir & L. Kozminsky (Eds.), *The construction of professional identity—processes of teacher education and professional development* (pp. 49-78). Tel Aviv: MOFET Institute. [In Hebrew: Histadrut Hamorim umorei hamorim: Toldotav shel ma'avak miktzo'i. In Havnayat zehut miktzo'it—tahalichei hachshara upituach miktzo'i shel morim beIsrael].

Hofman, A., & Kfir, D. (2012). Who shapes the teacher training? In R. Klavir & L. Kozminsky (Eds.), *The construction of professional identity–processes of teacher education and professional development* (pp. 13-25). Tel Aviv: MOFET Institute.[In Hebrew: Mi meatzev et hahachshara lehora'a? In Havnayat zehut miktzo'it–tahalichei hachshara upituach miktzo'i shel morim beIsrael].

Hofman, A., & Niederland D. (2010). The image of teachers from the perspective of teacher training: An historical glance. *Dapim*, 49, 43-86. [In Hebrew: Demut hamoreh bere'i hachsharat hamorim: Mabat histori].

Hofman, A., & Niederland, D. (2012). The autonomy of the academic colleges of education. In R. Klavir & L. Kozminsky (Eds.), *The construction of professional identity–processes of teacher education and professional development* (pp. 242-274). Tel Aviv: MOFET Institute. [In Hebrew: Ha'otonomya shel hamichlalot ha'academi'iot lechinuch. In Havnayat zehut miktzo'it–tahalichei hachshara upituach miktzo'i shel morim beIsrael].

Horin, A. (2004). *Educational philosophies and epistemological beliefs of teacher educators and their reflection in the instruction process.* Dissertation submitted for the Doctor of Philosophy degree. Tel Aviv: Tel Aviv University. [In Hebrew: Hashkafot chinuchiyot ve'emunot epistemologiyot shel morey morim vebituyan betahalich hahora'a].

Kainan, A., Asaf, M., Hoz, R., Elam, N., Bzalel, Y., & Back, S. (2004). *Pedagogical tutoring: Social and cultural aspects.* Beersheva: Ben-Gurion University of the Negev Press. [In Hebrew: Mi at hamadricha hapedagogit? Hebetim tarbuti'im vechevrati'im].

Kainan, A., & Hoz, R. (2007). The contribution of a teacher's college to social reproduction. In *The Fifth International Conference: Teacher Education at a Crossroads—conference abstracts* (p. 122). Tel Aviv & Beersheva: MOFET Institute and Kaye Academic College of Education.

Kfir, D., & Ariav, T. (2004). The reform in teacher education: A partial process and its results. *Megamot, 43*(1), 170–194. [In Hebrew: Hareforma behachsharat morim: mahalach chelki vetotzotav].

Kfir, D., Ariav, T., Fejgin, N., & Liebman, Z. (1997). *The academization of the teaching profession and teacher education in Israel.* Jerusalem: Magnes Press. [In Hebrew: Ha'academizatzia shel hahachshara lehora'a veshel miktzoa hahora'a].

Kfir, D., Liebman, Z., & Shamai, S. (1999). The role of research activities in academic colleges of education. *Dapim, 28,* 8–16. [In Hebrew: Tafkide'a vetrumata shel hapeilut hamechkarit bamichlalot ha'academiot lehachsharat morim].

Klavir, R. (2007). A research network at the MOFET Institute. *Shvilei Mechkar*, *14*, 42–73. [In Hebrew: Reshet amitei hamechkar bemachon MOFET].

Klavir, R., Cohen, N., Abadi, R., & Greinfeld, N. (Eds.) (2009). *Vision, theory and practice: The program for excellent students in Israeli Colleges of Education.* Tel Aviv: MOFET Institute. [In Hebrew: Halacha, ma'ase vechazon: hachsharat studentim metzuyanim lehora'a bamichlalot ha'akademiot lechinuch].

Kozminsky, L., Back, S., Klavir, R., Kfir, D., Levin-Rozalis, M., Kupferberg, I., Kaniel, S., & Niederland, D. (2007). New faces in the mirror: A research network on teacher education Israel 2007. In *The Fifth International Conference: Teacher Education at a Crossroads—conference abstracts* (p. 131). Tel Aviv and Beersheva: MOFET Institute and Kaye Academic College of Education.

Kozminsky, L. (Ed.) (2009). Joint Research. *Shvilei Mehkar*, *16*, 13–97. [In Hebrew: Mechkar meshutaf].

Kozminsky, L., and Klavir, R. (2010). The construction of the professional identity of teachers and teacher educators in a changing reality. *Dapim, 49,* 11–42. [In Hebrew: Havnayat zehut miktzo'it shel morim veshel morey morim bemetziut mishtana].

Kupferberg, I. (2000). *Text and discourse analysis: A RASHOMON of research methods* (2000) Beersheva: Ben-Gurion University of the Negev Press. [In Hebrew: Cheker hatext vehasiach: rashumon shel shitot mechkar].

Levy, D. (Ed.) (2006). *Action research: Theory and practice.* Tel Aviv: MOFET Institute. [In Hebrew: Mechkar peula: halacha vema'ase].

Levy-Feldman, I. (2008). *Perception of the accomplished teacher among teacher educators in 'research oriented' and 'teaching oriented' institutes.* Dissertation submitted for the Doctor of Philosophy degree. Tel Aviv: Tel Aviv University. [In Hebrew: Tfisat dmut hamore bekerev machshirey morim bemosadot im 'orientatzia mechkarit' vemosadot im 'orientatzia hora'atit'.].

Lidor, R., Fresko, B., Ben-Peretz, M., & Silberstein, M. (Eds.) (2005). *Crossroads in educational research: Researchers' deliberations*. Tel Aviv: MOFET Institute. [In Hebrew: Tsmatim bemechkar chinuchi: shikouley da'at shel chokrim].

Liebman, Z. (2011). Who "supervises" teacher training? Academic freedom and supervision mechanisms over academic institutions for teacher training in Israel. In D. Kfir (Ed.) *A fateful search: Israeli society seeking good teachers* (pp. 83–90). Tel Aviv: MOFET Institute. [In Hebrew: Mi 'mefakeach' al hachsharat hamorim? Chofesh academi vemangenoney pikuach al hamosadot ha'academi'im lehachsharat morim beIsrael. In Chipus goarli: hachevra beIsrael mechapeset morim tovim].

Margolin, A. (Ed.) (2010). *Crossing the beyond: A multi-track teacher education program—an ongoing discourse*. Tel Aviv and Jerusalem: MOFET Institute, Levinsky College of Education, The Ministry of Education—The Teacher Training Department and the Experiments and Initiatives Division. [In Hebrew: Me'ever laNH"R (Nativ hachshara rav-masluli)—Hachsharat morim kerav siach].

Margolin, I., & Zellermayer, M. (Eds.)(2005). *In the first person: Self-studies by participants of school-college partnership*. Tel Aviv: MOFET Institute. [In Hebrew: Beguf rishon: amitut michlala-sade—kovetz mechkarim atzmi'im].

Nir, A., & Inbar, D. (2004). Israel: From egalitarianism to competition. In I. C. Rotberg (Ed.), *Balancing change and tradition in global education reform* (pp. 207–228). Lanham, Maryland: Scarecrow Press.

Schanin, N. (1996). *The academic development of teacher education in Israel: Chapters in the history of David Yellin Teachers College*. Jerusalem: Magnes Press. [In Hebrew: Hatahalich ha'academi shel hachsharat morim beIsrael—prakim betoldot hamichlala lechinuch al shem David Yellin].

Shagrir, L. (2007). *Teacher education curricula in relation to changes in Israeli society, Dor LeDor, 28*. Tel Aviv: MOFET Institute & Tel Aviv University. [In Hebrew: Tochniot linudim bahachshara lehora'a bezika leshinuyim bachevra haIsraelit].

Shagrir, L., & Iram, Y. (2005). Demographic changes in Israeli society and teacher training curricula: A content analysis and a comparative historical analysis. In R. Lidor, B. Fresko, M. Ben-Peretz, & M. Silberstein (Eds.), *Crossroads in educational research: Researchers; deliberations* (pp. 301–322). Tel Aviv: MOFET Institute. [In Hebrew: Shinuim demographi'im bachevra haIsraelit vetochniot limudim behachsharat morim:nituach tochen venituach histori mashve. In Tzmatim bemechkar chinuchi—Shikuley da'at shel chokrim].

Shamai, S., Kfir, D., Liebman, Z., & Kainan, A. (2000). Factors affecting research activities and research culture at colleges of education. *Dapim, 30,* 150–167. [In Hebrew: Gormin hamashpi'im al hapeilut hamechkarit vetarbut hamechkar bamichlalot lehachsharat morim].

Shiloah, Y. (2004). *Teaching conceptions held by disciplinary teachers and disciplinary-pedagogical instructors in a teachers college*. Dissertation submitted for the Doctor of Philosophy degree. Jerusalem: The Hebrew University. [In Hebrew: Tfisot shel morim distziplinari'im vemadrichim pedagogi'im distziplinari'im legabey hahora'a bamichlala lehachsharat morim].

Shlasky, S., & Alpert, B. (2007). *Ways of writing qualitative research*. Tel Aviv: MOFET Institute. [In Hebrew: Drachim bektivat mechkar eichutani].

Silberstein, M., Ben-Peretz, M., & Greinfeld, N. (2006). *A new trend in teacher-training programs: Collaboration between colleges and schools—the Israeli story*. Tel Aviv: MOFET Institute. [In Hebrew: Megama chadasha betochniot hahachshara shel morim: shutafut bein michlalot lebein batey sefer—hasipur haIsraeli].

*Summary of Forums' Activity* (2007). Tel Aviv: MOFET Institute. [In Hebrew: Forumim, sikum peilut 2007].

Tohar, V., Asaf, M., Kainan, A., & Shachar, R. (2003). *Lecturing at a college: The personal story as key to learning about lecturers' world—a research report*. Beersheva: Kaye College, the Research & Evaluation Unit. [In Hebrew: Lihiyot martze bemichlala: hasipur haishi kemafteach lehakarat olamam shel martzim, doch mechkar].

Tomer, O. (2000). *Pedagogical mentoring in colleges of teacher education: The relationships between their role conception and supervisory style, and the supervision setting.* Dissertation submitted for the Doctor of Philosophy degree. Beersheva: Ben-Gurion University of the Negev. [In Hebrew: Madrichim pedagogi'im bamichlala lechinuch: hazikot shebein tfisot hatafkid shelahem vesignon hahadrach shelahem].

Tuinman, J. (1995). Rescuing teacher education: A view from the hut with bananas. In M. F. Widen & P. P. Grimmett (Eds.), *Changing times in teacher education: Restructuring or reconceptualization?* (pp. 105–116). London: Falmer Press.

Tuval-Mashiach, R., & Spector-Mersel, G. (Eds.) (2010). *Narrative research: Theory, creation and interpretation.* Tel Aviv & Jerusalem: MOFET Institute & Magnes Press. [In Hebrew: Mechkar nerativi: teoria, yetzira veparshanut].

Vardi-Rath, E., Horin, A., Greensfeld, H., and Kupferberg, I. (2010). Teacher education colleges at a crossroads: Teacher educators position themselves in an era of crisis. *Dapim, 49*, 87–118. [In Hebrew: Michlalot lehachsharat morim al parashat drachim: morey morim trmatzvim et atzmam be'et mashber].

Yogev, A. (2000). The stratification of Israeli universities: Implications for higher education policy. *Higher Education, 40,* 183–201.

Yogev, E. (2011). Back to the future: The dialectic of training educators in the Kibbutzim College of Education over time. In E. Yogev & R. Zuzovsky (Eds.), *Magnifying the glass: Pedagogical training under inspection* (pp. 15–47). Tel Aviv: Hakibbutz Hameuhad, MOFET Institute & the Kibbutzim College of Education. [In Hebrew: Bechazara la'atid: hadialektika shel hachsharat mechanchim beseminar hakibutzim betmurut hazman. In Hadracha bemabat choker].

Yogev, E., & Zuzovsky (Eds.) (2011). *Magnifying the glass: Pedagogical training under inspection.* Tel Aviv: Hakibbutz Hameuhad, MOFET Institute & the Kibbutzim College of Education. [In Hebrew: Hadracha bemabat choker].

Yogev, S., & Yogev, A. (2005). Teacher educators as researchers: Research in the colleges of education as opposed to research in the universities. *Dapim, 40,* 90–107. [In Hebrew: Morey morim kechokrim: hamechkar bamichlalot lechinuch leumat hamechkar buniversitaot].

Yuval, A. (Ed.) (2007). *Democracy in action.* Tel Aviv and Jerusalem: Seminar Hakibbutzim Teachers College, The Ministry of Education—The Experiments and Initiatives Division and the Teacher Training Department. [In Hebrew: Democratia bepeula:hatochnit hanisuyit-hademokratit bemichlelet seminar hakibutzim: hashanim harishonot].

Ziv, S., Katz, P., Silberstein, M., & Tamir, P. (1995). *Characteristics of the pedagogic supervisors' work in Israel's teacher training system: Research report.* Tel Aviv: MOFET Institute. [In Hebrew: Meafyeney avodatam shel hamadrichim hapedagogi'im bema'arechet hachsharat hamorim beIsrael: doch mechkar].

# *Chapter Four*

# Teacher Educators in the Midst of Scottish Educational Reform

Sally Brown

## SCOTTISH EDUCATION IN TRANSITION

Teachers' education is necessarily part of the system in which they are trained, and closely linked to what is going on in that system, even though they may spend their teaching careers in other parts of the world. In the past, as Scottish schooling has been reformed, individual teacher education institutions have been expected to work out for themselves how their practices should respond to the changes, and then get on with it. In the middle of 2012, things are different. Scottish education is undergoing substantial national changes, *including* those for teacher education. Teacher education in Scotland finds itself, therefore, in the throes of reinvention in the midst of at least four other kinds of key change or uncertainty that comprise a major transition in Scottish education. These reforms will take several years to implement at a time of financial stringency, so the focus in this chapter has to be on the challenges of the innovations and concerns about their progress, rather than evaluation of their successes.

## FOUR ASPECTS OF CHANGE

First, there are far-reaching *curriculum and assessment* innovations in school education. The new Scottish Government (May 2011), with Scottish Nationalists the majority party, is introducing the *Curriculum for Excellence (CfE)* for young people from age three to eighteen. The ideas behind this development emerged seven years ago,[1] imply significant changes in the educational culture, are backed by all political parties and many educationalists, but are still at the work-in-progress stage. Inevitably, such a marked curriculum change requires correspondingly substantial innovations in the assessment and qualifications system for young people in the years up to the school-leaving age[2] and this adds to the "new" features of education to be taken account of by teacher education.

Secondly, for *teacher education itself* there are significant uncertainties about funding for student teachers combined with recurrent concerns about possible freezes in the government-controlled numbers of teacher education places and/or reductions in the number of teacher education institutions. However, such changes are uncertain and a wide-ranging review of teacher education with recommendations for the future has been undertaken.[3] This has been largely welcomed by the universities; the General Teaching Council for Scotland (GTCS), which is responsible for teaching standards; the Scottish government; and teachers—an unusually wide and positive consensus.

Thirdly, for *teachers themselves*, a government-commissioned review of their terms and conditions of employment has been published[4] (the McCormac Report), and public sector pension rights are being revised. This coincides with concerns about the recruitment of beginning teachers into schools; recent figures suggest only 20 percent of the newly qualified are able to find permanent full-time posts. And for those with experience and ambition, the Chartered Teacher programs, introduced in recent years to enhance teachers' professionalism and pay, although initially welcomed, have now been seen as less than effective, indicating both financial constraints on local authorities (the employers of teachers) and, perhaps, a sense of anti-intellectualism in public thinking about teaching.

And fourthly, a crucial *systemic change* has arisen from the Scottish government's decision to merge *Her Majesty's Inspectorate for Education (HMIE)* with *Learning and Teaching Scotland (LTS)* to form *Education Scotland* from 1 July 2011.[5] The significance of this merger stems from the very different responsibilities of the two bodies. The former has had a role of inspection and assessment of educational capacity. In the past, HMIE's "overviews" have been powerful in policy terms, but also independent of and sometimes uncomfortable for government. LTS, in contrast, has responsibility for building and supporting curriculum and learning as directed by government. It is argued that this merger has fundamentally reduced the independence of the Inspectorate and undermined its ability to offer detached evaluations of the developments. Furthermore, there is little evidence of any other plans for independent evaluations of, or proper research on, the extensive educational changes.

The first and second of these areas of change have significant and direct impact on thinking about, and development of, teacher education, and this chapter aims to illuminate some of the ways they can be expected to influence practice for the future. The effects of the third and fourth may be less direct, but constitute an agitated background. Before discussing details, however, we should look at the nature of the existing teacher education that provides the starting point for what many believe are to be profound changes in Scotland's educational culture.

## SCOTTISH TEACHER EDUCATION OF RECENT YEARS—RIPE FOR CHANGE

A paper (Menter et al., 2010)[6] commissioned by the Scottish government, provides a very good overview of strengths and weaknesses in the Scottish system and comparisons with practice and research elsewhere. Since 1984, all entrants to primary and secondary school teaching have been graduates of degree programs (Marker, 2000). These qualifications have been achieved mostly at colleges of education, either through four-year BEd vocational programs (mainly primary teachers) or one-year postgraduate vocational diplomas (PGDE) after completion of university academic degrees. A minority of secondary teachers, however, have followed concurrent degrees at one university (Stirling), comprising studies of academic disciplines alongside professional education, and an even smaller group have followed part-time or distance-learning pathways.

In the 1990s, initial teacher education (ITE) moved firmly from the colleges of education into the Scottish universities (Kirk, 2003), with a few online and distance-learning developments, all sustaining traditional approaches of curricular studies, professional studies, and school experience (Hulme and Menter, 2008; Christie, 2008). Schoolteachers, however, have played rather minor roles in the mentoring and assessment of student teachers in comparison with some school-based teacher education developments in England.

On the one hand, developments such as Chartered Teacher programs initially looked promising, and the induction year for beginning teachers entering Scottish schools, which guarantees a paid year of teaching, protects professional development time, and provides support through mentoring, has been widely admired (OECD, 2007) On the other hand, continuing professional development (CPD) has generally been seen as in need of improvement with existing approaches frequently regarded as costly but ineffective in impact. The improvements needed imply more *career-long* approaches to teacher education, with closer collaborative partnerships among schools, universities, and local authorities, and a firmer focus on development, mentoring support, and research. And even the respected induction year could be improved by enabling newly qualified teachers to benefit from more continued contact with universities.

As the twenty-first century progressed, the focus of thinking moved to the enhancement of teachers' professionalism and status through improvement of their knowledge base and the introduction of standards frameworks for student teachers at the end of initial education, at full registration, for chartered teacher status and for headship (Doherty and McMahon, 2007). These standards, articulated by the GTCS, relate to the understanding, skills, values and commitments expected of teachers.[7] Notions of the professional teacher as effective, reflective, inquiring, and transformative have influenced official guidance on teaching (e.g., McCrone, 2000: *A Teaching Profession for the 21st Century*) and the school curriculum (*Curriculum for Excellence*, see note 1). The latter looks to develop four "capacities" in each young person as a *successful learner*, *confident individual*, *responsible citizen*, and *effective contributor*. Teacher education is expected to respond to, and enable the achievement of, these aspirations.

## THE CURRICULUM FOR EXCELLENCE (CFE) AND ASSOCIATED QUALIFICATIONS

### Curriculum Change

This school curriculum is moving away from traditional "subjects" with their disciplinary materials, prescriptive advice, and syllabuses. It envisages the inclusion of interdisciplinary work that focuses on real-life issues, much more autonomy for teachers and emphases on active learning, discussion, debate, and critical thinking. The substantive areas around which the curriculum is organized are: expressive arts, health and well-being, languages, mathematics, religious and moral education, sciences, social studies, and technologies.

The *CfE* has strong support from all the political parties in the Scottish Parliament and frequently is described as the most significant reform for a generation. Many argue that it is not a curriculum in the usual sense, but comprises starkly new teaching methods that must respond to a structure of identified "experiences and outcomes" rather than the traditional objectives, syllabus, and activities. There is an expectation that if the aims of this development to enable young people to develop the four central "capacities" are achieved, then twenty-first-century Scotland will be well served.

However, while the general philosophy of the curricular changes is seen by many as valuable, there have been serious questions about inadequacies of the implementation strategy, lack of attention to knowledge or proper pedagogical regard for the disciplines, and opaqueness of some of the proposals. For example:

- so far the meaning of interdisciplinary study seems to be conceptualized only in simplistic ways;
- historians are concerned that their subject's inclusion in social studies may mean that it is not taught by historians;
- computer scientists regret a continuing tendency to teach information technology but without proper inclusion of computer science;
- some parents are claiming bewilderment at the language used in children's reports.

Criticisms of the implementation express concerns about the absence of specialist leadership in its management, particularly the lack of involvement of those with classroom knowledge in the fundamental decision-making processes that have been dominated by civil servants. At later stages, however, groups with appropriate expertise have been brought together to prepare "excellence reports." But it is the dearth of proper planning and resourcing for CPD, together with totally inadequate independent monitoring of the learning that emerges from the new curriculum, that have been among the most serious concerns. In any educational development cries about insufficient levels of resource available to support the innovations are always heard; in times of acute financial constraints such as currently experienced by the UK, they are particularly evident.

## Changes in Assessment and Qualifications

Major challenges for teachers following the introduction of CfE are the uncertainties about assessments' structures, content, modes, and timing for new national qualifications in 2013–2014. From the point of view of young people entering teacher education or other university programs, something like the existing system based on awards of "Highers" and "Advanced Highers" will still be in place, although these are currently under revision (a second revision is likely as CfE develops to produce what education chatter refers to as "CfE Highers and Advanced Highers" for 2014–2016.)

At the complex level below this, Scotland's current national qualifications of Standard Grade General or Credit and Intermediate 1 or 2 will be replaced by National 4 and 5 (with other changes to lower Foundation and Access levels). Course specifications for the new assessments and qualifications are published by the Scottish Qualifications Authority (SQA).[8] It is proposed that the schools and local authorities will make local decisions about the number, range, and timing of qualifications. Concerns have been expressed by schools and universities, however, about how account will be taken of the inevitable diversity of practice across schools and regions, and whether the arrangements in place will lead to reduction in the currently valued breadth of the curriculum in Scottish secondary schools.

## "Teaching Scotland's Future"—Review of Teacher Education

The review of teacher education in Scotland, *Teaching Scotland's Future* (Donaldson, 2011), was published in December 2010 with a remit covering primary and secondary teaching and offering fifty recommendations "to build the professional capacity of our teachers and ultimately to improve the learning of our young people in Scotland" (p. iii). It received a warm reception and the universities' Scottish Teacher Education Committee (STEC) has particularly welcomed its key recommendations for university involvement in the *career-long* education of teachers. The government's response to the report[9] has also been remarkably positive, if somewhat bureaucratic, and this has placed the local authorities and the universities in relatively good positions to influence the implementation of new approaches.

A new National Partnership Group (NPG) has been formed as the locus for decisions about where responsibility lies for implementation of the report's broad recommendations. The group is cochaired by the local authorities' Association of Directors of Education (ADES), STEC, and the Scottish government. The implementation process, however, is a different animal from the traditional approach to the introduction of a more or less prescribed program and it might be better construed as action research and development. The role of the civil servants, representing the government on NPG, is difficult to forecast, not least because they lack professional teaching experience and there has been significant impact on continuity from changes in personnel. The NPG has very recently produced a report with recommendations to which the government has responded[10], and a new National Implementation Board to oversee the developments in teacher education has been established.[11]

Teacher educators have not been centrally involved in CfE developments, but are expected to take responsibility for preparing those who undertake the challenging innovations. There are inadequacies in teacher educators' own CPD, and academics, especially scientists, have concerns about the intellectual knowledge and conceptual understanding that beginning teachers will bring to their work, especially in the primary school. The model proposed for teacher education focuses firmly on its inseparability from teacher professionalism, and seeks a twenty-first-century change in the role of universities and local authorities in strengthening the culture of professional learning that is *sustainable for the indefinite future*. This replaces the *series of reforms* for curricula and approaches that characterised the second half of the twentieth century.

The fundamental question for this strategy is, of course, "What is the nature of the proposed enhancement of teacher professionalism?" In essence, the answer to the question argues that intrinsic to teaching there has to be a greater sense of teachers being accountable for:

- acknowledging their obligation to their own learning, that is, not waiting to be "trained" but taking responsibility for their own development and self-evaluation
- ensuring that they keep up-to-date with the subject matter of their teaching
- developing understandings of the nature of children's learning and how the environment in which they learn influences that learning
- emphasizing their explicit and increased responsibility for pupils' learning and enhanced achievements
- establishing more trusting relationships with pupils
- undertaking more interactive roles with parents and other professional groups
- enhancing their awareness of the importance of research (especially action research), reflection on practice, and active support for less experienced colleagues
- withdrawing from notions that teaching and leadership are distinctively different activities and seeing their role as encompassing both
- seeing those in more senior school positions as responsible for building capacity in the learning of pupils, staff, and student teachers using evidence-based innovations.

Most importantly professional teachers should see *themselves* as shaping the future and getting away from an assumption that they should be waiting to be told what to do and how to do it—described as the need to abandon their "learned helplessness."

A priority for teachers, student teachers, and teacher educators in working toward such changes concerns decisions about how to cope with new ideas (CfE and twenty-first-century teacher professionalism) that encompass ambitious aims, but lack fully theorized models or specific understandings of what these imply for implementation. For example, the increase in teachers' autonomy inevitably means much greater *diversity* in teaching and learning across the country, but the implications of that have neither been adequately conceptualized nor allowed for in current planning for assessment or inspections of schools. Furthermore, other perturbations in the system, such as the current review of teachers' terms and conditions of employment, may well have unpredictable impacts, especially on industrial relations.

By autumn 2012, NPG is expected to indicate the work to be done over several years, and to provide specific proposals, frameworks, and guidelines for developments, collaborations, and responsibilities. The intention is to make recommendations for three aspects of teacher education:

1. Early career: initial teacher education plus the first "induction" year.
2. Career-long continuing professional development.
3. Leadership in teaching.

## TEACHER EDUCATION AND THE UNIVERSITIES: NEW DEMANDS AND NEW RISKS

### Demands for Change and Increased Collaboration

The merging of the colleges of education into the universities in the 1990s did not result, as many had hoped, in the movement away from the culture of mono-technic institutions. For example, it appears that BEd degrees remained avowedly vocational, with student teachers impatient of those strands of their work that were not immediately relevant to school classrooms, and reluctant to undertake academic study in its own right. *Teaching Scotland's Future* proposes the demise of the essentially vocational BEd for primary teaching and envisages student teachers in the future spending about half their time on other academic disciplines. Inevitably, this has implications for decisions about the length of their degree programs, and the extension of the PGDE to run for two years rather than one is also mooted. At the same time, the government is anxious to create greater flexibility and wider access for all pathways into university education.

More generally, the intention is that the professional component in initial teacher education should address more directly areas where teachers have their greatest difficulties and that will require radical reappraisal of present courses and of guidelines provided by GTCS. But just as important are the proposals seeking stronger disciplinary study for all intending teachers, with other university academic departments involved in the planning and delivery of programs that currently are the sole responsibility of education departments. And that implies interdepartmental transfers of resources with the potential to increase tension. University education departments are often regarded by other disciplines, in many cases without good justification, as punching below their weight, especially in terms of research—in the UK systems research is a major determinant of university funding. In particular, the value of action research, which can be such an important strand of work in teacher education including CPD and development activities, is not always properly appreciated. It remains to be seen how the next national assessment of universities' research will respond to action research.

Clearly the new strategies require universities' senior managers, various academic disciplines and education departments to engage with each other in thinking about different ways to construe student teachers' learning. They are expected to ensure teachers of the future have, and maintain, much more solid knowledge backgrounds, especially in less familiar or interdisciplinary areas. This implies continual updating, stronger links between universities and schools, mentoring, and mentors' training (for teacher educators and schoolteachers). However, while CPD might be seen as the aspect of teacher education with most potential expansion and greatest urgency, increased funding for this from either central or local government seems unlikely.

Collaborations with schools will have to move on from individual institutions' current private and familiar arrangements for student teachers' school experience. The expectation is that clusters of schools from the local authority and the (much smaller) private school sectors will come together as "hubs" for, among other things, teacher education that engages with the universities. There is some pilot collaborative work on hubs, and one example involves Glasgow University with twelve schools (eleven primary and one secondary) and a dedicated full-time member of staff. However, Glasgow is Scotland's largest city and there are acute anxieties about how such collaborations could work in the country's many remote areas.

There is no agreement yet among government, schools, local authorities, and teacher education institutions on how the agenda for implementation of the new ideas will be paid for, organized and managed. Will all schools have the capacity, structure, procedures, and commitment that are required for the development of the new professional learning systems envisaged as integral to the totality of teacher education? For student teachers, school experience will have to provide opportunities not only to develop and hone classroom skills, but also to use practice as a way of exploring theory, examine research evidence, and develop essential habits of reflection, self-evaluation, and teamwork. And since the proposals imply much fuller integration than in the past of all the public services for children, teachers have to develop new relationships and ways of working with other professionals.

There will be developments requiring new regulations governing teacher education and influencing financial support for student teachers. These will affect many of the arrangements and decisions previously made autonomously by individual institutions, but now to be shared across the system. Not least of these will be a common approach to selection of students for teacher education programs, including tests of literacy and numeracy. It remains to be seen whether such tests will go beyond basic skills to test greater understanding of language and mathematics, and the universities are wary of the teacher education report's proposal for a national assessment center for the admission of students. There is no indication, however, that Scotland will follow England into the territory of psychometric testing for intending teachers. An issue that will have to be faced is that tariffs for entry to existing BEd degrees are significantly lower than those for the other academic departments that will now be involved in the teacher education programs.

Questions on the extent to which different strands of teacher education programs will confer master's-level credit are still to be resolved, but it is clear that such a requirement would be challenging for some existing courses. Current Chartered Teacher programs aspiring to this level have exhibited a wide range of quality. However, the integration of the different stages of teacher education not only implies greater challenges for teachers, but also means they will have increased expectations about the accrual of greater credit.

## Teacher Education's Risks and Insecurities

As well as *demands* on universities, the proposed new approaches to teacher education bring *risks and feelings of insecurity*. The consolidation into career-long development with very limited finance available could increase competition and tension among members of STEC, or even result in government decisions to reduce the number of teacher education institutions. Furthermore, requirements to bring the BEd route for primary education to a conclusion almost certainly means that some teacher educators, who themselves lack solid academic discipline foundations, may no longer be needed. Other staff losses may occur as the emphasis on research confronts those teacher educators who have little sound research experience. And finally changes in expectations about which aspects of learning will be best achieved in schools, rather than universities, suggests some staff will have to modify their teaching identities.

There remain questions about workforce planning. In 2011 there were extraordinary "last-minute" reductions in government quotas of student teachers. Such changes are destabilizing and make reductions in teacher education staff in some institutions more or less inevitable. The PGDE route is one particularly at risk of being seen by government as straightforward to turn off and on at short notice. Predicting teacher numbers and making informed decisions about the likelihood of employment are difficult, but teaching qualifications can have currency and credibility in other employment markets. In this respect, concurrent degrees that include achievement in other academic subjects as well as education have been more successful than the purely vocational programs. The review proposes that transferrable skills from education degrees should be highlighted to both students and a breadth of employers and, where qualified teachers have moved into other employment, the path of return to teaching should be eased.

## New Capacities for Teacher Educators

The centrality of the need for new perspectives on CPD in the efforts to change the culture of education in Scotland is reflected in the teacher education review's many recommendations for replacement of traditional in-service activities for teachers and for an emphasis on teacher education as a career-long experience. Three aspects of these proposals illustrate some of the distinctive features of the way changes are construed:

1. CPD should be planned and evaluated by teachers, schools, and teacher education in terms of its *direct impact on young people's progress and achievements.*
2. The GTCS's professional standards should be revised to create a coherent framework reflecting a reconceptualization of *career-long teacher professionalism.*
3. Because leadership is regarded as central to educational quality, a virtual college of school leadership should be developed to *improve leadership capacity at all levels* within Scottish education.

Perhaps the most constructive way to think about changes in the culture of Scottish teacher education for the future is to extend the use of the four "capacities" of *successful learner, confident individual, responsible citizen,* and *effective contributor* as set out by the CfE for young people in schools. It could be argued that such capacities also provide a powerful framework for the development of teachers and of teacher educators.

If we start with *effective learners*, then the ideas for teachers' future professionalism stress a stance whereby teachers take much more action and responsibility for their own learning and the extension of their role in education. While appropriate support has to be offered, it is the teachers who are held to account for their own progress. Because teacher educators are an essential element in the support for teachers' career-long process of learning, they also will have responsibilities for their own learning if they are to offer teachers what is sound and up-to-date in knowledge and skills. This implies active involvement in research and drawing much more widely on the knowledge of other university departments. The anticipated reward is one of enthusiasm for learning, determination to reach high standards, and openness to new thinking about teaching at all levels.

One example of teachers' and so teacher educators' learning, where they have been exhorted to ensure they keep up with that of young people, is information and communications technology. Significantly, as well as the capacity here of the *effective learner*, that of the *confident individual* is necessary but currently often absent. It is expected that with such confidence would come self-respect, a sense of well-being, secure values, and ambition for achievements and independence. Confidence of this kind will be particularly important for teacher educators in the increased engagement with other university academics. The same argument is made as it becomes clear that many teaching methods, that have been so comfortable for teachers and teacher educators in the past, have to be replaced by others for the CfE.

As well as extending collaboration to other university staff, local authorities, and schools, teacher educators have to support teachers throughout their careers as they are urged to increase their engagement with parents, other public services, cultural organizations and political bodies. This indicates a focus on the capacity for being a *responsible citizen* and developing understanding and respect for other political, economic, social, and cultural views. The task for the individual teacher educator is one of finding ways of becoming better informed and more engaged with and more constructively critical of a range of complex issues that characterize the modern world.

The fourth capacity, *effective contributor*, encapsulates the self-reliance and resilience of the enterprising teacher educator. The ability to think critically and communicate appropriately in different environments will provide the basis for creative contributions to the partnerships envisaged across Scottish education for the rest of this century.

But what conditions, in addition to adequate finance, have to be fulfilled for all this to become a reality? At the very least, there must be acceptance that:

- clearer and more concise conceptualizations are required for the *four capacities*, new *teaching methods with testable hypotheses* about their influence on young people's progress, and *leadership* at all levels of teaching
- GTCS and teachers carry responsibility for ensuring the *new professionalism* underpins the formal standards and reforms of classroom practice
- both teachers and teacher educators have *career-long CPD* needs
- universities and schools must take *wider responsibility* for teacher education and collaboration
- government must abandon the highly bureaucratic beginnings of its reforms and *devolve the big decisions* to experienced professionals
- teachers and teacher educators must ensure young people's achievements are *construed and reported to parents in straightforward understandable terms*
- a proper program of *independent evaluation and research* must be undertaken.

More fundamentally, however, the late Donald McIntyre (2006) provided a telling argument for four crucial ingredients that are necessary if we are to introduce new, effective and enduring collaborative partnerships among universities, schools and local authorities.

"First, there has to be genuine respect for the expertise of practicing teachers from academic teacher educators and recognition that, while each of them has important and rich but different expertise from which beginning teachers need to learn, it is the learning from teachers and in schools that is the more crucial. Second, to make that possible it is essential that substantial resources be specifically provided for this purpose. Third, there has to be a recognition on all sides that schools and teachers need to engage in new learning if they are to make more effective use of their expertise in teaching for helping beginning teachers to learn (and the expertise of university lecturers will be of only limited help in this). Finally, the center of gravity of ITE curricula has to move from the universities into the schools. This will mean the planning of new kinds of school-based curricula" (McIntyre, 2006, pp. 17–18).

Half a decade later the argument is as valid as it was then; I hope we are up for it.

## NOTES

I am very grateful to Graham Donaldson, Richard Edwards, and Ian Mentor for extremely helpful conversations of which I have taken full advantage.

1. www.scotland.gov.uk/Resource/Doc/26800/0023690.pdf.
2. www.sqa.org.uk/sqa/41278.html.
3. www.scotland.gov.uk/Publications/2011/01/13092132/6.
4. http://www.scotland.gov.uk/Resource/Doc/920/0120759.PDF.
5. www.scotland.gov.uk/News/Releases/2011/07/01114648.
6. www.scotland.gov.uk/Publications/2010/09/24144019/0.
7. www.gtcs.org.uk/standards/standards.aspx.
8. www.sqa.org.uk/.
9. www.scotland.gov.uk/Topics/Education/Schools/Teaching/SGresponse09032011.
10. http://www.scotland.gov.uk/Publications/2012/11/7834/0
11. http://www.scotland.gov.uk/News/Releases/2012/11/teaching06112012

## REFERENCES

Christie, D. (2008). Professional studies in initial teacher education. In T. Bryce & W. Humes (Eds.), *Scottish Education* (3rd ed.) (pp. 826–835). Edinburgh: Edinburgh University Press.

Doherty, R., & McMahon, M. (2007). Politics, change and compromise: Restructuring the work of the Scottish teacher. *Educational Review, 59*(3), 251–265.

Donaldson, G. (2011). *Teaching Scotland's future: Report of the review of teacher education in Scotland.* Edinburgh: The Scottish Government.

Hulme, M., & Menter, I. (2008). Learning to teach in post-devolution UK: A technical or an ethical process? *Southern African Review of Education.* Special Issue of *Teacher Education, 14*(1–2), 43–64.

Kirk, G. (2003). Teacher education institutions. In T. Bryce & W, Humes. (Eds.), *Scottish Education* (2nd ed.) (pp. 921–930). Edinburgh: Edinburgh University Press.

Marker, W. (2000). Scottish teachers. In H. Holmes (Ed.), *Education* (pp. 273–296). East Lothian, UK: Tuckwell Press.

McIntyre, D. (2006). Opportunities for a more balanced approach to ITE: Can we learn again from research and other experience? *Scottish Educational Review, 37 Special Edition*, 5–19.

McCrone G (2000) *A teaching profession for the 21st century.* Report to the Scottish Government, Edinburgh.

Menter, I., Hulme, M., Elliot, D., & Lewin, J. (2010) *Literature review on teacher education in the 21st century,* Report to the Scottish Government, Glasgow University.

Organization for Economic Cooperation and Development. (2007). *Quality and equity of schooling in Scotland.* Paris: OECD.

*Chapter Five*

# Teacher Educators as Agents of Change

## *A Hong Kong Perspective*

Teresa Tsui-san Ng, John Chi-Kin Lee, and Chun Kwok Lau

## CONTEXT OF CHANGE: THE EDUCATIONAL LANDSCAPE OF SCHOOL AND HIGHER EDUCATION IN HONG KONG

Narrative inquirers do not proclaim findings as universal truths. Rather, they tell stories constructed in specific time and places with unique personal and social signatures (Clandinin & Connelly, 2004). In this chapter, John and Teresa draw on their experiences as teacher educators and share their own puzzles and struggles in their professional journeys against a backdrop of the Hong Kong higher educational scene at a specific point in time.

Hong Kong had been a British colony for over 150 years, since 1842. On 1 July 1997, its sovereignty was handed over to the People's Republic of China (PRC) by the United Kingdom and it became a Special Administrative Region of the PRC. This history has furnished unique political and educational opportunities and challenges, and our concern is with the educational development of the city.

In the higher education sector, the University Grants Council (UGC), established in 1965 after the model of the British UGC, advises the government on the development and funding of the seven public-funded universities plus the Hong Kong Institute of Education (HKIEd), which is not yet a full-status university. The HKIEd was established in 1994 with the amalgamation of five former government colleges of education responsible for training of the majority of primary school and kindergarten teachers in Hong Kong.

For more than a decade Hong Kong has experienced an ambitious government-led school curriculum reform and this has included a greater emphasis on helping students to learn, promoting school-based curriculum development and pedagogical changes in classrooms through four main key tasks: reading to learn, information technology for interactive learning, moral and civic education, and project learning. The reform has also emphasized the development of students' generic skills, and especially the three core skills of communication, critical thinking, and creativity.

Further, the government has encouraged teacher educators to conduct research and development projects designed to inform curriculum policy and practice in schools, to share successful experiences of school-based curriculum development with colleagues in the school sector, and to strengthen preservice and in-service teacher education programs (Curriculum Development Council, 2001). In addition to the funding from the Education Bureau, the government set up the Quality Education Fund in 1998 to support educational innovations in schools and other educational institutions.

Elliott and Morris (2001, p.148) argued that the policy actions bringing about change, especially during the early stage of the reform, tended to ignore the assumption that "if teachers are to change the curriculum in action in their classrooms and schools, they require consistent support over a long period of time from a variety of sources, including policy-makers and government officials, school principals, parents, and *teacher trainers*."

During the decade of curriculum reform in the new century, much has been achieved in schools. Learning communities are being developed; team cultures have been nurtured through collaborative lesson planning and lesson observation; and teachers have developed their pedagogical content knowledge and enhanced their participation in whole school curriculum development. However, increasing teacher workload has been an enduring concern and there has been a call for capacity-building support and building up leadership capacity (Education Bureau, 2008, pp. 17, 24–25, 36–40).

Teacher educators engage actively or passively, shaping or being shaped by the sociocultural features of society and the externally imposed policies and institutional cultures in which we work. Each teacher educator has the capacity to encompass "individual beliefs, identity, values, subject area and pedagogic knowledge, past experiences with reform . . . , emotional well-being . . . and professional vulnerability" (Lasky, 2005, p. 901). Our focus is on the unique opportunities that external change might provide for teachers/teacher educators.

In the following stories, John and Teresa act as agents of educational change or advocates for innovations in teacher education. From being scholar-teachers and teacher educators, they move to being agents of change in their teaching and through engaging in partnership/action research projects with schoolteachers. During the process, they change teachers and they also change themselves.

## JOHN'S STORIES

### Scale New Heights in Career Development

John worked as a secondary school teacher for a few years before joining one of the colleges of education as a lecturer. In 1994, he started his academic career as an assistant professor in the Chinese University of Hong Kong (CUHK) and became a professor and the dean of the Faculty of Education in 2003. While he was in CUHK, he led several influential large-scale projects and published over a hundred academic articles and book chapters, and has edited and written more than twenty books while fulfilling his teaching, research, and administrative responsibilities and giving professional service to the community.

In 2010, John left the CUHK and became the vice president (Academic) of HKIEd, a teacher education institute that is still in the process of re-titling to a full-status university. While John has led a productive and fruitful professional career, he is not without his own struggles and puzzles when reflecting on his experiences at the CUHK.

### Escape from the Ivory Tower

On reviewing my professional career, I reflected that I do not want to stay inside the comfort zone of the ivory tower. For many years, I served as a consultant or a change facilitator in school curriculum reform through university-school partnership projects. As a curriculum scholar, I was strongly influenced by Schwab's practical curriculum theories, and while my work has strong theoretical underpinnings, it is not pure research in curriculum debates but scientific studies that seek to bridge theory and practice and solve practical problems and bring about improvement in schools.

I inquired into curriculum theories and practices through working closely with school teachers when the Faculty of Education first launched a "problem-based university-school partnership" program in 1997. I then engaged in school improvement and curriculum development projects following the launch of the Hong Kong government's Quality Education Fund in 1998. I advocated a "mutual adaptation," action research–oriented approach to curriculum development and implementation that took into account school realities.

In one of my projects, "Accelerated Schools for Quality Education Project" between 1998 and 2001, originating in the Accelerated Schools Project led by Henry Levin in the United States, I recognized that there were cultural factors to be taken into account in adapting a comprehensive school reform model to the context of Hong Kong where school-based management was still in its infancy in the late 1990s and teacher participation in local school curriculum reform tended to be hierarchical, arising from pragmatic needs rather than a call for democracy (Lee, 2006).

In another project that I codirected, "University School Partnership for Quality Education" (2000–2002), I initiated a 4-P teacher-friendly action research approach (a cycle of problem clarification, planning, program action, and progress assessment) which was applied in future projects and has attracted attention in China and Taiwan (Lee, 2010; Lee, Ma, & Ko, 2011).

I also disseminated the concept of the four Ps in my teaching on action research and I worked with colleagues in developing an MA program in "School Improvement and Leadership," where I shared my insights on school development from my past projects with students.

## The Man in the Middle

Working in the interface between the school and university, I was always sensitive to the voices of teachers and shared their concerns. I always took the practitioners' experiences seriously and felt the professional, research, and publications tensions and confusions in my roles as a scholar, educator, and teacher.

During the process of working with schools to initiate school-based curriculum change, some teachers had concerns over their excessive workloads and sometimes questioned the rationale of the curriculum reform. However, the government hoped that we could help to disseminate the positive aspects of the reform and equip the preservice and in-service teachers to understand and implement the change.

I often faced the tensions between the roles of teacher educators as supporters of curriculum reform that nurture and train teachers to cope with the curriculum reform and teacher educators as independent critical analysts that cultivate teachers as critical, independent professionals (Elliott and Morris, 2001).

I sometimes felt confused, asking myself: Shall I cultivate my students, who are in-service schoolteachers, to question the inadequacies and impracticality of the reform and criticize the government for offering inadequate support? Shall I share my vision of the reform that change is possible with the schoolteachers and enlighten them to be vanguards of the reform?

Upon reflection on my experience in the university-school partnership projects, I found strong resonance with John Goodlad's remark (1988, p. 11): "education professors eschew both the preparation of teachers . . . and sustained involvement with schools, their prime source of reward being publication in refereed journals. But schoolteachers and administrators rarely read these journals and, indeed, inhabit a culture that values action over reading, reflection, and dialogue about alternatives."

## Standing at the Crossroad

The anxieties of teacher educators may be associated with losing the respect of practicing teachers while not gaining the respect of senior academics in universities. For example, school subject teachers see a lecturer becoming increasingly outdated and out of touch. Senior academics see that lecturer becoming overly concerned with school and classroom realities and not sufficiently immersed in "pure" theories and academic research, often of very little interest to professionals. And one's career path is determined not by professionals in the field of school education but by academics in the ivory tower.

I feel that the university lecturer is squeezed between the professional audience (highly critical and often not convinced that an academic has anything worth listening to) and a university audience (highly critical and dismissive of professionally oriented efforts). Despite my successful endeavors, I faced some challenges as an academic in a research-intensive university. Like academic colleagues in many Western universities with a strong "publish or perish" culture, I faced the demands for publishing high-quality research findings in high-impact international refereed journals (i.e., in nonlocal languages). It also proved difficult to publish case studies of school-based curriculum development in those journals where the local context might not be familiar to or of interest to an international audience and the insights might not be easily transferred to other settings in different sociocultural traditions.

While my passion and mission of being a teacher educator is in applied and action research, it is considered by some scholars as lacking the respectability and rigor of basic/empirical research involving sophisticated statistical analysis in the context of acknowledged theories, and more importantly, I faced the challenges of taking up another role (action researcher and school consultant) in the school setting in addition to that of university teacher educator. Teachers in school may sometimes question whether university professors understand their real situations and the suggested measures and strategies could really work in schools and their classrooms. From the perspective of a scholar in curriculum and school improvement, teachers and scholars could not expect a "quick-fix" panacea for curriculum change, which requires cultural changes in schools, mind-set changes of teachers, and concerted efforts between university colleagues and teachers.

## TERESA'S STORIES

Teresa is an assistant professor at the Hong Kong Institute of Education (HKIEd) with strong personal interest and experience in drama education and creativity teaching. She is keen on innovative teaching practices. She shares her personal stories below on how a strictly disciplined schoolgirl became a creative educator and the challenges she encountered as she faced a demand to change her course on creativity, which aims to provide participants with the experience to develop sensitivity, fluency, flexibility, originality, and elaboration inherent in creativity. Teacher creativity, as a crucial component of teacher competence in recent education reform, will be nurtured and cultivated through specifically designed performance tasks and activities in the course. Participants are expected to develop teaching strategies relating to their subject areas to foster active and meaningful learning.

### Circling in a Weird Spiral

The current reforms are sending shock waves across the education community, exerting pressure not only on schoolteachers, but also on teacher educators in the tertiary institutions. I have the feeling that the weight of research and teaching is always on my shoulders, strangling me, leaving me grasping for my breath, and my wretched soul striving to meet the challenges from all directions. I have to exert all my physical and mental effort in facing this challenge while fatigue and anxiety have sapped my energy. I always cried out, "Keep up the effort," as a way to motivate myself. But time and again I am overcome by the feeling of being lost and alone, and that I am circling in a weird spiral.

### Embarking on a Journey of Creativity

Looking back to my time as a student, I have been brought up in the traditional way of learning. I used to sit perfectly still in class facing the teacher and immaculately postured with my back pinned to the backrest. I learned not to raise questions and not to challenge the teacher. Studying meant taking exams and learning standard answers by heart.

Creativity was a concept that was totally alien to me at the time. After finishing high school, I had a chance to continue my education in the United Kingdom, where my study habit was completely knocked over. For the first time, I learned I did not have to maintain the same stiff posture for the entire lesson. I, for the first time, was aware that I could raise questions as they came to mind. For the first time, I consulted the work of classmates without being suspected of copying by the teacher. I even achieved an A+ in Mathematics (my weakest subject) without learning standard answers by heart. To my surprise, I was praised by my teacher, for the first time in my life! All of these "first times" have been rather unusual experiences for me.

These "first time" experiences inspired me to embark on my further studies in creativity upon returning to Hong Kong. My enthusiasm for creative teaching did not wane and I was deeply captivated by the subject in my teaching and research.

After joining the HKIEd, I was involved in different projects related to creative teaching, including modifying the existing courses, leading several research projects, and coordinating and developing new MEd programs on curriculum and innovative teaching.

Apart from my teaching at HKIEd, I provided staff development workshops for teachers in schools to promote creative teaching in the field. At the same time, I published academic papers and books that documented my experiences in creative teaching. These steps, taken with great enthusiasm, made me even more adept at teaching the creativity course.

As the course became one of the most popular courses in the HKIEd, I felt I had gradually entered a comfort zone where it seemed improbable that changes could be made. An encounter in 2009 completely overturned my experience.

## Defeated by Outcome-Based Learning?

In August 2009, two weeks before the commencement of the new semester, I received a notice from my department that I had to implement outcome-based learning (OBL) in my teaching. At that time, OBL was being promoted in all higher education institutions in Hong Kong not because of any academic findings or discussions from within. Instead, it originated in the UGC, advocating that teaching in the tertiary institutions could be improved by focusing on accountability and by adopting an outcome-based approach to student learning. Since the UGC controls government funding, its decisions and initiatives have strongly influenced the operation of the publicly funded higher education institutions in Hong Kong.

I recalled the panic I felt: Facing a course that started in two weeks, I had no idea of the direction to take. Why was the reform necessary? What kind of class arrangement would fulfill OBL? What would I have to do to ensure a smooth transition to OBL?

These questions kept swirling in my head, and incapable of coming up with solutions, I pushed myself into a dead end. In panic, I read extensively and attended all workshops and meetings on OBL. I spent nearly all my time trying to change my course into the OBL mode. Without adequate guidelines and experience of implementation, I could only struggle alone in getting the OBL course ready.

I struggled to prepare the course without much progress despite repeated attempts at exploring new methods. As the deadline drew near, I was charging in various directions, not having a clue about how the course I had taught for more than six years could be linked with OBL.

One evening, while working alone in my office preparing for the OBL course, I stumbled upon an article written by Biggs and Tang (2007). The article provided a summary of outcome-based learning. It emphasized the interlocking relationships between intended education outcomes, teaching/learning activities, and teaching assessments. The article was a revelation to me. Immediately I followed the guidelines in the article and threw out whatever I had done with my effort to reconstruct the OBL course.

However, things did not turn out as I had expected. Reconstructing the course was still fraught with difficulties. At the time, I had a sense that the obstruction to a complete overhaul of the course had come from my reservations about change.

Since joining the Hong Kong Institute of Education, I have been developing and teaching the creativity course. The course was not only well received by students, but, after years of adjustments and integration, it had developed into a very mature one. I was convinced that my creativity course had been meticulously arranged and thoroughly tested. All components of the course were closely interconnected with one another. A minute adjustment in any part would affect the whole. So I had difficulty convincing myself of the need for change.

As I was unable to clear the doubts in my mind, two weeks of preparation passed quickly and I decided to follow my original teaching plan. In the premise of guaranteeing the teaching quality, I continued to search for the path to reform through the course of teaching.

The three-month course started without a glitch and I worked tirelessly to finish all my tasks in the limited time I had, uneasy about taking rest. Fortunately I received the usual high praise from the students that semester. It was at that moment that a turning point suddenly arrived, and the turning point came with a sharp warning.

One day, I was invited to share my "successful experience" in OBL with the colleagues in the faculty. Good heavens! As I was still in my search phase, where would I find "successful experience"? What successful experiences could I possibly share? Although the sharing session was warmly welcomed by my colleagues, deep down inside, I felt that I had not achieved what I had set out to accomplish.

To be honest, it felt like I was passing off a half-hearted attempt as a genuine effort to undertake OBL. Facing my students, I was consumed by guilt. I repeatedly asked myself whether I would allow myself to be defeated by OBL. I was given the opportunity to learn OBL, and I sincerely wished to help my students learn better, which was what I had always believed. I was convinced that the only thing that kept me going was that I loved what I did, I just had to keep going. Hence, I made up my mind and swore that I would successfully implement OBL in my course in the next semester.

## An Unexpected Breakthrough

In the next three months, I read extensively with an aim to reform my course. It seemed to me that OBL was a necessity in setting up courses. I was also convinced that OBL, starting with clear teaching objectives, adjusting the content by taking into account the students' previous knowledge and capacity to learn, would allow a more sensible adjustment to the course arrangement. The second semester arrived quickly. The department stopped pushing me on the OBL reform. But instead I put in a greater effort to tackle the challenge. I devoted all my effort and time to collating and reflecting on the material I had previously collected.

For the course I taught in that semester, I first adjusted my teaching objectives. I took steps to standardize the course content and rearranged and redesigned class activities with more games and classroom discussion. More importantly, I wanted to ensure that the teaching content met the teaching objectives. A Q&A session was added at the end of each class and the idea was to check if my planned teaching objectives were achieved through soliciting students' opinions and the material learned in that class.

In order to have a better understanding of students' backgrounds and their previous knowledge, I asked them to fill out a questionnaire in the first class of the course. I found from the collected questionnaires that most students had heard about the basic theory of creative teaching and were familiar with many of its concepts. This finding did not match with my previous assumption that students did not have basic knowledge of creative teaching. Based on the increased knowledge level of the target, I made the bold move to expand the depth and breadth of the teaching content, and supplemented contents that would otherwise be excluded in the original course and these include the relationship between intelligence and creativity, the myths of creativity, and so on.

With changes in the teaching material, I have correspondingly increased or adjusted the teaching activities. In the fourth session, on finding the students have not gotten to know each other as in previous years, I added a number of "ice-breaking" activities to strengthen the relationships among the students. I also modified the pace of teaching and its contents through observing the subtle reactions of students in the class.

## Changing Myself to Change Others

With the completion of thirteen classes, this course, which I have taught for more than six years, has changed considerably in many ways, including course content as well as class activities. I have invested more effort into each class. As seen from the pre- and the post-test on creativity, students' creative ability, which includes fluency and sensitivity, has been raised appreciably. They are gradually becoming aware that they can be creative teachers, and this has boosted their confidence in teaching. Hence, the course has changed the students' beliefs and they have come to realize the close connection between creativity, teaching, and their daily lives.

From my observation in class, students become more enthusiastic about learning and eager to voice their own opinions; their critical thinking skills have also been improved. Over 80 percent of the students believed that the course had changed their concept of creative teaching in two main areas: (a) "students who excel academically are not necessarily creative" and (b) "creativity can be nurtured through training." These two points are the two most common misconceptions about creativity, which demonstrates that the students have developed the right ideas about creativity.

It is gratifying that all of the students have stated that the course has helped them acquire the attitude for nurturing creativity in a person. They have proactively reflected what they have learned in their daily lives and teaching, and have begun to adopt different teaching strategies to stimulate students' enthusiasm for learning, hoping that their own and students' creativity can be enhanced from different perspectives.

All these changes provide ample evidence that the creativity course has accomplished the planned teaching goals. I am delighted that the results have far exceeded my original expectations. Students have told me upon completion of the course that they were very satisfied with this approach of OBL learning, and would recommend the course to their friends. In fact these gratifying results are the reward for the painstaking care and effort I have put in during the semester. My OBL course is at last successful.

After the second semester, once again I attended an OBL experience-sharing session at the request of my faculty. This time, I was very clear about the meaning behind the data presented. I believe I have genuinely applied the essence of OBL into curriculum reform. Although the path is treacherous, the rewards are equally rich.

I rejoice each time I think back on the experience. If I had simply given up during the arduous breaking-in period in the first semester, I would have been stuck at the same place, forever clinging on to what I had originally thought was a perfect course design, and ignoring the needs of students. However, I have taken one step forward to change; with all my effort I have achieved the beliefs I have so firmly held on to. Most importantly I am clearly seeing changes not only in myself, having the courage to face adversity and accept challenges but also my students, becoming better and more active to learn.

### Secrets for Successful Change Agents

At the end of the semester in December 2010, I had an opportunity to share my experience in OBL at an international symposium. Quite a number of schools invited me to establish an OBL course for their units and programs. I see myself transformed from a passive adaptor of education reform into an active promoter.

This change of role has led me to believe that in the face of adversity in implementing education reform, teachers from primary to secondary schools to tertiary institutions, from local regions to other areas across the world, can take inspiration from my personal experience in OBL and convert the pressure of the reform to an impetus for personal change, and the energy can be projected outward to influence others. Only then will our students truly benefit from the reform.

Any reform must come from within. Teachers should be ready to discover the need for reform. Through gradually putting in effort, changes can be made in areas previously thought to be unchangeable. We should bravely persist, not for the chance to gain anything, only for wishing the students can learn more effectively. In confronting change, if the teacher reluctantly accepts education reform without attempting to change, the resultant reform would only lead to a low quality or a negative one.

On the contrary, change that comes from within is an incentive for change, a source for progress. Time and space are both required in reform; honestly, these are luxuries for the scholar-teachers in the tertiary institutions. But if we are willing to change, it would add to the chances of self-reflection. If we have a pressing desire to change for self-improvement and not accepting responsibility in frustration, positive energy would flow.

## REFLECTIONS ON EXPERIENCES AND IMPLICATIONS FOR TEACHER EDUCATION

In this chapter, both authors have recounted the pressure and hardship faced by their profession in the Hong Kong education reform. John's experience illustrated multiple identities of a teacher educator: a facilitator of curriculum and teaching reforms through working collaboratively with schools; and a scholar-teacher bridging theory and practice and teaching-research nexus through program development and action research. There are many external demands on a teacher educator, sometimes the expectation in a changing world could be somewhat impossible (Ben-Peretz, 2001). John's experience highlighted the importance of balancing and synergizing competing demands on a teacher educator under the principles of making teacher educators' work relevant to educating teachers to teach and supporting the development of educational community including the school.

Teresa's experience revealed the three internal conditions for a teacher educator as a change agent in the twenty-first century: innovative space, intrinsic drive, and self-reflection, which also serve as the impetus for high-quality change in education. Making space for reflection will give us as teacher educators the chance to solve problems effectively and we will have more courage to face future challenges. This is not only for teaching more effectively but also to grasp the opportunity to improve ourselves through reflective practices.

It is important to note that both of them have displayed some "explicit modeling" of teaching practices (Lunenberg, Korthagen and Swennen, 2007), such as adapting the four Ps and using OBL, and have ridden on the opportunities from reform to make a difference: John applied for funding from the Quality Education Fund and the Education Bureau to conduct university-school partnership projects; Teresa made use of the promotion of the Outcome Based Learning within the Institute as an opportunity to reform her own teaching and learning practices. After all, only the momentum and self-inspection that comes from within and the pursuit and enjoyment of success, would allow us to persevere. These are the attitudes we should have when facing our common predicament in curriculum reform and becoming a successful change agent as a teacher educator in the twenty-first century.

Both authors hope to share candidly their internal struggles in facing the challenges with peers in the education sector. The "never give up" attitude and sense of responsibility, as well as the positive message, are indeed an inspiration for all in the areas of professional development of teachers and teacher educators.

## REFERENCES

Ben-Peretz, M. (2001). The impossible role of teacher educators in a changing world. *Journal of Teacher Education, 52*(1), 48–56.

Biggs, J., & Tang, C. (2007). *Teaching for quality learning at university*. Buckingham, UK: Open University Press/McGraw-Hill Education.

Clandinin, D. J., & Connelly, F. M. (2004). *Narrative inquiry: Experience and story in qualitative research.* San Francisco, CA: Jossey-Bass.

Curriculum Development Council. (2001). *Learning to learn—Lifelong learning and whole-person development.* Hong Kong SAR: Printing Department.

Education Bureau. (2008). *Improving learning, teaching and the quality of professional life in schools.* A midterm report on curriculum reform to school heads and teachers. Hong Kong SAR.

Elliott, J., & Morris, P. (2001). Educational reform, schooling, and teacher education in Hong Kong. In Y. C. Cheng, K. W. Chow, & K. T. Tsui (Eds.). *New teacher education for the future: International perspective* (pp. 147–166). Hong Kong: The Hong Kong Institute of Education and Kluwer Academic Publishers.

Goodlad, J. (1988). School-university partnerships for educational renewal: Rationale and concepts. In K. A. Sirotnik & J. I. Goodlad (Eds.), *School-university partnerships in action: Concepts, cases, and concerns* (pp. 3–31). New York: Teachers College Press.

Lasky, S. (2005). A sociocultural approach to understanding teacher identity, agency and professional vulnerability in a context of secondary school reform. *Teaching and Teacher Education, 21*, 899–916.

Lee, J. C. K. (2006). Hong Kong: Accelerated Schools for Quality Education Project (ASQEP) Experiences. In J. C. K. Lee & M. Williams (Eds.), *School improvement: International perspectives* (pp. 159–174). New York: Nova Science Publishers, Inc.

Lee, J. C. K. (Ed.). (2010). *School-based curriculum development, teacher development and partnerships*. Beijing: Educational Science Publishing House [in Chinese].

Lee, J. C. K., Ma, H. T., & Ko, M. L. (Eds.). (2011). *Building up professional learning communities for the subjects of Chinese language and mathematics: Theory and practice.* Nanjing: Nanjing Normal University Press. [in Chinese]

Lunenberg, M., Korthagen, F., & Swennen, A. (2007). The teacher educator as a role model. *Teaching and Teacher Education, 23*, 586–601.

*II*

# A Look into the Future: Societal Issues in Teacher Education

## *Chapter Six*

# Teacher Education as Drama

## *Possible Roles for Teacher Educators*

Miriam Ben-Peretz and Efrat Toov Ward

*All the world's a stage,*
*And all the men and women are players :*
*They have their exits and their entrances;*
*And one man in his time plays many parts*
—Shakespeare, *As you like it*, Act 2, Scene 7

The role of teacher education is to provide professional education for student teachers. Teacher educators are responsible for this endeavor and are, therefore, conceived as key players in the education system. This chapter deals with the different ways that teacher educators fulfill this important role. The chapter starts with a brief review of relevant literature concerning the work of teacher educators. The major part of the chapter introduces a view of teacher education programs as "drama" and the different roles teacher educators might play in this context. Several basic concepts of drama are discussed in relation to this metaphor. The implications of this view on the work of teacher educators and their professional development are suggested.

The question addressed in this chapter is: What are some possible roles for teacher educators? Some sub-questions are:

- What are some typical roles assigned to teacher educators at present?
- What circumstances require the adoption of new roles by teacher educators?
- In what ways might the world of drama and theatre suggest new roles for teacher education?

## REVIEW OF LITERATURE RELATED TO THE ROLES OF TEACHER EDUCATORS

Much of the literature concerning the role of teacher educators focuses on their role as teachers: "Teachers who educate teachers are the people who instruct, teach and provide support to student-teachers, thus making a significant contribution to the development of future teachers" (Koster et al., 2005, in Ben-Peretz et al., 2010, p. 113).

The role of teacher educators is confounded by their need to act in two different scenarios: (1) assisting student teachers in developing knowledge and skills for their future role as teachers, and (2) fulfilling the exemplary role of models of teaching. In the concrete situation of teacher education programs, these two scenarios are interwoven into a complex play that unfolds over time.

In programs of teacher education, teacher educators might teach subject matter courses, disciplines of education, and method courses. While accompanying student teachers in their practicum, teacher educators are expected to share knowledge and experiences about the practice of teaching. According to Tillema (2004), teacher educators function as mentors or coaches, role models, and monitors of the professional standards of teaching quality.

Several scholars who have studied teacher education suggest that teacher educators play an exemplary role for their students. The impact of teacher education on the practice of future teachers may be achieved through modeling, especially in promoting new visions of learning (Lunenberg, Korthagen, & Swennen, 2007).

Due to the academization of teacher education, teacher educators are expected to be researchers as well as teachers. According to Cochran-Smith (2005, p. 224) "a major part of the work of the teacher educator has been working the dialectic of research and practice by blurring boundaries and functioning simultaneously as both researcher and practitioner." Cochran-Smith (2005) emphasized the value of transforming local knowledge to public knowledge by teacher educators research, thus making it accessible and usable in other contexts.

Day discusses the role of teacher educators in contexts of social and economic change, the "standards" agenda, present-day expectations of teachers, and the division between the role of teacher and academic. Day suggests that teacher educators must broaden their roles as research and development consultants to teachers, and that the relationships between teacher educators and teachers "need to extend beyond the current narrow range of course provision and institution centered research to embrace an agenda that recognizes the importance of sustained collaboration, teachers roles as knowledge producers, their need to manage change and a mutuality of moral purpose" (Day, 2004, p. 145). Grant and Gillette, as well, claim that effective teachers have to take into consideration "the larger social context in which they are working . . . take into account that academic and social achievement does not occur in a vacuum" (Grant & Gillette, 2006, p. 293).

Massanari, Drummon, and Houston (1978) suggested different roles for teacher educators from which several categories emerge: instructor, advisor, designer and researcher. The teaching role is not prominent, while counseling and advising on an interpersonal level are conceived as important. Moreover, teacher educators are assigned an active role in the development of programs and in research on teaching, learning, and teacher education. These roles are linked to the status of teacher educators as faculty members in higher education who are expected to be involved in knowledge use, but also in the creating of knowledge (Murray, 2011).

Once teacher educators are moved out of the classroom, to develop programs and instructional materials, their ability to shape teacher education, and influence how student teachers become teachers, grows. The question is whether teacher educators are offered opportunities to fulfill this role, or whether they are expected to teach according to pre-determined programs. This approach has limitations.

Teaching at all levels has to adapt itself to a globalized world, which is characterized by more heterogeneous societies, a changing economy, rapidly revolutionized technology, and a growing threat for ecological sustainability (Ben-Peretz, 2009). Teacher education has to prepare teachers to respond to these new needs.

Reforming teacher education programs to suit a changing world requires great flexibility and creativity. Institutions of teacher education tend to view student teachers as a homogeneous population and do not necessarily consider the great variability of cultural contexts. Teacher educators' knowledge and experience, as well as their intimate understanding of student teachers, might be the basis for planning of programs that match the specific needs of local contexts.

Much has been written on teachers' roles as curriculum planners (Connelly & Clandinin, 1988; Ben-Peretz, 1990). School-based curriculum development (SBCD) is considered to be an important tool for responding to local needs, interests, and priorities of diverse populations. Similarly, the involvement of teacher educators in the planning of programs would contribute to the relevance of programs for different audiences, especially in times of growing heterogeneity of populations. The world of theatre and drama might expand our perceptions of this role, as awareness to dramatic structures like plot, theme, unity, and catharsis might serve teacher educators in the planning of programs.

## THE DRAMA AND THEATRE METAPHOR AND TEACHING

The theatre metaphor has been used to describe and understand the work of teachers in comparison with the work of actors in the theatre (Grumet, 1978; Bolton, 1984; Verriour, 1994). According to Schonmann (2005): "Realization of the theatre metaphor is much more than simply thinking one thing (pedagogy) in terms of another (theater). Realization of the theatre metaphor establishes a basic attitude toward pedagogy as enactment, toward teaching as performance. The use of a metaphor permits a passage from one concept to another, while the realization of the metaphor permits action within the new world of concepts" (p. 307).

One of the advantages of using metaphors in relation to phenomena is their potential for raising new issues and questions. Thus, the metaphor of "sea" in relation to "air" provided the basis for searching for aerodynamic, parallel to hydrodynamic, forms.

We suggest using the theatre metaphor for understanding teacher education programs for raising new questions about programs and the role of teacher educators. In an attempt to realize the theatre metaphor, several central concepts of the theatre world will be discussed and their relevance to the planning and implementation of teacher education programs will be presented.

The idea of using the theatre metaphor for understanding curriculum development has been presented by Schonmann (1996). Schonmann suggests a view of curriculum development as a process of staging a play, a performance. Schonmann argues that the theater metaphor is a starting point for changing our conception of curriculum. Basic classic components of curriculum are: Subject matter, teacher, student, and milieu, jointly constructed in a certain place and time (Schwab, 1973). Once you identify teachers and students as participants in a play, subject matter as text and milieu as context, the following curricular elements are obtained: time, place, participant, text, and context. These elements are, as well, the basic elements of theatrical performance.

The understanding of classroom situations as performance leads to a perception of curriculum development as the process of cocreation of lived-in curriculum, which blurs the distinction between the written curriculum and curriculum in use.

## APPLICATION OF THE THEATRE METAPHOR IN TEACHER EDUCATION PROGRAMS

How far is this approach appropriate for developing teacher education programs?

Teacher education programs are expected to give student teachers a common body of professional knowledge, language, and skills. For these commonalities to be expressed in teacher education programs, the text of these programs has to include curtain basic elements, such as knowledge in the subject matter domain, some foundation disciplines like psychology, basic principles of pedagogy, and practical experiences. Such a common text requires maintaining a distinction between curriculum and curriculum in use. The implementation of the common text constitutes the curriculum in use. Teachers play a major role in the interpretation of the common text of curricula and their adaptation to local, unique, classroom situations.

In the hands of teacher educators, teacher education programs require the same kind of interpretation and adaptation. Moreover, teacher educators who are familiar with student teachers, and the context in which the teacher education program is implemented, might be in an appropriate position to develop programs and not only to use externally determined ones. Teacher educators may fulfill a role as "playwrights."

It is claimed, herewith, that the theatre metaphor is highly productive in the context of teacher education programs and its realization in the development endeavor has significant advantages. The realization of the theatre metaphor presented in this chapter accepts the distinction between curriculum and curriculum in use, but sees both through the lenses of theatrical concepts. The focus of this chapter is on the curriculum of programs of teacher education with teacher educators as "playwright developers" as well as program users, comparable to "directors" of plays.

In her insightful and stimulating paper "Theoretical Representations of Teaching as Performance," Schonmann presents several applications of theatrical concepts with regard to teacher education. One interesting definition of drama, suggested by Schonmann is: "a series of unexpected and surprising events occurring in social situations in which people experience some confrontation or struggle" (Schonmann, 2005, p. 286).

One might claim that the essence of effective professional education is the confrontation of learners with unexpected and even surprising situations. This statement contradicts what one might view as the usual way of learning about teaching. According to Lortie, teachers learn about teaching through their own experience as students in school, "the apprenticeship of observation" (1975). Lortie claims that "It may be that the widespread idea that 'anyone can teach' (a notion built into society's historical reluctance to invest heavily in pedagogical research and instruction) originates from this; what child cannot, after all, do a reasonably accurate portrayal of a classroom teacher's actions?" (1975, p. 62). What student-teachers have learned about teaching is imitative rather than explicit and analytical and not based on pedagogical principles. Lortie concludes that the apprenticeship of observation is "a potentially powerful influence which transcends generations, but the conditions of transfer do not favor informed criticism, attention to specifics, or explicit rules of assessment" (1975, p. 63).

Teacher education programs have to present student teachers with unexpected and surprising events related to the actions and behaviors of teachers and students in order to diminish the influence of past experiences. Thus, the cycle of imitating these experiences might be broken and new ways of being a teacher might be perceived and tried. Through the prism of drama, one can find a different way of preparing teachers that breaks away from this typical "apprenticeship of observation."

In chapter 8 of this book, Richert and Rabin present several cases in which student teachers faced unexpected and surprising interpretations and behaviors of their students around the subject of race. Richert and Rabin suggest the importance of preparing student teachers to such events: "[W]e must prepare them . . . to imagine how different children might respond, which would help them determine what steps they need to plan to move the children's responses toward their curricular goals." Richert and Rabin describe student teachers facing racist comments made by their students as "being caught off guard" and stress that "the preparation of student teachers for dealing with the emotional side of such occurrences and the educative requirements is a necessity." Such preparation should include an intentional and well-planned confrontation of student teachers with similar situations as part of the process of teacher education.

## Drama of Discussion

Vaughn describes another type of drama, the "drama of discussion," as "a type of play in which the characters discuss their problems and their situations, thereby engaging the audience's attention and ideas rather than in emotions" (1978, p. 66). This type of drama invites the audience to an intellectual experience that requires an exploration of the playwright's ideas. In a drama of discussion, ideas are put in the mouth of the characters rather than in the form of theoretical or conceptual writing. Moreover, these ideas can be brought into conflict and are used to represent real-life situations. In teacher education, the student-teacher experience can be engaging and challenging in the domain of ideas beyond involving emotional response.

The idea of a drama of discussion is especially relevant to teacher education programs because it requires the presentation of ideas and concepts that are different in their approach and might lead to coping with conflict and possibly reaching some resolution. It is important to link these ideas to classroom experiences and practices.

## Teacher Educators as Playwrights

"Playwrights" are obviously central figures in the world of drama and theatre. Adopting the drama metaphor for teacher education programs, the program is analogous to the written play.

The role of teacher educators as playwrights is conceived herewith as crucial for the future of teacher education in a changing world. Teacher educators, whose aim is to adapt teacher education programs to specific student audiences and cultural situations, are viewed as playwrights who create their own *drama*. In order to create a drama it is important to be aware of *dramatic structure*.

In the following section we draw on basic theatrical concepts based on Aristotle as follows: *Dramatic structure* "the system of organization and arrangement of elements that is unique to the drama as a literary genre works, regardless of period, style, or national origin" (Vaughn, 1978, p. 62). In analogy, there exists a system of organization and arrangement of elements that is unique to teacher education programs regardless of time or place. The classical elements of teacher education programs are: foundation disciplines, like psychology or sociology; subject matter domains, like mathematics or language; general principles of pedagogy; as well as the special pedagogic knowledge required for teaching diverse subject matter domains.

A central and crucial element of teacher education programs is the practicum, namely the opportunities for observing classroom practices, and therefore conducting such practices. A different list of elements of the knowledge of teaching was proposed by Shulman (1978) as follows: content knowledge, general pedagogical knowledge, curriculum knowledge, pedagogical content knowledge, knowledge of learners, knowledge of educational contexts and knowledge of educational ends, purposes and values and their philosophical and historical grounds. These elements might be perceived as elements of teacher education programs.

The organization and arrangement of these elements is in the hands of developers of teacher education programs, and there is no predetermined sequence. Teacher educators as "playwrights" might arrange these elements in a manner they deem appropriate to their own teaching situation. This brings us to the notion of plot.

*Plot* might be understood as the story of the play. Usually plot is evaluated by the clarity, or coherence, of the storyline. According to Aristotle, plot must exhibit *wholeness*, having a beginning, middle, and end. In presenting the concept of drama as a guiding metaphor for the realization of teacher education we chose the Aristotelian conception of plot as most appropriate for educational purposes, requiring a beginning, middle, and end.

In the beginning of a teacher education program, student teachers have to be introduced into a dual role, as students who are learning new content and new skills, and, as future teachers who are responsible to teaching to others the same material they have learned themselves. For instance, student teachers learn mathematics but also have to learn how to teach mathematics. Following this beginning, several events have to occur in order for the drama of teacher education to reach an end where all the learning that came before comes together to create a coherent image of teaching. Like a drama that, according to Aristotle, portrays actions that effect a change, teacher education programs have to demonstrate a similar movement from a beginning leading to an envisioned end.

For Aristotle, another principle of plotting is *unity*, which Vaughn describes as "the essential organizing principle in a drama that assures its cohesiveness, its completeness, and its oneness" (Vaughn, 1978, p. 207). Unity exists when all parts of the plot are necessary elements and the removal of any part of the plot will cause the story to become unclear. It would be interesting to study what the term unity means for the storyline of teacher education. What parts of the program are interchangeable while the removal of some might cause chaos and loss of meaning? For instance, the practicum seems to be a necessary element in the plot of teacher education, removing it might cause loss of meaning. But what about courses like "philosophy of education"? Are they part of the unity of the program? The comparative analysis of different teacher education programs might uncover the secret of their unity. This is a relevant question, especially in times when there is a call for alternative ways to acquire a teacher education license. The question of unity arises in the context of the general outline of the teacher education program. Teacher educators are in the best position to judge whether the program they develop or implement represents unity in the sense of cohesiveness, completeness, and oneness. Unity might exist in the whole program as well as in specific courses.

*Theme* is basically "the central or dominating ideas with which a drama is concerned" (Vaughn, 1978, p. 197). Such a central idea of drama is analogous to the "big idea" that characterizes curriculum material (Shulman & Sherin, 2004; Cohen, Lotan, Whitcomb, Balderrama, Cossey, & Swanson, 1995). A big idea of a teacher education program might be social justice or the role of teachers as inquiry guides. Big ideas of the teacher education program at Mills College include, for instance: teachers as agents of change, constructivism, and ongoing inquiry.

Themes might be decided a priori by the playwright or be uncovered through the analysis of plays. For example, one might perceive *Othello* as a drama of jealousy or *A Doll's House* as concerned with the status of women. In the curriculum field, big ideas, or themes, might be identified in different ways. Shulman and Sherin (2004) suggest that "substantive ideas" like evolution, or "syntactic ideas" like the design of an experiment, might guide the development of curriculum materials. Big ideas might also apply to ideological/theoretical constructs such as equity, ecological sustainability, or active learning.

Big ideas in teacher education programs might be related to the future work of teachers, such as "reflection and inquiry" because of their importance in teachers' work. Big ideas in education, like themes in the theatre, might be part of the planning of curriculum and instruction and might emerge through analysis of programs.

## Catharsis

A most intriguing theatrical concept is *catharsis*, found in Aristotle (*Poetics* chapter 4). Catharsis is associated with the affective power of drama, spectators are expected to feel a flood of emotions. Boyce (1987) maintains that this emotional response has therapeutic and educational value. "Catharsis is perceived as supporting one's emotional life and can help a person function better outside the theatre doors" (Ben-Peretz & Schonmann, 2000, p. 45).

Catharsis might be viewed as a response to a therapeutic need through the release of emotions. Viewing drama as having the potential of raising strong emotional responses in the audience might be relevant to teacher education programs. Such programs might, indeed, cause strong emotional reactions, for instance, in the realm of learning about the conditions of student lives. The purpose of introducing catharsis explicitly into the language of developing and implementing teacher education programs is to direct attention to these phenomena as part of the process of teacher education.

In contrast with the emotional aspect of catharsis there exist cognitive catharsis theories. Bohart suggests that a process of change in attitude or understanding of personal phenomena requires a dialogue between feeling and cognition. "Cognitions carry forward what is implicit in feelings" (1980, p. 199). That means that teacher educators have to provide student teachers with opportunities to discuss their feelings concerning various emotional experiences that are part of their learning process.

Another perspective concerning the catharsis impact of drama is based on Brecht's notion of "Verfremdung" or the "alienation affect." According to Brecht the audience has to distance itself from the dramatic events in order to be able to consider social realities and reach appropriate conclusions. "The new alienations are only designed to free socially-conditioned phenomena from that stamp of familiarity which protects them against our grasp today." . . . [For the spectator] "to transform himself from general passive acceptance to a corresponding state of suspicious inquiry he would need to develop that detached eye" (Brecht, 1964, p. 192).

In notes written by Brecht to his play *Die Mutter*, he describes the play as a "non-Aristotelian drama" that "makes nothing like such a free use as does the Aristotelian of the passive empathy of the spectator; it also relates differently to certain psychological effects, such as catharsis" (1964, p. 57). Brecht believed that this kind of theater can cause the audience to change their attitude, which may lead them to changing the world "to teach the spectator a quite definite practical attitude, directed towards changing the world, it must begin by making him adopt in the theatre a quite different attitude from what he is used to" (1964, p. 57). On the other hand, Verfremdung might reach a point where the spectators will view the dramatic events as not applying to them (Bach & Bach, 1963).

Brecht's notion of dramatic alienation suggests important implications for teacher education programs. Alienation, according to Brecht, requires a movement from passive acceptance of a situation to what he calls "suspicious inquiry." In the context of teacher education programs as drama, that means the confrontation of student teachers with the harsh realities of students' lives, for instance, extreme poverty. Student teachers have to be moved by the program to raise questions, and to inquire into the roots of these situations, in order to take steps to prevent them.

One of the expected outcomes of teacher education is assisting teachers in identifying with their students and developing empathy with their students' problems and difficulties. Introducing relevant texts into the literature for student teachers, and creating experiences that could lead to emotional catharsis might serve these goals. Beyond that, teacher education has the potential of becoming a revolutionary power for improving society, diminishing gaps, and serving equity. For teacher education to become a significant part of the future of human life it is not enough to be able to identify with students and the conditions of their lives. Teacher educators have the moral obligation to include ideas of equity and justice into their practice. One of the ways of achieving this goal is by distancing oneself from specific instances of societal wrongs and injustices and trying to adopt a meta-level stance seeking for appropriate solutions.

These components of teacher education programs are consistent with approaches that view teachers as levers for social change and reform in the spirit of the desire to improve and repair the world. These ideas are expressed by educators like Cochran-Smith (1991). Cochran-Smith argues that teachers should be accountable for reforming teaching and schools. She suggests that education is a political enterprise, with teachers and teacher educators having the potential to shape the future of education. "Teaching and teacher education are unavoidably political enterprises and are, in that sense, value-laden and socially constructed. Over time, they both influence and are influenced by the histories, economies, and cultures of the societies, in which they exist, particularly by competing views of the purpose of schools and schooling. Like it or not, more of us in teacher education and in the policy communities will need to engage in these public and political debates if we are to have a real voice in framing the questions that matter for the future of teaching education" (Cochran-Smith, 2000, p. 165).

Teacher education programs should suggest possible solutions for societal problems. The programs must give hope and a sense of competence and power to make an impact. They cannot settle for introducing the wrongs but have to encourage to work toward creating a better reality.

The question is how to introduce the notion of catharsis in teacher education programs. One possibility is to use case literature of teaching episodes (Shulman & Sato, 2006). Another way is to analyze student teachers' own experiences (Ben-Peretz & Schonmann, 2000).

## TEACHER EDUCATORS AS CURRICULUM USERS

In the life of schools the use of externally prepared curriculum materials requires adaptation to specific local contexts. It is the role of teachers using such materials to uncover their potential for diverse student populations and classroom situations, as well as their own pedagogic orientations and priorities (Ben-Peretz, 1990). Adopting the theatre metaphor provides an important lens for this process.

The notion of "curriculum potential" (Ben-Peretz, 1990) provides a conceptual link between the curricular text and its use by teachers. According to this notion teachers might use curricular texts in ways and forms beyond the intentions of curriculum developers. Comparing programs of teacher education to drama provides an intense relationship between the text and its enactment in the same way that the written text of drama allows a great variety of interpretations when put on stage. For instance, the role of Hamlet might be played very differently by different actors, or, a play might be moved from its original context into another time or place. *Romeo and Juliet* is a good example of the transformations of dramatic text into multiple enactments. Usually in these transformations the text stays the same but its potential is expressed in various modes. Viewing a program of teacher education through the lens of the metaphor of drama might enrich the developing process by aiming at constructing multidimensional, multisensory performances to be enacted by teacher educators. As users of teacher education programs, teacher educators might try to uncover their potential for transformation into specific local contexts. Possible enactments of the texts of teacher education programs are analogous to the use of curriculum potential in curricula designed for schools.

## DRAMATIC CONCEPTS AS TOOLS FOR ANALYZING AND EVALUATING TEACHER EDUCATION PROGRAMS

Present-day research on teacher education programs faces difficulties in providing evidence for their effectiveness. Notions of drama, dramatic structure, plot, unity, theme, and catharsis might provide relevant tools for analyzing and evaluating teacher education programs.

Curriculum analysis is an accepted way of uncovering the nature and meaning of curriculum materials. Categories for analysis might be curriculum goals, linguistic aspects of the text, as well as a way that the curriculum relates to the role of students or the introduction of the basic concepts in the discipline. Similarly, programs of teacher education might be analyzed by using dramatic categories mentioned above. Following the plot of the program, or opportunities for catharsis, might yield important insights into the nature of the program and its potential uses. Such an analysis might uncover, as well, the null curriculum, namely, missing elements in the program that could be complemented by users. The analysis of teacher education programs might yield summative evaluation outcomes or be used in a formative manner to improve programs. Teacher educators could be involved in these forms of analysis.

## CONCLUSION

In this chapter, an examination of relevant literature showed that the role assigned to teacher educators focuses on providing student teachers with the knowledge and dispositions required for classroom practice. Attention was directed, as well, to other roles that teacher educators play, and their obligations to conduct research and contribute to the knowledge base of teaching and learning.

Using the metaphor of teacher education as drama, additional potential roles are suggested for teacher educators. Several concepts related to the world of drama and theatre were presented and discussed, providing the basis for a variety of roles for teacher educators, for instance, as "playwrights," developing programs of teacher education. This role might lead to programs that are significant for changing contexts of schooling. The "themes" of these programs could represent central, big ideas in education like equity, constructivism, or cultural sustainability. Dramatic concepts like plot, unity, or catharsis, were suggested as guiding frameworks for the development and use of teacher education programs. The drama of teacher education programs deserves a central place in the education system. This chapter proposes to use dramatic concepts not only for designing teacher education programs and for extending the anticipated roles for teacher educators, but also as a framework for the critical analysis, and comparison of existing programs.

## NOTE

We thank Shifra Schonmann for her invaluable help and advice in writing this chapter.

## REFERENCES

Bach, M., & Bach, H. L. (1963). The moral problem of political responsibility: Brecht, Frisch, Sartre. *Book Abroad, 37*(4), 378–384.

Ben-Peretz, M. (1990). *The teacher-curriculum encounter: Freeing teachers from the tyranny of texts.* Albany: State University of New York Press.

Ben-Peretz, M. (2009). *Policy-making in education: A holistic approach in response to global changes.* Lanham, MD: Rowman & Littlefield.

Ben-Peretz, M., Kleeman, S., Richenberg, R., & Shimoni, S. (2010). Educators of educators: Their goals, perceptions and practices. *Professional Development in Education, 36*(1–2), 111–129.

Ben-Peretz, M., & Schonmann, S. (2000). *Behind closed doors: Teachers and the role of the teachers' lounge.* Albany: State University of New York Press.

Bohart, A. C. (1980). Toward a cognitive theory of catharsis. *Psychotherapy: Theory, Research and Practice, 17*(2), 192–201.

Bolton, G. M. (1984). *Drama as education: An argument for placing drama at the center of the curriculum.* London: Longman Group.

Boyce, S. N. (1987). *Welcome to the theatre.* Chicago: Nelson Hall.

Brecht, B. (1964). *Brecht on theatre: The development of an aesthetic.* New York: Hill and Wang.

Cochran-Smith, M. (1991). Learning to teach against the grain. *Harvard Educational Review, 61*(3), 279–310.

Cochran-Smith, M. (2000). Teacher education at the turn of the century [Editorial]. *Journal of Teacher Education, 51*(3), 163–165.

Cochran-Smith, M. (2005). Teacher educators as researchers: Multiple perspectives. *Teaching and Teacher Education, 21*, 219–225.

Cohen, E. G., Lotan, R. A., Whitcomb, J. A., Balderrama, M., Cossey, R., & Swanson, P. (1995). Complex instruction: Higher order thinking in heterogeneous classrooms. In R. J. Stahl (Ed.), *Handbook of cooperative learning* (pp. 82–96). Westport CT: Greenwood Press.

Connelly, F. M., & Clandinin, D. J. (1988). *Teachers as curriculum planners: Narratives of experience.* New York: Teachers College Press.

Day, C. (2004). Change agendas: The roles of teacher educators. *Teaching Education, 15*(2), 145–158.

Grant, C. A., & Gillette, M. (2006). A candid talk to teacher educators about effectively preparing teachers who can teach everyone's children. *Journal of Teacher Education, 57*, 292–299.

Grumet, M. R. (1978). Curriculum as theatre: Merely players. *Curriculum Inquiry, 8*, 37–64.

Koster, B., Brekelmans, M., Korthagen, F., & Wubbles, T. (2005). Quality requirements for teacher educators. *Teaching and Teacher Education, 21*, 157–176.

Lortie, D. (1975). *Schoolteacher: A sociologic study.* Chicago: University of Chicago Press.

Lunenberg, M., Korthagen, F., & Swennen, A. (2007). The teacher educator as a role model. *Teaching and Teacher Education, 23*, 586–601.

Massanari, K., Drummond, W. H., & Houston, W. R. (1978). *Emerging professional roles for teacher educators.* Washington, DC: American Association of Colleges for Teacher Education and ERIC Clearinghouse on Teacher Education.

Murray, J. (2011). Towards a new language of scholarship in teacher educators' professional learning? In T. Bates, A. Swennen, & K. Jones (Eds.), *The professional development of teacher educators* (pp. 202–213). London: Routledge.

Schonmann, S. (1996). Curriculum planning by staging a play, *Halacha Le'maashe Be'tichnun Limudim, 11*, 35–48. [In Hebrew: Tahalichey Hafakat Htzaga Kederech Leyetzirat Tochnit Limudim].

Schonmann, S. (2005). Theatrical representations of teaching as performance. In J. Brophy & S. Pinnegar (Eds.), *Learning from Research on Teaching: Perspective, Methodology, and Representation, Advances in Research and Teaching, Vol. 11.* (pp. 283–311). Bingley, UK: Emerald Group Publishing Limited.

Schwab, J. J. (1973). The Practical 3: Translation into curriculum. *School Review, 81*, 501–522.

Shulman, J. H., & Sato, M. (2006). *Mentoring teachers toward excellence: Supporting and developing highly qualified teachers*. San Francisco: WestEd & Jossey-Bass.

Shulman, L. S. (1978). Knowledge and teaching: Foundations of the new reform. *Harvard Educational Review, 57*(1), 1–22.

Shulman, L. S., & Sherin, M. G. (2004). Fostering communities of teachers as learners: Disciplinary perspectives. *Journal of Curriculum Studies, 36*(2), 129–135.

Tillema, H. H. (2004). The dilemma of teacher educators: Building actual teaching on conceptions of learning to teach. *Teaching Education, 15*(3), 277–291.

Vaughn, J. A. (1978). *Drama A to Z*. New York: Frederick Ungar Publishing.

Verriour, P. (1994). *In role: Teaching and learning dramatically*. Markham, ON: Pippin Publishing.

# *Chapter Seven*

# Feminine Culture and Teacher Education

Michal Zellermayer and Esther Hertzog

## QUESTIONS WE NEED TO ASK OURSELVES

In light of the feminization of teaching (the fact that the teaching profession has become a "women's profession"), several intriguing educational, feminist, and social issues should be investigated. Are we, teacher educators, aware of our special responsibility and powerful role in society? Are we aware of the gendered characteristics of the educational system, of the teachers, the teacher educators, and of the potential stemming from the overwhelming presence of women in education? As our students will interact intensively and continuously with wide-ranging populations (citizens, professionals, family members) in the years to come, are we aware of the impact we have (or can have) on our students, as women, and its far-reaching consequences? Can we, feminist teacher educators, contribute to the beginnings of an essential change in the content, shape, and structure of the educational system, with the aim of constructing "a feminine culture"?

Indeed, much work has been done on both the theoretical and the practical levels, with regard to feminist perspectives of educational issues at large and of feminist pedagogy (Noddings, 1984, 1988, 1995; Leck, 1987; Weiler, 1988, 1991; Blackmore, 1996; Thompson & Gitlin, 1995; Hollingsworth, Cody, & Clandinin, 1994). Feminist research in the Israeli educational context is also rapidly expanding, since it began more than three decades ago (Ben Zvi-Mayer, 1976; Avrahami-Einat, 1989; Shlasky, 2000; Zellermayer & Peri, 2002; Hertzog & Walden, 2010). However, only very limited research has been performed on feminist issues with regard to the work of teacher educators, most of whom are women (Alpert, 2010; Dvir, 2007; Fishbein, 2010; Kehat, 2010).

In elaborating on gendered perspectives of the "feminization" of teacher education in Israel, we will discuss several issues that, while predominantly relevant to the Israeli context, may, at the same time, contribute to wider understandings and prompt a more general analysis of the connection between feminine culture and the feminized teacher education.

Examining the Israeli educational system from a critical feminist perspective, we shall follow both the political feminism and the caring approach. The first is focused on a gender transformation that entails women's collective awareness of male domination (McCall, 1994) and the construction of a new social order, namely a partnership of men and women (Eisler, 2000), while the caring approach (Noddings 1992, 1995) emphasizes the ethics of empathy, generosity, and the empowering of the other, which are widely attributed to women's socialization.

Several unique characteristics of the Israeli educational context are relevant to our analysis. One of its features is, for instance, the profound gender bias, which is symbolically and socially accentuated through masculinized language. Thus, for example, Hanna Kehat (2010), a teacher educator in a religious teacher education college, complains about her female students, who express themselves in Hebrew in the masculine form. This is clearly not unique to the religious sector. A striking illustration of this phenomenon is the fact that even feminist scholars relate to teachers and teacher educators in the masculine, in spite of the fact that teachers in Israel are predominantly women. Thus, teacher education should take this significant aspect into account in the planning and implementing of teacher education. The Israeli educational system is also characterized by its sectorial fragmentation, the main expressions of which are the Jewish-Arab and the religious-secular divides. The gendered quintessence of the sectorial structure has a far-reaching impact, for instance, on boys and girls who, in the religious and orthodox Jewish parts of the system, are separated and study different subjects, adjusted to their gender. This separation serves to preserve, enforce, and strengthen the gendered socialization and the taken-for-granted gender segregation (El-Or, 1994; Ayalon & Yogev, 1998; Kehat, 2010). "War culture" (Hiller & Sandler, 2007) is yet another conspicuous characteristic of the Israeli state. It is a "man's culture" due to the fact that the country is constantly engaged in military activities and the military enjoys a prominent status and a priority in the country's allocation of its financial resources. The obligatory military service and the constant necessity to defend the existence of the nation against external and internal threats entails a significant influence on the gendered socialization of boys and girls from a tender age through high school. They are exposed to the militaristic culture through national narratives, "the most important of these are narratives of power, fighting and masculinity" (Gurr & Mazali, 2001), and through the history curricula, field trips, and school ceremonies. It appears that the education system "normalizes war and military service" and instills the belief that no alternative exists to the state of war (Gurr, 2005; Gurr & Mazali, 2001; Hiller & Sandler, 2007). In the militaristic reality of Israel, feminine discourse and women's struggle for equality and partnership assume special importance.

Thus, our challenge, as feminist teacher educators and scholars who accompany women teachers on their academic journey, is to commit ourselves in our professional activity to the feminist and human efforts to challenge a reality governed by concepts of power, authority, domination, competition, and materialism. We shall therefore discuss the significance of gendered forms of speaking, thinking, and acting, as reflecting a wider gendered social order, as well as preserving and reinforcing it. We shall illustrate from our work with graduate students who are veteran teachers how we attempt to introduce feminine concepts and practices, which will contribute to enhancing a feminine culture of schooling. We assume that, as the school system is a part of the wider society, if these changes evolve in schools, they may be followed by a much greater impact on the wider society. In what follows, we will elaborate on the concept of "feminine culture," discuss its implications for education and illustrate it from our work with graduate students at the Levinsky College of Education in Israel. The exemplars that will be presented focus on two main elements of the feminist and critical pedagogy: caring and partnership. Michal's exemplar demonstrates how behaving "femininely," by introducing the teacher's inclusion, support, and caring of a rejected child into their relationships, affects both the adult and the young persons. Esther's exemplar stresses the recognition by academia of invisible experiences and silenced voices of women (as a marginalized group). Elaborating on the subject of "leadership" in terms of the students' "women's" world in the kindergarten, the students offer the academic-hegemonic context their own interpretation, and they are being accredited by it.

## What Is and Is There a "Feminine Culture"?

Our understanding of feminine culture has been inspired by Riane Eisler's work and particularly *The Chalice and the Blade* (1987) and *Tomorrow's Children: A Blueprint for Partnership Education in the 21st Century* (2000). Her futuristic work begins with a comprehensive description of the dynamic evolution that has taken place in the last five thousand years, according to the findings of archeologist Marija Gimbutas (1982). Eisler contends that a world based on partnership between men and women existed until five thousand years ago; a world in which both men and women cocreated life conditions for evolutionary survival, adaptiveness, and reproduction. This world was destroyed with the invasion of Europe by Indo-European nomadic tribes (or the "Kurgan culture"). These tribes brought with them values of competition, hierarchical domination, fighting, oppression, and cruelty, which prevail throughout the world to this day, representing the shift of power from Old European matrilineal cultures to Kurgan culture. Gimbutas believed that the expansions of the Kurgan culture were a series of essentially hostile, military incursions where a new warrior culture imposed itself on the peaceful, matriarchal cultures of "Old Europe," replacing it with a patriarchal warrior society, a process visible in the appearance of fortified settlements and hill-forts and the graves of warrior-chieftains.

The power shift of five thousand years ago resulted in the creation of hierarchies. As Goerner (2000) notes, hierarchies were crucial when they first arose because they added social coherence and the ability to mobilize group resources and energies in focused ways. Now, however, the pace of change and level of complexity of a twenty-first-century world is too much for this ancient command-and-control system. Bonds break vertically and absurdity is common.

Various kinds of exploitation and abuse of power became widespread because the culture that arose with hierarchy was based on imperialism (war for profit, power, and empire-building). This culture is responsible for many (perhaps most) of the convoluted calamities we now face: from materialism, inequity, and environmental degradation, to democratic processes dominated by financial interests.

Eisler suggests that the feminist vision of peace, equality, and partnership can save the male-dominated world from its demise. She claims that we are on the verge of social transformation, which means a transition (or return) from a society based on domination, power, and control to a society built on social equality and gender partnership. Eisler's model of partnership is based on the eminence of values such as compassion and concern for others, on which women are raised. This does not imply an essential difference between women and men, but rather two sets of values instilled in the patriarchal society that create binary and dichotomous hierarchical control.

## DEVELOPING A CULTURE OF CARING AND PARTNERSHIP IN EDUCATION

Following Leck (1987), Noddings (1995) and Eisler (1987, 2000, 2002), we contend that the feminization of the educational system can contribute to changing human society from an androcratic society (controlled by men) to a gylanic society that binds and liberates men and women, and "actualize(s) a partnership society" (Eisler, 1987, p. 170). This change will be from a reality that is based on patriarchal, capitalistic, and militaristic fundamentals, to one that is based on equality, caring, and social and environmental sustainability.

Eisler (2000) compares between two contradictory educational models, the dominator and the partnership. The latter enables children to realize their human potential and enhances their supportive, caring, and creative capabilities that characterize partnership in all spheres of life. The dominator model subjects children to "negative, uncaring, fear, shame, and threat-based treatment or other aversive experiences such as violence or sexual violation." As a result, children "develop responses appropriate for this kind of dominator environment. They become tyrannical, abusive and aggressive or withdrawn and chronically depressed, defensive, hypervigilant, and numb to their own pain as well as to that of others" (Eisler, 2000, p. 8).[1]

Eisler (2000) suggests that education in the twenty-first century can make teachers and children partners in the cultural transformation from domination to partnership—not only in gender relations but in the creation of a more effective, humane, and sustainable economy and social welfare. When teachers and children reach an understanding of the two models, it would result in "educational methods, materials, and institutions that foster a less violent, more equitable, democratic, and sustainable future" (p. xiv). While the dominator model characterizes the teacher as the sole source of information and knowledge and where relations are based on teacher control, in the partnership model "teacher and student knowledge and experience are valued; learning and teaching are integrated and multidisciplinary; curriculum, leadership and decision making are gender balanced; the multicultural reality of human experience is valued and tapped as a source of learning; social and physical sciences emphasize our interconnection with other people and nature; mutual responsibility, empathy and caring are highlighted and modeled" (p. 23).

The two examples that are presented below illustrate, through our teaching of graduate students who are veteran teachers, how we attempt to incorporate the feminist approaches of caring and partnership into our teaching.

## COMPASSIONATE EDUCATION—DOING ACTION RESEARCH WITH TEACHERS IN THE CONTEXT OF LITERACY EDUCATION: *MICHAL'S EXEMPLAR*

Like Eisler, Khen Lampert (2003) criticizes the way in which schools create, exacerbate, and ignore the distress of children, when in fact schools are supposed to provide a humane response to that very distress. His work points to the organizational, psychological, and functional difficulties of today's public schools, which prevent the adults working there from taking responsibility for and acting to alleviate the children's distress. As graduate students, teachers voice their concerns about children's distress and their lack of engagement in learning. Many of their action research studies attempt to find ways to change this situation in their classrooms and to develop, through action research, compassionate, partnership teaching. For example, take the case of Shoshana, a sixth-grade veteran teacher with more than thirty years of teaching experience. In the beginning of the academic year, she raised the concern that in her new class of thirty-four pupils, with an equal number of boys and girls, there were five children with special needs: Asperger's syndrome, ADHD, PDD, and one with difficult behavioral problems. She asked: "How can I involve five children with special needs in my teaching?" And soon afterward she provided an answer: "I will begin my action research with Nathan (a pseudonym), the boy with the behavioral problem."

In her research diary, she described Nathan as a short twelve-year-old boy who is not well cared for physically, wearing sloppy clothes that are often inadequate for the weather. Dragging his feet as he walks, he looks withdrawn and depressed. She noticed that he comes to school without the necessary books and school supplies and without lunch. Nathan is the son of an immigrant family from Russia, who lives with his mother and fifteen-year-old sister near his grandparents' home. His mother works in the office of a public health clinic and is barely able to support the family. His father lives and works in another town. He rarely contacts the family and does not support them financially. When Nathan called him, he promised to come but did not show up, not even for parent-teacher conferences or for Nathan's birthday. Nathan's case was transferred by the school counselor to the attention of the municipal department of social services.

Shoshana described the numerous reports that his teachers wrote over the previous five years about Nathan's many class disruptions, violent arguments with other children that sometimes escalated into fist fights. Apparently, in a questionnaire administered by one of his former teachers, about two-thirds of the class mentioned that he ruins the class climate and that they refuse to share a desk with him.

From Shoshana's notes, one got a clear picture of an at-risk pupil with low self-esteem, who was lonely at school and at home. The family believed they could provide for all of his physical and emotional needs, but, as his mother sometimes said to Shoshana whenever she showed up at school, they still hoped that the school would provide a better future for him and were disappointed that he was making very limited educational progress and was too often involved in at-risk behavior. Shoshana wrote that she was drawn to Nathan because of his strong need for love, support, and guidance. She felt profoundly responsible for him: "He made his way deep into my heart. I want to save him and change his image. I want to reveal his good and strong features. And most of all, I want him to be happy and laugh like the rest of the children and be accepted to a good junior high school." When she began her study, she had already established a close relationship with him. She described this relationship in detail:

> Every morning I check his attendance. Whenever he is absent I call his home to find out why. When he comes, I approach him and inquire about his health and about how he slept. Before he goes to other teachers' classes, I check his backpack to see whether he has the right supplies, I remind him to mind his behavior and to listen to the teachers.
>
> We have an agreement that he stays late after school and I check his backpack. I help him prepare for the next school day. I make sure the he eats a warm lunch with the children in the afterschool program. I get him new clothes from contributions that the school gets and I managed to get him a used computer from the municipality. Every day, I ask him about the kind of day he had.

Thus, since the beginning of the school year, Shoshana was significantly present in Nathan's life. She was engaged in his learning and felt committed to his well-being. On the basis of this relationship, she began collecting data while planning an action research asking the question: How can I change Nathan's situation from risk to hope? While considering her first research cycle, she noted that Nathan was good with computers, and his free writing was rich and interesting. On this basis, she decided to start writing to him in a dialogue journal, in which she invited him to share with her his personal experiences and emotions. They exchanged writing on a daily basis for several weeks and they decided on a secret place where they would leave the journal for each other.

Here are some quotes from his journal entries that demonstrate Nathan's genuine emotional bonding with Shoshana:

> I was happy to stay with you this afternoon and I was glad to see you. Thank you for giving me another wonderful day. . . . I think that my afternoon meetings with you are really useful. And that they really help me with my studies. . . . I was sad that you lost your voice. It hurts me to see you suffer and I try to help you by making the pupils quiet. I hope that you feel better soon and return to the way you were before. . . . I am sorry that I raised my voice at you. I was nervous about something that happened to my sister yesterday. I hope that there will be no more days like that.

In the dialogue journal, Nathan provided considerable evidence of self-reflection, readiness for guidance, and empathy with Shoshana as a significant adult in his life. Consequently, Shoshana decided to upgrade their partnership and tie it to the current curriculum-based learning task—book writing for the annual book show. Shoshana invited Nathan to participate in the book show and publish his own life story. He began doing so by writing a short paragraph that eventually, under her guidance, developed into a seven-chapter book about Roy (a pseudonym). In these chapters, he introduced himself, told about his hobbies and his daily routines, and then about his immediate family, about their immigration to Israel, the separation of his parents and their present relationship. He ended his book with a chapter describing his last birthday, at which his father had not shown up, and concluded with a happy description of his extended family, his mother's sister and her husband and children, who served as a model of a functional family and with whom he celebrated his birthday.

When Shoshana reflected on Nathan's autobiography, she noted that "as Freire argues, writing was liberating for Nathan, enabling him to identify his own abilities and to construct a positive self-image." Yet, she regretted that he did not allow her to display his book in the show and was not yet able to gain public recognition of his writing abilities. Still, her work with him gave her the power and motivation to redesign a more inclusive and accessible learning environment for the rest of her students.

In the third action research cycle, she constructed an integrative teaching unit on the topic of the prophet Elijah. She divided the pupils into five groups. Each included one of the special needs children and at least one of their personal friends. She invited each of her students to contribute something to the collaborative display of their learning, according to his or her special interests and skills. Nathan, for example, made a clay figure of the prophet and dressed it in a blue Superman-like robe. All of the projects were publically displayed and presented by the group members at the school.

Following the public presentations, Shoshana wrote:

> That's it. I can now see Nathan gradually changing for the better. I feel that I fought for him and won. It was a fascinating experience for me. I learnt that I should never give up on a child even if the prospect of progress is very limited. Inclusion is not an impossible project for me anymore. I learnt that I can plan a learning environment for all my pupils, including the at-risk children.

Shoshana's story is not complete without describing a study by Naomi, her peer teacher and a student in the same graduate program. Both teachers took the same seminar with me and Naomi decided that her research project would consist of twelve shadowing observations of Shoshana's lessons that were part of the unit on Elijah and of her conversations with Shoshana following these sessions. Her research question was: How is Shoshana's caring and compassion manifested in her teaching? Drawing on the work of Noddings (1984, 1988) and van Manen (1991), she identified the following categories in her data:

- Personal attention: Shoshana listens to the children, as she moves among the groups, she caresses and encourages them.
- She is authoritative and draws limits.
- She draws on the children's experiences and knowledge, and invites them to display their particular interests and skills.

- She gives voice to a marginalized child.
- She models caring and compassion.
- She encourages the pupils' personal commitment and voluntary service activities.
- She is optimistic and communicates hope for everybody.

In her study, Naomi acted not as Shoshana's peer but as her critical friend, accompanying her in the three cycles of her action research. Their partnership served as a scaffold for Shoshana's learning on how to overcome her fear of at-risk children and how to create an inclusive learning environment for all, including herself, in which they all learned to identify and acknowledge their own self-worth. This process enabled Shoshana to construct an interesting study of her own. And so they became each other's mentors.

The rest of the graduate students who acted as a support group for Shoshana and Naomi gained a rich narrative that showed the possibility of a relational, conversational learning environment, told from a local classroom-context point of view. Against this background, throughout the academic year, we heard Nathan's voice getting stronger and, through Naomi's observations, saw the class becoming increasingly collaborative and engaged in learning. Without knowledge of Eisler, Shoshana and Naomi constructed a partnership model for veteran teachers, one that may help to provide a new generation of teachers with understandings and experience in a partnership way of interaction and thinking (Eisler, 2000, p. 134). They engaged with each other and with the children in partnership conversations (Eisler & Garrick, 2008) characterized by

- discernment instead of judgment
- compassion instead of judgment
- appreciation over criticism
- generosity in place of self-interest
- reconciliation over retaliation

Together, Shoshana and Naomi illustrate in practice Eisler's (2000, p. xv) vision of partnership education that prepares teachers for a relationship with children and with each other in which

- each child's intelligences and capabilities are treated as unique gifts to be nurtured and developed
- students have a real stake in their education
- teachers act more as mentors and facilitators than as lesson dispensers and controllers
- caring is an integral part of teaching and learning

- young people are learning to work together instead of continuously competing with each other
- they are offered the opportunity for self-directed learning and peer teaching
- education is not merely a matter of filling an "empty vessel"; students and teachers are partners in the adventure of learning

## THE PARTNERSHIP APPROACH IN GRADUATE TEACHERS' CLASSES: *ESTHER'S STORY*

The concept of partnership (and caring for that matter) in education is not unique to the feminist pedagogy, and many education theorists and practitioners (a few of the most prominent are John Dewey, Maria Montessori, and Paulo Freire) have elaborated on it in various ways (defined, for instance, as: humanistic, dialogic, democratic, emancipatory, critical). However, the feminist perspective emphasizes the partnership learning as opening up a wide range of topics and perspectives that are profoundly embedded in women's lives and are absent from the public and academic discourse. It underscores Weiler's (1991) argument about the importance of personal experience as a source of knowledge for women. Such learning is essentially political because it is invested in changing the gendered power structure in the educational system as well as in the larger society. This agenda necessitates the raising of awareness of educators and educated with regard to the existing social order. The gender change is expected to derive through a bottom-to-top resistance, which will emerge from personal awareness of collective discrimination and oppression. Feminist teacher education can contribute its part to this process by unveiling power structures and mechanisms that preserve patriarchy as well as other hierarchies. Its dialogic or partnership approach empowers and legitimizes the voices/experiences/insights of the women teachers.

In what follows, I shall illustrate from my teaching how I attempt to implement the partnership approach and then examine its implications and prospects with regard to the formal education system.

### What Is Leadership? Discussing Marshall Sahlins's Article

As a feminist, my teaching aspires to encourage dialogues among my students in which I am an equal participant. Each week I assign the reading task to two of my students. I expect them to present their reading to their classmates and lead conversations with the other students and me about the main ideas. I never know in advance how the students will connect the anthropological text to their daily experience and the kind of connections they will make between the personal and the political. For example, when we discussed "Leadership," two graduate students, kindergarten teachers, presented Marshall Sahlins's article, "Poor Man, Rich Man, Big Man, Chief" (1963),[2] comparing leadership in Polynesia and Melanesia. While Melanesia is characterized by relatively isolated and independent villages populated by small groups, Polynesia comprises relatively interconnected large villages that are part of a pyramidal structure. Sahlins describes Melanesia as an underdeveloped social system and Polynesia as a developed system, which enjoys relative economic prosperity and better infrastructures and explains differences between the leaders in these two societies and how these differences are reflected in their physical bearings. The Melanesian "big man," according to Sahlins,

> seems so thoroughly bourgeois, so reminiscent of the free-enterprising rugged individual of our own heritage. He combines with an ostensible interest in the general welfare a more profound measure of self-interested cunning and economic calculation.
>
> The historical caricature of the Polynesian chief, however, is feudal rather than capitalist. His appearance, his bearing is almost regal. (1963, p. 288)

Following Sahlins's analysis, the students identified two leadership types in public versus private kindergartens in Israel. They showed that in private kindergartens, almost everything depends on the "big man"; that is, on the kindergarten's director, on her personality, her charisma and the characteristics she presents in the kindergarten's social environment and to potential clients. She decides how the kindergarten will be run, and those who are unhappy with what it has to offer are entitled to leave and find themselves another "big (wo)man" of their liking. This leadership type depends on geographical, demographical, economic and other circumstances, and emerges from them rather than from the leader's "personality." Similar to the big man, the kindergarten's director needs to demonstrate a magnetizing personality or else her organization will crumble.

Like the Melanesian big man, the private kindergarten's director offers her services and expects to be rewarded for them, mainly by accepting her leadership (and being paid). This implies a "give-and-take" relationship. As long as the leader's followers (the group of parents) receive what they expect, they reciprocate (by paying and spreading the word about her excellence). Thus, the kindergarten director must please the parents, who are her customers, and preserve a balance between the educational and the economic interests, between her interests and those of her clients. This situation may cause the private kindergarten teacher to become exhausted and worn out, which may explain the instability of private kindergartens. As a result of the intense competition, private kindergartens frequently open and close. The students' comparison implied that private kindergartens can flourish in an economically richer environment and in urban areas with a competitive orientation.

On the other hand, leadership in the large public educational system is similar to the political system of Polynesia. The Polynesian leader's achievements and status do not necessarily derive from the dimensions of his body, brains or personal achievements but rather from his position in the tribe and his connections with the big "chief." It is a stable system. When the leader is replaced, the system continues to function smoothly by crowning a new chief. The weakness of this political structure stems from its inflated ruling institutions, which cause constant exploitation of the public by increasing taxes needed to fund the extensive staff (including the security forces that protect the chief and the regime).

Directors (or leaders) of kindergartens in the public sector do not inherit their position, nor are they appointed by a religious authority, but, like in the Polynesian political structure, once they are appointed, they cannot be removed unless they want to leave or because they move to a higher position in the hierarchy. They are not "chiefs" like in Polynesia, but are often perceived as "bosses."

The presentation and discussion that followed served well to illustrate one of the main theoretical issues of the course, namely, that early education frameworks are, in many ways, bureaucratic social enterprises. In this context, Max Weber's "bureaucracy" was found relevant even to the seemingly "family-like" kindergarten. The students referred to the relative stability of the "Polynesian political system/Israeli public education system" in Weber's (1968/1921) terms: "From a purely technical point of view, a bureaucracy is capable of attaining the highest degree of efficiency, and is in this sense formally the most rational known means of exercising authority over human beings" (p. 223).

The critical comparative analysis carried out during the discussion raised the students' awareness to the fact that women teachers are leaders no less than men; that Sahlins, like many other scholars, did not reflect on the gendered aspect of the leadership he studied; that the female students' managerial skills (just like those of male managers) are less important than the structured conditions of the relevant socioeconomic environment; that in the bureaucratic context, power relations characterize their prospects for success more than their "feminine" skills; and that kindergartens are comparable to any other political and bureaucratic social entity in terms of their hierarchy, authority, competition, efficiency, and so on. Hence, thanks to the students' insightful interpretation of a taken-for-granted social framework, they (and I) became aware of the price one needs to pay for economic and professional independence and of the rewards one gains from functioning within a bureaucratic-hierarchic system. The students exposed the power relations, especially in the privatized kindergartens' social surroundings, between the director and the parents.

In my listener position I recognize academic value of the students' arguments and their legitimacy. As a result, the dichotomy between scientific and practical knowledge, theory, and practice, academic and grassroots activity is significantly decreased. When the students engage in "a collective exploration" (Weiler, 1997, p. 637), all of us act as "partners in the adventure of learning" (Eisler, 2000, p. xv).

At times, the students arrive at the understanding that their experience in the graduate program can be applied to their own teaching in class. In these instances, the collaborative practice contributes to the reduction of power distance in classes and encourages pupils to bring their own life perspectives to the classroom.

## CONCLUDING REMARKS

It appears that "not much is new under the sun." The dialogue-partnership learning goes back to Socrates' times—conducting dialogues/conversations, rather than "lectures." or in Weiler's (1997) terms carrying out "a collective exploration" (637), or "a continuation of a conversation" as Weiler and Middleton (1999, p. 1) phrase it. Socrates' collective brainstorming took place anywhere, in the streets and public places, and not in closed rooms, avoiding the "student-teacher dualism" (Freire, 1970) and the bureaucratic-hierarchized setting.

Yet it seems that the efforts (of all educational reformist movements) to introduce the partnership model and the caring approach, to reduce authoritative power in the educational system, and to deconstruct its hierarchical structure, have had a very limited impact. As the educational system is an integral part of a hierarchized society, the democratic/humanist/feminist approach can thrive only negligibly. However, nurturing the feminist-liberal approach of caring-partnership/dialogue in teachers' education institutions can become the seeds out of which a far-reaching social change will hopefully emerge.

We suggest that our feminist and pedagogical task should be oriented at unveiling domination mechanisms in the education system and beyond and at searching ways to overcome the strategies of the hegemonic power that preserve the student-teacher dualism and hierarchy. The examples we drew from our teaching experiences provide some evidence to the potential of encouraging teacher-student dialogue, in which all share their personal and professional experiences and interpretations. We assume that, through similar and other venues, teachers can, as Clark suggests (2001, p. 173), learn to articulate their implicit theories, beliefs and practices.

In our experience, most teachers who apply to the graduate school are interested in personal and professional advancement. We offer them our support in facing their hesitations with regard to "the powerful draw of the disconnected life" (Palmer, 1998) that separates head from heart, facts from feelings, theory from practice, and teaching from learning, distancing themselves from their students as well as from the subjects they teach. We do so by treating our students as partners in the exciting excursion to the feminine culture.

Finally, following Goerner (2000) we perceive the role of education in building an integral civilization as crucial, and we identify with his warning that "we will all pay the price if we fail."

## NOTES

1. Eisler's analysis derives support from neuroscientists' work; one of these is Perry, Pollard, Blakley, and Viglante (1995).
2. I am grateful to Ms. Talia Rotshtein and Ms. Michal Tuvia for permission to use their contribution to the discussion in class, as part of their presentation, in this chapter.

## REFERENCES

Alpert, B. (2010). Feminist pedagogy as an approach in education and teachers' training. In S. Shlasky (Ed.), *Sexuality and gender in education* (pp. 29–62). Tel Aviv: Ramot [In Hebrew: Pedagogia feministit kegisha beshinuch ubehachsharat morim. In Miniyut umigdar bachinuch].

Avrahami-Einat, Y. (1989). *She and he in the classroom: Teacher*. Ben Shemen: Modan [In Hebrew: Hi vehu bakita].

Ayalon, H., & Yogev, A. (1998). Knowledge and courtesy (*Tora ve'derech eretz*): The alternative world view of national-religious high-school education. In H. Ayalon (Ed.), *Curricula as social constructions* (pp. 33–54). Tel Aviv: Ramot [In Hebrew: Tochniot limudim kehavnaya chevratit].

Ben Zvi-Mayer, S. (1976). The girl in the formal education. *Iyunim Be'chinuch, 12*, 107–144 [In Hebrew: Habat bachinuch haformali].

Blackmore, J. (1996). Breaking the silence: Feminist contributions to educational administration and policy. In K. A. Leithwood, J. Chapman, P. Corson, P. Hallinger, & A. Hart (Eds.), *International handbook of educational leadership and administration* (pp. 997–1034). Netherlands: Kluwer Academic Publishers.

Clark, C. M. (2001). *Talking shop: Authentic conversation and teacher learning*. New York: Teachers College Press.

Dvir, N. (2007). The place of feminist conceptions in the professional identity of a student teachers' supervisor—a case study. *Dapim, 44*, 91–122. [In Hebrew: Mekoman shel tfisot feministiot bezehuta hamiktzo'it shel madricha pedagogit—cheker mikre].

Eisler, R. (1987). *The chalice and the blade: Our history, our future*. San Francisco: Harper Collins.

Eisler, R. (2000). *Tomorrow's children: A blueprint for partnership education in the 21st century*. Boulder, CO: Westview Press.

Eisler, R. (2002). *The power of partnership: Seven relationships that will change your life*. Novato, CA: New World.

Eisler, R., & Garrick, L. E. (2008). Holding partnership conversations. *Integral Leadership Review, 8*(3). Retrieved March 23, 2012 from: www.archive-ilr.com/archives-2008/2008-06/2008-06-article-eisler-garrick.php.

El-Or, T. (1994). *Educated and ignorant: Ultraorthodox Jewish women and their world.* Boulder, CO: Lynne Rienner. [In Hebrew: Maskilot veburot: olamam shel nashim charediot].

Fishbein, Y. (2010). Women-teacher education: Feminist perspectives. In E. Hertzog & T. Walden (Eds.), *At teachers' expense: Gender and power in Israeli education* (pp. 73–90). Jerusalem: Carmel. [In Hebrew: Hachsharat morot: hebetim feministi'im. In Al gav hamorot: koach vemigdar bachinuch].

Freire, P. (1970). *Pedagogy of the oppressed.* New York: Continuum.

Gimbutas, M. (1982). *The goddesses and gods of old Europe: 6500–3500 B.C.: Myths, and cult images.* Berkeley: University of California Press.

Goerner, S. (2000). Rethinking education in light of great change. *New Horizons.* http://education.jhu.edu/newhorizons/Transforming%20Education/Articles/Rethinking%20Education/index.html.

Gurr, H. (2005). *Militarism in education.* Tel Aviv: Babel. [In Hebrew: Militarizem bachinuch].

Gurr, H., & Mazali, R. (2001). Man, woman, war and peace. *Panim, 17.* Retrieved March 23, 2012, from www.itu.org.il/Index.asp?ArticleID=1217&CategoryID=503&Page=1 (the website of the teachers' organization in Israel) [In Hebrew: Gever ve'isha, milchama veshalom].

Hertzog, E., & Walden, T. (Eds.). (2010). *At teachers' expense: Gender and power in Israeli education.* Jerusalem: Carmel [In Hebrew: al gav hamorot: koach vemigdar bachinuch].

Hiller, R., & Sandler, S. (2007). A matter of conscience: Militarism and conscientious objection in Israel. In M. Polner & S. Merken (Eds.), *Peace, justice, and Jews: Reclaiming our tradition* (pp. 207–214). New York: Bunim & Bannigan.

Hollingsworth, S., Cody, A., & Clandinin, J. D. (1994). *Teacher research and urban literacy education: Lessons and conversations in a feminist key.* New York: Teachers College Press.

Kehat, H. (2010). Female teachers' training in religious colleges from a gender perspective. In E. Hertzog and T. Walden (Eds.), *At teachers' expense: Gender and power in Israeli education* (pp. 267–288). Jerusalem: Carmel. [In Hebrew: al gav hamorot: koach vemigdar bachinuch].

Lampert, K. (2003). *Compassionate education: Prolegomena for radical schooling.* Lanham, MD: University Press of America.

Leck, G. M. (1987). Review article—Feminist pedagogy, liberation theory and the traditional schooling paradigm. *Educational theory, 37*(3): 343–354.

McCall, A. L. (1994). Rejoicing and despairing: Dealing with feminist pedagogy in teacher education. *Teaching Education, 6*(2), 59–69.

Noddings, N. (1984). *Caring: A feminine approach to ethics and moral education.* Berkeley: University of California Press.

Noddings, N. (1988). An ethic of caring and its implications for instructional arrangements. *American Journal of Education, 96*(2), 215–231.

Noddings, N. (1992). *The challenge to care in schools.* New York: Teachers College Press.

Noddings, N. (1995). *Philosophy of education.* Boulder, CO: Westview.

Palmer, J. P. (1998). *The courage to teach: Exploring the inner landscape of a teacher's life.* San Francisco, CA: Jossey-Bass.

Perry, B. D., Pollard, R. A., Blakley, W. L., & Viglante, D. (1995). Childhood trauma, the neurobiology of adaptation, and "use dependent" development of the brain: How "states" become "traits." *Infant Mental Health Journal, 16,* 271–291.

Sahlins, M. D. (1963). Poor man, rich man, big man, chief. *Comparative Studies in History and Society, 5*(3), 285–303.

Shlasky, S. (Ed.)(2000). *Sex and gender in education.* Tel Aviv: Ramot [In Hebrew: Miniyut umigdar bachinuch].

Thompson, A., & Gitlin, A. (1995). Creating spaces for reconstructing knowledge in feminist pedagogy. *Educational Theory, 45*(2), 125–150.

van Manen, M. (1991). *The tact of teaching: The meaning of pedagogical thoughtfulness.* London, ON: Althouse Press.

Weber, M. (1968/1921). *Economy and society*. New York: Bedminster Press.
Weiler, K. (1988). *Women teaching for change: Gender, class and power*. New York: Bergin & Garvey.
Weiler, K. 1991. Freire and a feminist pedagogy of difference. *Harvard Educational Review, 61*(4), 449–475.
Weiler, K. (1997). Reflections on writing a history of women teachers. *Harvard Educational Review, 67*(4), 635–658.
Weiler, K., & Middleton, S. (Eds.). (1999). *Telling women's lives: Narrative inquiries in the history of women's education*. Buckingham, UK: Open University Press.
Zellermayer, M., & Peri, P. (Eds.). (2002). *Women teachers in Israel: A feminist perspective*. Tel Aviv: Hakibbutz Hameuchad [In Hebrew: Morot beIsrael: mabat feministy].

## *Chapter Eight*

# Preparing Teachers for Teaching Dilemmas Raised by Race and Racism

## *One Case Example of Teacher Education for Social Justice*

Anna E. Richert and Colette Rabin

> *Social justice practices promote social and emotional development as well as academic learning through the creation of caring and just classrooms and by consciously avoiding creating a wedge between students and their families and communities . . . Social justice practice is guided by the principle of making equity/inequity and respect/disrespect for individuals and social groups explicit parts of the curriculum and allowable topics in the classroom. This supports the development of critical thinking and deliberative skills as well as the inclination to participate in a democratic society and an increasingly interdependent global society.*
>
> —Cochran-Smith, 2008, cited by Pedulla et al., 2008, p. 9

How do we prepare teachers to create the caring and just classrooms suggested by Cochran-Smith in this quote from her paper, "Towards a Theory of Teacher Education for Social Justice" presented at the American Education Association Meeting in 2008? Cochran-Smith suggests that teachers need to consciously avoid creating a wedge between students and their families and communities—a strategy she describes further by highlighting the importance of making equity and respect explicit parts of the curriculum.

A factor we have found persistent in creating the wedge that Cochran-Smith alludes to here—especially in settings like ours, a large metropolitan west coast city in the United States, is race—or better said, racism. Given the inherent inequities that exist in the United States, where people continue to be privileged or not based on the color of their skin, race functions to separate people and build animosity. Both make their way through the schoolhouse door and into the classrooms where we teach. Preparing teachers to recognize how race and racism impact teaching and learning, and to create safe and productive learning environments for all children given that reality, are critical components of social justice teacher education.

## CONSIDERING RACE AND SCHOOLING IN THE UNITED STATES

Our society sorts people by the color of their skin and subsequently offers differential opportunities for access to society's riches. Schools mirror these conditions of inequity for children of color. One does not need to look hard for evidence. The growing achievement gap, suspension records, standardized test scores, college entrance rates, expulsion, and drop-out and graduation rates all point to the discrepancies that exist between the school experiences and success of children of color as compared with their white peers. In spite of laws that mandate equity, schools seem to "work in the best interest" of some children more effectively than others. Because the institution of school as we know it privileges some children over others by race, teachers must learn to take race into account when making pedagogical decisions. Race is a critical factor to consider when examining the moral imperative of teaching in the United States today.

Of all the contextual factors teachers need to consider when making decisions, the most important is the students they serve—who they are, what they know, what they care about, what languages they speak, what ethnicities they represent, what funds of knowledge they bring with them to the classroom. Coming to grips with this aspect of learning to teach—that of learning about one's students—is increasingly challenging given the changing demographics of U.S. schools and classrooms. According to a 2004 report prepared by the National Collaborative on Diversity in the Teaching Force only 60 percent of the school population in the United States was white in 2001 while 90 percent or more of the teaching force was white (Clowes, 2005). In California, where the teacher education project described in this paper took place, close to one-half of the students in the state's schools and more than half the babies born in the state are Latino (Gándara, 2009). In Oakland, California, in particular, the student population in the schools where our students student-teach is almost entirely African American, Latino, and Southeast Asian. Our students—the majority of whom are white—must learn to establish relationships with their students across race and class lines.

Learning to understand one's students is critically important to good teaching. Teachers who know their students are better able to meet their needs and make decisions that will serve them well (Villegas & Lucas, 2002; Ladson-Billings, 1997; Bartolomé & Balderamma, 2001; Nieto, 2000; Delpit, 1995). Part of learning about one's students in our multicultural multiracial society is learning how race impacts the child's life. Since we know that race functions to systematically disadvantage people in our society and our schools, learning to grapple with issues of race and racism is an important component of morally responsible, socially just teaching practice as well.

### Preparing Teachers for Morally Responsible Practice

How then do we prepare teachers to meet the challenges outlined here? The Ethical Dilemma Case Assignment is one of several strategies in our Introduction to the Profession of Teaching Diverse Learners class directed toward this goal. We locate this assignment under the umbrella of our program principle "teaching is moral work" and argue that learning to "read "students and their school experiences accurately and then act on their behalf are both central to one's moral responsibility as a teacher. Acting in the best interest of students is extraordinarily difficult for all teachers, even if they have done the work of knowing their students well. For new teachers the challenge can be paralyzing.

What does it mean to act in someone's best interest? What is *best* and for which child? As we have argued above, the teacher must decide which of many possible actions will serve her students well. The choice is seldom clear. It is more likely that in facing a teaching dilemma there are several possible "good actions" and yet none can the teacher make with assurance that it will be the *best* for her students in the end. Teachers must sort through the cacophony of messages regarding students' needs and teacher actions. They must develop the knowledge and skills of moral reasoning as well as the courage to act. Our role in teacher education is to help them to do that. We designed the Ethical Dilemma Case Assignment to help our students recognize the moral content inherent in their work and develop their skills of moral reasoning so that they can act with moral intent.

## THE ETHICAL DILEMMA CASE ASSIGNMENT: AN EXAMPLE OF SOCIAL JUSTICE TEACHER EDUCATION

The Ethical Dilemma Case Assignment has two iterations in our course—one each semester. The fall assignment asks the novice teachers to select and write about a teaching dilemma raised by the diversity of the student population of the schools where they teach. During the spring, when they consider the moral nature of teaching as a course component, the focus of their case can be on any aspect of teaching that requires the kind of moral deliberation we are discussing here. Both semesters the assignment begins with a case write-up for which students choose an instance of practice from their student teaching that raises a dilemma for them.

After presenting a brief statement describing the *context* where the incident took place, they describe in narrative form the situation that led to their dilemma by providing as many details as they can to elicit a vicarious experience of the events in the reader. Their framing of the dilemma and how they reasoned it through (including the various actions they might take to resolve the dilemma and the consequences of each possible action for the various people involved) are all part of the *case narrative*. For the *case analysis* that follows, students are asked to look back at the story as written and reflect on how the dilemma was resolved (if it was—it need not be at the time of the case writing) as an additional step in this sense-making/learning process. These cases are short—two to four pages long. The only criterion as far as content goes is that they are true.

On the day of the Case Conference, students bring four copies of their cases to share with their credential peers. They are randomly assigned to cross–grade level, interdisciplinary groups of four. For each of the four cases, students follow a protocol for reading and discussing the case. The orientation of the discussion is to *understand* the case rather than to solve it; we emphasize that this work is not about solving problems, but rather understanding them. Whereas this is challenging for students at first, it is a powerful learning outcome for them ultimately.

## Ethical Dilemmas and the Matter of Race

Given the urban, multicultural context of the school districts for which our students are being prepared to teach, it is not surprising that race features frequently and powerfully in the dilemmas students describe for this case assignment. Whether it's a question of coming to know one's own racial identity, knowing how to function in settings where racist policies seem to be in place, knowing how to deal with claims of racism by students, knowing what and how to teach children about race, or knowing how to help them talk about it in productive ways—the dilemmas raised by race are of central importance. Because of our desire to understand the dilemmas race raises for our novice colleagues, we analyzed a collection of thirty-nine cases written in the last several years that focus on teaching dilemmas raised by race specifically. Our first step was to read through the full set of cases and select out those that met our race criterion. This first step resulted in our thirty-nine-case data set. We proceeded with a content analysis of these thirty-nine cases aimed at determining the domains of teaching where the dilemmas occurred; the kinds of dilemmas race raised for these novice teachers and how the teachers framed them; and finally, what aspects of race and/or ethnicity they highlighted in the case write-up.

## WHAT WE LEARNED: OUR FINDINGS

The moral questions teachers face are ubiquitous. Whether it's about what to teach, how to teach, which children need extra help, which parents to call, how much to reveal about one's self, how to best approach a colleague—the teacher must be prepared to reason through her purposes and what she determines are possible consequences as she moves toward action.

In analyzing the thirty-nine cases for this project we were quick to note how, like the larger umbrella of moral decision making, issues of race and ethnicity also appear in all the different domains of teaching practice. We found many examples of how race factors into curricular decision making, for example, and how it appears frequently as a defining factor between students at every grade. The cases we read suggest race filters relationships between colleagues just as it is a starting point between teachers and parents. Whereas the content of the cases we analyzed covered the broad spectrum of the decisions teachers must make, we were able to cluster those we analyzed for this project according to a set of teaching domains into one or more of which each case fell: curriculum, student expressions of race and racism, school structures, and teacher identity. Some cases were coded for two or three of the teaching domains.

### Race and Curriculum

In line with Cochran-Smith's assertion that issues of equity and inequity need to be built into the curriculum directly, we decided to focus our analysis on the *curricular dilemmas* race raised for our student teachers. Our program emphasizes the teacher's role as curriculum developer. We want our students to recognize that working toward equity in schools involves creating and enacting a thoughtful, rigorous curriculum aimed at academic engagement and success for all students. Given our equity goal, learning how race intersects with curriculum is an important knowledge domain. By analyzing the cases about curriculum we hoped to learn about the challenges our students face in doing this curricular work. In the pages that follow we will describe the case situations as the teachers presented them and characterize how they framed their dilemmas. Both the situations the teachers describe and the dilemmas that emerged from them suggest new directions for our own practice of preparing teachers for this challenging work.

We clustered the cases that pointed to curriculum and race into two subcategories. The first set describes situations where the teachers incorporated questions of race and ethnicity into their curricula but were not prepared for the ways their students responded. The teachers felt they were not able to take the needed steps to build on their students' ideas. We termed this category "race and curricular inclusion." The second set also describes situations where the teachers were uncertain how to respond to their students' questions and concerns. But in this second category the students raised questions about race independent of any curriculum designed to elicit this topic. The curriculum became about race as the teachers charted a path of response. These cases we termed "race as curriculum."

## Race and Curricular Inclusion

Throughout our program—including the class where this project occurred—there is considerable focus on the teacher as curriculum developer and the teacher's responsibility for creating an inclusive curriculum that reflects the cultural, ethnic, and racial backgrounds of the students. Our content analysis revealed that the teachers took this challenge to heart. Across the K–12 continuum there are case examples of the teachers developing curricula that represent African American, Asian, and Latino history and experience. Whereas our teachers created curricula that were inclusive in this way, our analysis revealed that they fell short in anticipating their students' responses and were caught without a plan for how to guide their students from this initial exposure to a deeper understanding of race. For many, this is where the dilemma began.

Sarah's case provides an example. Sarah is a second-grade teacher who began her case by explaining that the "school-wide curriculum" at her school "focuses on using multi-culture history as a context for Language Arts." Aligned with this goal, Sarah and her cooperating teacher filled their book corner with books about the lives of people from all the different ethnic and racial groups in the class. In their classroom the morning begins with time for silent reading when the children choose books and proceed to read on their own. Sarah describes Kalema, an eager, precocious student in her class who chose to read a book about George Washington Carver. Sarah explains that she was not surprised by Kalema's engagement in reading Carver's story, or her desire to share what she learned. She was surprised, however, by Kalema's interpretation of what she read. She explains:

> Kalema began silent reading, part of the morning routine in our room. She was reading a biography of George Washington Carver. During silent reading, Kalema is often eager to share what she's learned with me and her other group members. This day was no different. Kalema began telling us about how George Washing Carver was a strong believer that black and white people could and should live together cooperatively. . . . Before I could get a word in, Kalema said something that caught me off guard. She said that she didn't understand why Carver would want to be nice to white people. After all, she continued, white people had discriminated against him and if she was Carver, she would not have wanted to be around "those white people."

Sarah's dilemma was how to respond to Kalema's reading of this text. She pondered what Kalema meant by these comments and if "she understood what she was saying." She asked herself whether Kalema's expression reflected a general feeling against white people or perhaps it was a reaction to this particular story. She writes,

> I think we've made a conscious effort to be honest and direct about painful realities in U.S. history, while trying to emphasize that many of these realities are in the past. So, is this subject not appropriate for her developmentally? Or have we not scaffolded the material enough? Are other students feeling like this? I feel a responsibility to teach my students about their history as U.S. citizens, but how do I do this in such a way that students become more knowledgeable and wiser from it?

We learn from Sarah how anticipating student response is an important part of curriculum development. As we prepare our student teachers to build a curriculum that is inclusive, we must prepare them as well to imagine how different children might respond, which would help them determine what steps they need to plan to move from the children's responses toward their curricular goals. Knowing how race and culture impact learning is one knowledge domain that is essential for preparing teachers (Ladson-Billings, 1997; Nieto, 1992/1999; Gonzales & Moll, 2005).

Similarly, preparing teachers to have a clear grasp of the underlying content goals of their lessons would also help them manage situations like the one Sarah faced here. If teachers have a deep understanding of the subject matter concepts underlying their curriculum they will have an anchor to which they can turn when they are caught off guard by the responses and connections their students make. Sarah describes her goal as wanting her students to "develop an appreciation for all cultures," while also learning about the "realities of the past." We might begin by asking when we teach children about the "realities of the past," what we want them to know about history. How do experiences of the present relate to stories from the past? What have we learned from George Washington Carver's stance? Why might he have assumed the stance he did? With a clear understanding of the *historical significance* of Carver's work, Sarah could build on Kalema's poignant observation and guide her toward a deeper understanding of race and racism in the United States. At the same time she would be working toward her goal of appreciating the contributions of peoples from different cultural backgrounds.

Susan's case is similar to Sarah's in her determination to "not teach watered-down half-truths" but rather provide her third-grade students a broader and more accurate picture of American history. Within a schoolwide curricular unit on the Underground Railroad, Susan chose to include the story of Nat Turner, whom she describes as a brave leader of the slave rebellions in 1831. Early in the unit one of Susan's students asked, "Why didn't the slaves just fight back?" Susan writes:

> Well, they did. Many organized through the network of the Underground Railroad itself, many organized within abolitionist movements, many slaves simply testified to life in the sheer act of survival and cultural preservation—but some slaves did revolt outright. I feel it is my responsibility within culturally responsive teaching to counter the "happy slave" archetype with source texts that provide for other, more culturally true archetypes, including that of the rebel. I feel it is my responsibility to answer such an important question.

According to Susan, the Underground Railroad curriculum went well, so well, in fact, that her cooperating teacher decided to document the students' ideas and then share the lesson with her colleagues. Susan reports, "All of the children showed maturity that impressed me and my head teacher, and they participated with an overall quality of the read-aloud strategy that was far richer than anything they had done before."

At the same time, like Sarah, Susan's unit left her pondering a number of pedagogical questions. She wondered about the different students in her class and noted how by race they responded differently to the text. She explained that the thirteen of her twenty students who were black engaged in the lesson more fully than usual. She noted four boys in particular who, through their posture and whispered phrases "that's right," signaled to her that they were "visibly proud." She learned while teaching the unit that one of the thirteen was "a direct descendent of one of Nat Turner's rebels who was hanged for his part in the rebellion"—a fact that brought the content close to home.

The white children, on the other hand, were "more physically and vocally subdued than they have been during other readings." The Nat Turner story "includes slaves recruiting other slaves to kill slave owners and their families, including the white children." One of the white students asked why the slaves killed the white children. Susan explains, "When the children wanted to think about this—with some calling out—I took three different insightful answers, all volunteered by Black children with no White children volunteering." Whereas both Susan and her cooperating teacher marveled at the children's maturity in the discussion and took note of what they perceived as good comprehension of the material as evidenced in student writing, Susan finished the unit wondering how to balance her deep commitment to teach history in an intellectually honest way (Bruner, 1977), and still care for all her students at the same time.

> I sill have questions about different children's reactions. What was my responsibility to the six White children? To the Asian child? To the two mixed-race children? Are these the same as my responsibility to the Black children? Again, I have no interest in glorifying violence or in overcompensating for the

> ways in which history has been taught. I am mindful of my responsibility to the emotional safety of all children. But, when given this unit, I must find ways to talk about race and violence or (instead I will) teach watered-down half-truths. Is it okay that this lesson rendered some of the more outgoing White children quieter? Where does the racial and cultural pride of an oppressed group, such as these Black children belong to, fit into a mixed class?"

Susan's case provides a second example of the group of cases that describe dilemmas raised as a result of curricular inclusion. The cases reminded us that preparing inclusive curricula necessarily involves not only defining carefully one's subject matter goals for the curricular inclusion and preparing a curriculum that will guide students toward those goals, but also anticipating how students will respond and then preparing a way to move students from these points of entry toward these goals. The cases raise the role of emotions in learning as well, and point to how likely it is that students will respond emotionally to texts that reflect their lives and cultures. The role of emotions is another aspect of the curricular inclusion puzzle that we need to consider in teacher education as we help students develop a curriculum that does not sidestep the significance of race within the subject matters we teach.

## Race as Curriculum

While Susan's and Sarah's cases represent situations where the novices purposefully planned inclusive curricula that address the diverse backgrounds of their students, the data present several other case examples where students surprise their teachers with questions about race that suggest the need for a curricular response. In those instances race *becomes* the curriculum—a curriculum, we learned, the teachers feel they are not fully prepared to teach. Our analysis of the case examples in this "race as curriculum" category shows that it is not uncommon for children to ask questions about race—or make comments about race—even when the curriculum is not about race, at least not intentionally so. When confronted with student questions about race that emerge unexpectedly, the teachers ask: "Where do I take this?" "How do I respond to my students' questions?" "What should I teach them about race?" "What is appropriate to teach at this grade level?" The dilemmas make it clear that race is on students' minds even when the curriculum is designed to accomplish other academic goals. Their questions are many and varied; teachers must be prepared for that reality.

The occurrences in Rachel's fourth-grade classroom provide a compelling example. Rachel planned a unit for her students on personal narratives. She began the unit by reading excerpts of memoirs to illustrate the personal narrative form before sending her students off to work on their own narratives. She provided additional examples that students could select and read during their silent reading time. The children involved themselves in the reading and writing and were eager to share what they were learning with the others in their class.

The second day of her unit, Rachel asked the students what they had learned about personal narratives from their exploration thus far. She noted their responses on the board and added an insight of her own about personal narrative form:

> The one I added to the list was that the experiences authors had affected their lives in profound ways. I gave the example that for Maya Angelou, growing up poor and black in the segregated south helped shape the woman she would become.

The news that Maya Angelou was black surprised Lana, one of Rachel's students who had selected Angelou's writing during silent reading and "had taken a shine" to them. Prior to this all-class discussion, Lana asked Rachel if she had any more of Maya Angelou's work. Rachel was delighted with Lana's interest. She quickly located several passages from *I Know Why the Caged Bird Sings* and began the search for additional "age appropriate" examples.

On the day of this class discussion and Rachel's Maya Angelou example, Lana was the first to respond. She burst out with an incredulous "She's black?! But she never said she was black!" Not anticipating this response Rachel explains, "I froze for a second and then replied, 'Well, she never said she wasn't black. . . . When you write a story do you start out by stating what your skin color is?'" She (Lana) replied, "'No, but that's different.'" In the moment Rachel found herself grappling with numerous questions about how to respond to this turn of events in her classroom. She wondered, "Why was that different? Why did Lana assume the author was white unless told otherwise? Would a black student have made the same assumption?" She decided to open the floor to a full class conversation about the children's experiences "around race." She states, "We never made it back to writer's workshop that morning, and instead spent the next half hour talking about skin color and how people talked about it or ignored it."

In Rachel's classroom race emerged as a curriculum even though Rachel had not planned for it in advance, nor did she feel fully prepared to develop or enact this curriculum as she wished she had been able to do. She explains:

> Before I could answer Lana I had several decisions to make, the first one being, where did I want to take that class? The students clearly wanted to discuss the issue, but did I consider that an appropriate use of class time? The answer was and remains yes. I hope I will always consider social issues raised by my class to be of the utmost importance. The second decision had to do with figuring out where I as a teacher was comfortable in discussing race and finding ways to be comfortable when students' reactions or responses threw

> me. I wanted this discussion to be safe for everyone, but I had to feel secure with what we were discussing before I could effectively guide it. Was I prepared for that conversation? Not really.

Rachel's story is only one of several where students raise questions of race that the teachers feel open a curricular opportunity to teach about it. At the same time, they feel not yet prepared to guide these discussions or do this curricular planning on the spot. Whereas these examples occur typically in the language arts or social science subject areas, they occur in math, science, and art as well. As we think about such principles of teaching as "connecting the curriculum to the child," "knowing the learner in preparing to teach him or her well," "drawing on the students' funds of knowledge," and "creating an embodied curriculum," we must keep in mind that we all are racial beings who will respond to the work of school in racialized ways.

Importantly, white students—and white teachers—are less likely to raise issues of race unless theirs is not the story being told by the curriculum as was the case in Susan's dilemma described above (Howard, 1999; Lawrence, 1997; Sleeter, 2001; Cochran-Smith, 1995). Because the "grand narrative" of the school subjects is typically white in origin, white students are less disequilibrated by the lessons they encounter in school. As we make it safe for our students of color to ask questions and offer different points of view, we must prepare ourselves for a curriculum that will grow in new ways. These case narratives make clear that race is a lens through which we view the world. As teachers and teachers of teachers we must not overlook the significance of race, and learn to open the conversation in our different subject areas to questions of race that will surely emerge. For the teacher educator, preparing students for these conversations becomes a curricular imperative as well.

## Racism and Curriculum

The ethical dilemma cases raise another kind of curricular concern, which occurs when students make racist comments in the classroom. Like the questions about race that emerge as children engage with the academic work of school, student comments that are blatantly racist—sometimes connecting with the curriculum directly and sometimes not—also require a response from teachers that could take a curricular form. A tenet of the Mills program is that racism in school must be interrupted whenever it occurs. The cases reveal a number of examples of teachers taking actions when they heard racist slurs, or perceived racist attitudes. Whereas the act of interruption was one the teachers seemed uniformly willing to make—assessing the situation, knowing what would be an appropriate response, and deciding how to take action (and what action to take)—all presented dilemmas for the novice teachers.

Monica is a middle school teacher who teaches a combined sixth-, seventh-, and eighth-grade Sheltered English class. Most of Monica's students are Mexican or Mexican American. Their language proficiency covers the full range from almost no English to fairly good English oral proficiency. There are a few Asian immigrant students in the class and one boy from Africa whose first day at school was the day Monica's dilemma occurred.

Monica describes her classroom as a very friendly place where "students frequently come . . . early, before the bell rings, because they like to hang out." Hector is one of Monica's students, who like his peers, enjoys the "horsing around and good-natured play" that starts the day in this classroom. Monica describes Hector as "a limited English speaker (who) loves to latch onto a word or phrase in Spanish or English and repeat it again and again." On the day of the incident, Hector chose the word "chango" to repeat over and over again as he sailed around the room jostling with his friends. Monica had a sense that "chango" might be a derogatory word so she asked one of the fluent English speakers what it meant. When she learned it means "monkey," she approached Hector immediately:

> I decided that this was leading in a bad direction, so I got Hector to sit still for a moment and told him he could not call anyone "chango." He looked confused, so I switched to my (admittedly bad) Spanish and explained that it was *not okay* to call anyone by that word. He asked me if he could call someone burro (donkey), to which I shook my head and then he asked about other animal names, to which I replied that he could not call anyone *any* animal name. He walked away from me as fast as possible and continued playing.

Still unsettled, Monica decided to talk this situation over with her cooperating teacher (her CT) who wondered if Hector might be using the term chango as a racial epithet. Based on what she knew of Hector's good nature, Monica didn't think he was, but she was unsure. Later in the morning Monica and her CT noticed that Hector was still running around using this term. Fearing that this could be Hector's way of responding to the new student from Africa, they decided to take action. They asked their colleague Luchita—a Spanish speaker who was in the room using their computer—if she would "have a serious talk with Hector about his language." In the meantime, the teachers decided to begin the morning with a speech from the CT about the use of inappropriate language in the classroom. Monica reflects,

> Some students became confused by her speech, and later I talked to Jose and David, two fluent English speakers who wanted to know why Hector was pulled out of the group. I explained that he was calling people "monkey" and Jose exclaimed that it wasn't a bad word. I agreed, but explained that people

> have historically called people monkeys as a way to insult them and it was used as a racial insult to insinuate a lack of intelligence and evolution. David, who tends towards complex thinking, said, "I don't want to be joking or anything, but weren't we descended from apes? Why would calling someone a monkey be an insult?"

Monica tried to answer his question but was pulled away by other classroom demands. In the meantime, her colleague Luchita reported that Hector was, in fact, using the term chango as a racial slur after all.

Monica frames her dilemma in two ways. First, she wonders how she can effectively deal with racist comments and teach her students about racism when she doesn't speak the same language as they do. Since she doesn't speak Spanish, she was unable to ascertain that Hector was using offensive language in the first place. Beyond the language issue, Monica questioned whether or not, once she did know what her students were saying, she would be able to explain the implications of actions across the language divide:

> I wondered about the difference in explaining the implications of using a racial slur to proficient English speakers versus non-proficient English speakers in *only* English. Hector understood that he couldn't call anyone any kind of animal name, but I wasn't able to explain the larger implications of calling someone a monkey. . . . I could explain why it's insulting to Jose and David because they really understand the English, whereas the students like Hector might need to have it completely translated because it's a very hard topic.

Monica's second concern was about her own lack of awareness of the students' propensity to reflect racism in the classroom. She says, "I think that I just didn't want to believe that he would be mean-spirited and it bothers me that I missed it because it puts other students at risk to be insulted." Later she follows up with:

> I was disturbed that Hector was holding these racist thoughts about some of the students in the class, and disturbed mostly because I knew that someone had taught him these stereotypes and it would be very difficult for me to unteach them.

Alongside the challenge Monica faces in understanding Spanish or in students' use of slang, is learning to predict a student's racist behavior and then learning how to respond to it. Of the latter she said, "I wasn't able to explain the larger implications of calling someone a monkey."

We can learn from Monica's case the importance of anticipating that students will make racist comments in the classroom. As young people in a racist society, they will undoubtedly hear and inherit racist attitudes that must be dealt with in the school context. Schools become important institutions for interrupting racism and teaching children about race. Knowing how race and culture frame the social context of students' lives is another knowledge domain crucial for preparing teachers. Developing a deeper understanding of racism as it is transmitted in our society could help Monica begin to consider how to "unteach" racist attitudes when she confronts them in her classroom. She wrote, "I want to know what I can do to affect the thinking that causes the insults." In important ways, Monica's questions are curricular: What and how should I teach antiracism in the context of my middle school Sheltered English classroom?

A similar situation occurred in Kathy's fourth-/fifth-grade classroom in the context of a unit she was teaching on the Civil War. Her case began with Kathy describing her students "working together on projects about ways to improve inequities in our society that they identified with or had seen others experience"—a topic that works well for children at this age given their concern with issues of fairness and justice. In the midst of what Kathy described as an "incredible discussion," she heard Will, a white male student, call Devon, the African American girl sitting in front of him, his slave. Not only was Kathy caught off guard by Will's comment, ("my mouth dropped and I froze") but so were the other students sitting close enough to Will to hear it. Kathy described the uproar that ensued. There was much commotion including several threatening comments directed at Will. Kathy felt at a loss to regain calm: "Within seconds the whisper chain had spread the news and there was an attack against Will. Students were yelling, threatening, and physically advancing."

Things happened quickly as they do in classrooms. All at once Kathy had to calm the class and take up the matter of racism at the same time. Although unsure what she should do, she knew her students were counting on her.

> I had to figure out how to calm the class and turn this into an educative experience. . . . I had no idea how to do this. . . . In this moment I really felt the power of teaching when all eyes were on me and I knew that these children were going to observe exactly how I would react to this situation and internalize how their teacher either protected them or disappointed them. . . . The pressure was incredible, but I didn't realize the extent of it until much later.

Kathy recognized the different dimensions of the responses the situation required but felt at a loss as to what exactly she should do. As with all of the cases where racist comments were made, Kathy's case raises the emotional impact of racism and the need for teachers to respond to that as well as handle the substantive matters of race and racism with students when these circumstances arise.

Both Kathy and Monica's representative cases show us how student teachers encounter expressions of racism in school in ways that they did not expect or plan for. Their cases teach us the necessity to help them anticipate that racism will be expressed by students of all ages and to respond to the emotional fallout that will most likely occur as a result. They must also learn how to turn these experiences into educative ones that will involve teaching students about race. These two cases that describe encountering students' racist language are examples of a subcollection of our thirty-nine cases that describe students making racist comments in the classroom. In all instances the teachers report being caught off guard. Whereas experience itself will help these novices anticipate the emergence of racism in their classrooms, preparing them at the preservice level for dealing with the emotional side of such occurrences and the educative requirements that follow is a necessity we realized from studying our students' work.

These cases where explicitly racist comments were made emerged in classrooms from first grade through high school. In addition to noting the grade range for these incidents, we noticed also (as might be expected) that as the students grew older, their racist actions became more intentional.

We learned from this that the challenge of responding well to racism requires an understanding of identity development—in particular development as it frames students' abilities to understand issues of race and ethnicity—as well as an understanding of race and racism themselves (Helms, 1990, 1994; Tatum, 1997). Framed this way, we see the need for helping our novice colleagues to develop their pedagogical content knowledge about how to teach issues of race and racism to children across the K–12 curricular time span (Shulman, 1986; Wilson, Shulman, & Richert, 1987).

## CLOSING THOUGHTS

Our analysis of these dilemma cases left us with the understanding that as teacher educators concerned with social justice, we have more to do to prepare our student teachers to make decisions that support their students' best interests and life chances in the racialized context of today's schools. On the one hand, the cases help us see that our student teachers have committed themselves to creating an inclusive curriculum reflective of students' cultural, ethnic, and racial backgrounds. The cases also clarify much about what these novices do not yet feel prepared to do when they encounter their students' reactions to the many ways in which race emerges in their classrooms. We need to support them as they learn to both develop clear curricular goals for inclusion and also to predict students' possible responses concerning issues of race. We must also support them as they learn to decenter white experience as the frame for doing the work of school. How might we begin?

One starting point would be to rethink how we introduce the notion of curricular inclusion so that our students connect their inclusion and subject matter goals more clearly. This way the subject matter base will be established before the teacher grapples with how to include examples that reflect their students' lived experiences (which will provide them with a curricular way to raise questions of culture, ethnicity, and race). Clarifying their purposes will help the teachers respond to students' questions in ways that simultaneously accomplish the inclusion and subject matter goals. For example, when Sarah's student caught her "off guard" by her question about why Carver considered it important "to be nice to white people," Sarah could have drawn on her reasons for including Carver in her history curriculum. This would both provide a means to engage her student in grappling with the racial content of her question and teach her about the history of racial relations (including racism).

We noticed that Sarah was not alone in her surprise over her students' responses around racial issues. Rachel was surprised by her student's alarm upon learning that Maya Angelou is black. Susan was surprised by her white students' response to the Nat Turner curriculum, and so forth. In all these cases, the questions students raised about race could be tied back to the curriculum and thus provide a way to legitimate the students' questions and concern, discuss race and racism, and provide the context for a deeper exploration of these important issues that impact their lives.

Preparing our students to make decisions concerning how to respond to issues of race and curriculum depends on not only supporting them in clarifying their curricular goals, but also offering them opportunities to practice predicting how students might engage with racial content and acting on those predictions. The cases revealed that the novices were taken aback by the emotional nature of their students' responses to issues of race—both when race was intentionally included in the curriculum and when students brought up race on their own. The fact that the teachers were startled by their students' emotional expressions concerning racial issues such as we witnessed in Kathy's case when her students became enraged with their classmate's racial slur, points to the need for novices to consider the "emotional geographies" of teaching (Hargreaves, 2001). We can see from these dilemma cases that by growing up in a racialized (and many would argue racist) world, children bring race with them to school. Teachers must be prepared to manage both the emotional and substantive issues that surface when they do.

While students spontaneously introduce race as a curriculum topic when they ask questions about it in class, they also bring race to the fore when they make racist comments. Helping our novice teachers anticipate racist thinking, even from young children, is another way we can prepare them for the work ahead. Monica described how her lack of foresight and naiveté concerning her students' potential expression of racism contributed to her "missing" a student's racial slur. Unless we prepare our students for how their students' learned racism may manifest at various developmental stages, they may be unprepared, as was Monica, to even notice it, let alone respond to it in productive ways.

Also along the lines of how racial identity plays out in school, is the issue of whiteness and how to decenter the white experience in schools. Rachel's example, in which a student assumed Maya Angelou was white because she had not indicated otherwise, teaches us that we need to increase our students' awareness of how whiteness serves as the default perspective in the grand narrative of school. We must plan with our novice colleagues how to begin this decentering process. As authors of this chapter and white teacher educators ourselves, we might begin by preparing both ourselves and our white student teachers to notice how our white lenses filter our understanding and experience of school—and how other lenses do the same for students and teachers of color. In so doing we might become better at anticipating the circumstances that led to the dilemmas our students wrote about in the cases reported here.

In sum, we learned from our teachers' case dilemmas that race assumes a central role in their students' identities, and therefore in the way students perceive themselves, their teachers, the curricular content, and their experiences in school. Race comes into play—whether it is an explicit aspect of a teacher's curriculum or not—in ways that challenged our teachers and left them not fully prepared to decide how to act in their students' best interest. We began this project assuming the stance that teachers' decisions have a moral component because of the consequences of those decisions for students. The teacher dilemmas we analyzed for this paper help us understand the depth of *our* moral responsibility to take the lessons learned here into our curricular planning. The project has given us new insights about how race functions in the context of school and how teachers might manage the dilemmas that race and racism raise. As we incorporate what we have learned into the curriculum and pedagogy of our teacher education practice, we hope that our classrooms will better support our social justice goal by preparing our teacher candidates to deal with issues of race and racism in their own classrooms. In this way, we join forces with our novice colleagues to better serve the children of the communities where we live and work.

## REFERENCES

Bartolomé, L., & Balderrama, M. (2001). The need for educators with political and ideological clarity. In M. de la Luz Rehes & J. Halcon (Eds.), *The best for our children: Critical perspectives on literacy for Latino students* (pp. 48–64). New York: Teachers College Press.

Bruner, Jerome. (1977). *The process of education.* Cambridge, MA: Harvard University Press.

Clowes, George A. (2005). Ethnic and gender diversity lacking in the teaching profession. *School Reform News: The Heartland Institute.* Retrieved from *http://news.heartland.org/newspaper-article/2005/01/01/ethnic-and-gender-diversity-lacking-teaching-profession.*

Cochran-Smith, M. (2008, March). *Toward a theory of teacher education for social justice.* Paper presented at the Annual Meeting of the American Educational Research Association, New York.

Cochran-Smith, M. (1995). Color blindness and basket making are not the answers: Confronting the dilemmas of race, culture, and language diversity in teacher education. *American Educational Research Journal, 32*(3), 493–522.

Delpit, L. (1995). *Other people's children: Cultural conflict in the classroom.* New York: The New Press.

Gándara, P. (2009). Immigration, language, and education: How does language policy structure opportunity? *Teachers College Record, 111*(2), 750–782.

Gonzales, N., & Moll, L. (Eds.). (2005). *Funds of knowledge: Theorizing practices in households, communities, and classrooms.* Mahwah, NJ: Lawrence Erlbaum Press.

Hargreaves, A. (2001). Emotional geographies of teaching. *Teachers College Record 103*(3), 1056–1080.

Helms, J. (Ed.). (1990). *Black and white racial identity: Theory, research, and practice.* Westport, CT: Greenwood Press.

Helms, J. (1994). Racial identity and "racial" constructs. In E. Trickett, R. Watts, & D. Birman (Eds.), *Human diversity* (pp. 285–311). San Francisco: Jossey-Bass Publishers.

Howard, G. (1999). *We can't teach what we don't know: White teachers, multiracial schools.* New York: Teachers College Press.

Ladson Billings, G. (1997). *Dreamkeepers.* San Francisco: Jossey-Bass.

Lawrence, S. (1997). Beyond race awareness: White racial identity and multicultural teaching. *Journal of Teacher Education, 48*(2), 108–117.

Nieto, S. (1992/1999). *Affirming diversity: The sociopolitical context of multicultural education.* New York: Longman.

Nieto, S. (2000). *Affirming diversity: The sociopolitical context of multicultural education* (3rd ed.). Boston: Pearson, Allyn and Bacon.

Pedulla, J. J., Mitescu, E., Jong, C., & Cannady, M. (2008, March). Observing teaching for social justice for teachers from two pathways. Paper presented at the Annual Meeting of the *American Educational Research Association,* New York City, New York.

Shulman, L. S. (1986). Those who understand: Knowledge growth in teaching. *Educational Researcher, 15*(2), 4–14.

Sleeter, C. (2001). Preparing teachers for culturally diverse schools: Research and the overwhelming presence of whiteness. *Journal of Teacher Education, 52*(2), 94–106.

Tatum, B. (1997). "*Why are all the black kids sitting together in the cafeteria?*" New York: HarperCollins.

Villegas, A. M., & Lucas, T. (2002). *Educating culturally responsive teachers: A coherent approach.* Albany: State University of New York Press.

Wilson, S. M., Shulman, L., & Richert, A. E. (1987). 150 different ways of knowing: Representations of knowledge in teaching. In Calderhead, J. (Ed.), *Exploring teacher thinking* (pp. 104–124). Sussex: Holt, Rinehart, and Winston.

## *Chapter Nine*

# Environmental Education for Sustainability as Values Education

## *The Challenge for Teacher Educators*

Sara Pe'er, Bela Yavetz, and Daphne Goldman

This chapter was written at a time in which the world is preparing for the Rio+20 Earth Summit. The year 1992 marked the first United Nations Conference on Sustainable Development, known as the Rio Earth Summit, to address the state of the environment and human development. This landmark, in which over 178 governments participated, produced the first plan of action (Agenda 21) to address human impacts on the environment at global, national, and local levels. Twenty years later, the United Nations Environment Programme (UNEP) report prepared toward the upcoming summit states,

> Maintaining a healthy environment remains one of the greatest global challenges. Without concerted and rapid collective action to curb and decouple resource depletion and the generation of pollution from economic growth, human activities may destroy the very environment that supports economies and sustains life. (United Nations Environment Programme, 2011, p. iii)

While the role of education in coping with the environment-development challenges was already addressed in Agenda 21, the current state of the world emphasizes that the necessity to educate a generation of environmentally responsible citizens, educators, professionals, and decision makers still remains crucial. Worldwide, educators, researchers, and academicians are dealing with similar questions and bottlenecks when addressing sustainability in education. This chapter constructs a link between environmental and value education in order to highlight the relevance of environmental education for sustainability (EEfS) for all teachers and teacher educators.

Stemming from the environmental crisis and consensus that this ecological crisis is a symptom of a deeper social, ethical crisis, the first section of this chapter focuses on the characteristics required of people, as individuals and communities, in order to live in a sustainable manner as a progressive society, and the role of education in promoting an environmentally literate citizenship. The second section constructs the link between environmental education for sustainability and values education. This link makes EEfS all the more relevant to all teachers and teacher educators, since it can provide a meaningful tool to promote wider educational goals. The third section focuses on the many challenges of and constraints to *reorienting teacher training to sustainability and the implications of these for teacher educators*. It addresses different aspects of empowering teacher educators so as to function as leaders of change in integrating education for sustainability within teacher education. These ideas are based on experience and insight gained through case studies of institutions that have undergone such a process and selected major guidelines that have been developed for addressing sustainability in teacher preparation.

## ENVIRONMENTAL CITIZENSHIP: THE CHALLENGE FOR TOMORROW'S EDUCATION

What are the characteristics required of people, as individuals and groups, in order to live in a sustainable manner as part of a humanistic society? Stemming from the ecological crisis and consensus that this is a symptom of a deeper social, ethical crisis, the first section of this chapter will focus on the characteristics of environmentally literate people.

> Our vision is a world . . . where a skilled population makes informed decisions in their home, community, and working lives and in their leisure activities. A world where people understand and take responsibility for the impact they have on the quality of life of other people, locally and globally." (Sustainable Development Education Panel, 1999, p. 11)

Earth's environment is being transformed. Environmental change began centuries ago, but this has undergone profound acceleration in the second half of the twentieth century due to the numbers and activities of people. Increasing rates of resource harvesting and waste generation that have enabled economic growth and consumption levels of the industrialized nations are depleting nature faster than it can replenish. There is wide agreement that Earth's ecosystems cannot sustain current levels of economic activity and material consumption, let alone increased levels (Millenium Ecosystem Assessment, 2005). These changes are affecting the basic functioning of the Earth system. As a result, we are facing an almost overwhelming array of challenges—

nationally and globally—resulting from the deteriorating condition of our environment, which is exacerbating economic and social problems. Bright (2003) categorized these environmental threats into five major groups: (1) *Geochemical flux*: The magnitude of certain forms of pollution is such that they are altering global chemical cycles that "regulate" key ecosystem processes. The carbon cycle is the best known of these. Increasing concentrations of this greenhouse gas are linked to climate change. This is highly relevant for all people, through health, food supply, and living areas; (2) *Long-term risks associated with toxic chemicals*: Global production of hazardous waste is in the scale of hundreds of million tons per year. Other materials moving through our economies, such as pesticides or hormones, while not classified as hazardous waste, are also major pollutants. The final destination of all these materials, whether in their original form or as breakdown products, is the environment and our bodies. Cancer, immunodeficiency, hormonal abnormalities, and birth defects are among the health risks associated with exposure even to trace quantities of these materials—in people and in wildlife; (3) *Genetic mixing*: Increasing numbers of organisms are moving through the global trade system, for example in packing materials and crop shipments, into regions that are not their native environment. The few of these exotic species that succeed in establishing colonies can trigger many outcomes, from launching epidemics to a cascade of ecological effects that may profoundly change the invaded community by altering its nutrient cycles, simplifying its structure and homogenizing its species composition; (4) *Ecological decline and loss of biological diversity*: The world is in a state of deforestation, reduction of wetlands, loss of soil fertility, decline of coral reefs, overfishing and trashing of oceans, species extinction, and many other threats to natural ecosystems; (5) *Social inequity*: Increasing numbers of people lack the means for a decent life. In the developing countries nearly a quarter of the world's population is classified by the World Bank as living in "absolute poverty." Most future population increase will occur in these countries where resources are already under serious strain and people are already vulnerable to disease, drought, or food shortage. Hence, conventional approaches to economic development are being severely questioned in view of growing awareness to social equity issues. Global economy, as it has been conducted to date, has not leveled these differences, rather it is paralleled by increasing social inequity.

Why should this worry us? Human health and well-being, economic vitality, social justice, and national security depend on healthy functioning of the Earth's ecosystems. This was clearly illustrated by the Millenium Ecosystem Assessment (2005) which empirically illustrates how natural systems function as humanity's "life-support system" (ecosystem services), and thus links between the health of earth's ecosystems to human survival and well-being.[1] Today, few would deny that the future of the environment determines the future of our existence. It is, therefore, not surprising that environmental issues are receiving increasingly more attention. Global problems challenge the individual and whole society in everyday life matters. The following text box demonstrates how routine decisions we make in our daily lives have complex environmental-social implications.

When in the store purchasing any of our daily commodities—clothes, toys, food, household products, and so forth, do we give any thought to the long list of environmental, social, health, ethical, or political implications that result from our seemingly mundane act of choosing a daily product? Is the product we chose imported or produced locally? If it is imported, most likely from a third world country, what were the working conditions of the workers who labored over this product? Were their wages fair? What are the health effects of their working conditions? Was this product produced through child labor? Regardless of where this product was produced, what are the environmental effects of its life cycle? Did manufacture of the product utilize nonrenewable energy resources and release of greenhouse gasses? Was it transported over long distances to reach this store, thus exacerbating this problem? What is the fate of the materials embodied in this product after we've finished using it? Does the product or any of the processes in its life cycle (from manufacture to use) involve materials that endanger our health? Have we considered purchasing an alternative product that may be a bit more expensive but supports local economy and contributes to social welfare of the local community?

These are but a few of the considerations most of us probably don't give thought to. The environmental crisis requires a dramatic change in human relationships with the environment. A main challenge modern society faces is to find the way to enable a balanced interrelationship between human and natural environments.

The concept of sustainability in relation to human development and the state of the environment emerged in the 1980s (International Union of Conservation of Nature, United Nations Environment Programme, World Wildlife Fund, 1980). The Brundtland Report reinforced the concept and defined sustainable development as "development that meets the needs of the present without compromising the ability of future generations to meet their own needs" (World Commission on Environment and Development, 1987, p. 8). Since then, "sustainable development" (SD) has been the accepted overarching concept for development aimed at finding a balance between providing the needs of present and future human society and protecting the environment. SD is development that can sustain itself since it does not degrade the resources it is based on. It is about "improving the quality of human life while living within the carrying capacity of supporting ecosystems" (IUCN, UNEP, WWF, 1991, p. 10). Sustainability issues deal with the complex social-environment interface and emphasize that environment, economics, and human development are inherently interconnected; therefore a holistic and integrative approach is required in order to create long-term and lasting solutions.

Although public awareness of environmental issues is growing, understanding of these issues and the ability to solve them are not (Yavetz, Goldman, & Pe'er, 2009). Potter (2010) contends that in the United States, the message of personal responsibility, involvement and action, and exhibiting stewardship is still not yet widely accepted or understood.

> In the long run, environmental quality is not determined solely by the actions of governments, regulated industries, or non-government organizations. It is largely a function of the decisions and behavior of individuals, families, businesses, and communities everywhere. (Science Advisory Board, 1995, in Potter, 2010, p. 5)

The challenge of education is to develop environmentally literate citizens who embrace the concept of stewardship and demonstrate environmentally (and socially) responsible attitudes and behaviors in their daily lives and consumption patterns. What does it means to be a citizen? What are our responsibilities as citizens to our society? Environmental literacy (EL) is viewed as a part of responsible citizenship. As stated by the Society for Community Development (1997) in Potter (2010, p. 13), a responsible citizen "participates in activities that promote the public good by understanding economic, political, social and environmental systems."

While there are many definitions of EL, there are elements that are common to all (Simmons, 2001): The environmentally literate person possesses the knowledge as well as the values, attitudes, and skills that motivate and enable conversion of this knowledge into action. A person's EL will be reflected in his or her behavior concerning the environment, and developing EL is equivalent to developing responsible environmental behavior (Roth, 1992). Responsible environmental behavior reflects a number of interacting components (Sia, Hungerford, & Tomera, 1986). The *cognitive* component refers to environmental knowledge that includes understanding of: (1) ecological principles and processes basic to comprehending the impact of humans on natural systems, (2) the interrelationship between social systems and natural systems and environmental issues that arise from these complex interactions, and (3) environmental action strategies including the ability to identify and critically evaluate alternative options for remediation. The *affective* domain is concerned with the attitudes and values that motivate people to the changes in personal lifestyle reflecting responsible environmental behavior (Hines, Hungerford, & Tomera, 1986/1987; Morrone, Mancl, & Carr, 2001; Sia et al., 1986; Roth, 1992; UNESCO-UNEP, 1978).

So, the question is: what will it take to achieve an environmentally literate public and an improved environment in the twenty-first century? A new way of thinking is needed—a profoundly different thinking about how we organize our lives and how our educational systems address this challenge. In this process toward sustainable living, education, and therefore teachers, plays a crucial role (IUCN, UNEP, & WWF, 1980; IUCN, UNEP & WWF, 1991; UNESCO, 1992; UNESCO-UNEP, 1996; WCED, 1987). "[E]ducation must be a critical element of a national strategy for environmental protection, a sustainable economy and a secure future." (National Council for Science and the Environment, 2008, in Potter, 2010, p. 6).

It is important to note that the ideas of SD and sustainability, as evolving concepts with many local interpretations, and their educational implications, are debated in the literature (Fien & Tilbury, 2002; Gough, 2006; Huckle, 2000; Suavé, 2002;).

The dilemmas raised in the textbox demonstrate the need for the ability to see the whole picture surrounding a problem—the history; the processes that caused it; the values, alternatives, and actions to solve it; and the ability to consider the implications of alternative courses of action. Developing this capacity is one of the foundations of a number of environmental educational approaches: Environmental Education, Education for Sustainable Development, Education for Sustainability, and Environmental Education for Sustainability (EEfS). These approaches receive substantial attention in the literature with respect to the similarities and distinctions in their content and underlying pedagogical dimensions (Gough, 2006; McKeown-Ice & Dendinger, 2000; Suavé, 2002; Wals & Kieft, 2010). Based on the understanding and characteristics of EEfS as provided by Tilbury (1995), we view this approach as the most encompassing. EEfS is relevant education. Through EEfS, we may better understand that social, economic, and environmental dimensions are all part of the same system—interconnected, influencing, and impacting each other. Hence EEfS offers a holistic and integrative educational approach. It is education that promotes the outcome we are trying to achieve: educated citizens who take an interest in and active part in their communities and country. Hence EEfS is relevant for all learners. It should not be limited to specific age levels or to specific disciplines. It is, by nature, a key to social change and can shape the required new way of thinking. Such education is one that imparts not only information (general and specific) and teaches different skills, but promotes a worldview that looks to the process of change guided by values.

## ENVIRONMENTAL EDUCATION FOR SUSTAINABILITY: SUSTAINING VALUE EDUCATION

Values are generally defined as standards that people use when evaluating the "worth of things," whether these are objects, ideas, or behavior toward these objects. Therefore, values can be defined as principles, beliefs, and ideals, and as such provide a reference point that guides an individual's position on different issues and hence his decision making or behavior (Maslovaty & Iram, 2002; Smith & Schwartz, 1997). It follows that values are a profound influence, shaping our lives, defining each one of us as a person, and guiding the decisions we make. Values function as an organizing and regulating device, not only at the level of the individual but also at the societal level. As Milbrath (1984) notes "What people value governs the way they behave and what they expect from society" (p. 1). Therefore, values, and educating for values, are a central focus of public discourse, philosophical thought, and the pedagogy of education and educational practice in any society or educational system. Developing values is a fundamental goal and component of education: society strives to ensure, through education, not only its continued physical existence but also a continuation of its value system (Kleinberger, 1961). It follows that educating for values is not a choice for society to make but rather its obligation. This should be reflected in curricula that "promote the spiritual, moral, cultural, mental and physical development of pupils" in order to prepare them for "the opportunities, responsibilities and experiences of adult life" (National Curriculum Council, 1990, p. 1). Such preparation includes promoting the "moral development of pupils, but also the moral development of society" (Tate, 1997, p. 10).

"Perhaps fewer of us are sensitive to what we might call the moral or ethical environment. This is the surrounding climate of ideas about how to live" (Blackburn, 2001, p. 1). Decisions we make in every aspect of our daily lives are a reflection of our personal value system. This is all the more relevant with respect to the environmental context: the decision to actively participate in either improving the environment or preventing its deterioration entails willingness to make changes in our lifestyle, and this may sometimes require compromise and sacrifice. Therefore, it is largely dependent on personal motivation, a sense of responsibility and commitment. These, in turn, are both dependent on and the outcome of development of a personal ethic (Tilbury, 1995). EEfS, described in the first section of this chapter, is, in essence, value education. Environmental education is the process of recognizing values and clarifying concepts in order to develop skills and attitudes necessary to understand and appreciate the inter-relatedness amongst man, his culture and biophysical surroundings (IUCN, 1970). Unlike many other areas of the curriculum, environmental education is directly and overtly concerned with influencing (some suggest fundamentally changing) learners' attitudes and behaviors, and it is widely held that values education is central to this process (Scott & Oulton, 1998).

The link between values and EEfS can be demonstrated using "The Theory of Universal Content and Structure of Value Systems" (Schwartz, 1992; Schwartz & Bilsky, 1990). Briefly, this theory identifies ten types of values that compose a value system of four higher-order value types: *conservation* (security, conformity, tradition), *openness to change* (stimulation, self-direction), *self-enhancement* (achievement, hedonism, power) and *self-transcendence* (universalism, benevolence). These value types can be organized on two opposing bipolar dimensions: *conservation* versus *openness to change*, and *self-enhancement* versus *self-transcendence* (Schwartz, 1992; Schwartz & Bilsky, 1990). Using this theory as a framework, EEfS, by essence, strives to move individuals from values of *conservation* to values of *openness to change* and from values of *self-enhancement* to values of *self-transcendence*, without compromising personal development. In line with this, Milbrath (1984) suggests that a more sustainable society requires a shift in values away from justice for self, aggression and competition, toward justice for all, empathy and compassion.

For such change to occur, values education needs to be more central in the curriculum. Since all images of the future are underpinned by differing value assumptions about human nature and society, it follows that in a democratic society, pupils need to be able to begin to identify such value judgment before they can themselves make appropriate choices between alternatives. In this context, EEfS provides a meaningful tool for educating for values since it addresses concrete issues that are relevant to the learners and confronts them with dilemmas. In their paper on the role of environmental values education in the school curriculum, Scott and Oulton (1998) offer a list of values relating to *humanity* (for example: democracy, human rights, equalizing opportunities) and to *sustainability* (for example: equitable sharing of resources, biodiversity, rights of indigenous peoples) which educational systems might actively promote.

Based on the above premises, EEfS, as education for values, can provide a meaningful tool for promoting a wide range of educational goals. The following goals exemplify what environmental values and EEfS can bring into education, with emphasis on the professional development of preservice and in-service teachers:

*Developing competencies to deal with complex situations*: The constructivist theory of teaching-learning-evaluating emphasizes social construction of knowledge as an alternative to "transfer" of knowledge (Richardson, 1997). Derived from this, teachers, student teachers, and teacher educators need to focus more on the developing and strengthening of capacities for dealing with complex situations for which there is no one ultimate solution. This educational approach is inherent to EEfS. Environmental issues (such as alternative versus conventional energy resources, development versus conservation, and consumer patterns) are situated at the environmental, social, economic, and political interphase. Through direct experience with such issues, teacher trainees and teachers are challenged to cope with the dilemmas of value preferences related to complex and contested situations.

*Enhancing self-efficacy*: Teachers, and therefore teacher educators, are required to influence and develop their students at the intellectual, moral, and behavioral levels. Effective teaching with respect to these depends largely on the teacher's self-efficacy (i.e., teacher's confidence in his knowledge, skills, and abilities needed to teach effectively) (Bandura, 1977 cited in Moseley, Reinke, & Bookout, 2002). EEfS can contribute to this since it is, by nature, interdisciplinary and integrative, and it encourages direct experience with local authentic issues that are relevant to the learners and, as such, has the potential for contextualized learning. Haney, Wang, Keil, and Zoffel (2007) examined teachers' beliefs and classroom practices during a professional development program. They found that active participation of the teachers in the developing and implementing of a problem-based interdisciplinary curriculum on locally relevant environmental health issues had significant positive impact on the teachers' self-efficacy. This increase in self-efficacy was also reflected in the teachers' implementation of teaching pedagogies that comprise reform-based best practices currently promoted by educational systems, such as inquiry-based, hands-on, cooperative, problem-based teaching for depth of student, assessing performance-based tasks, and contextualized learning. These are inherent pedagogical principles of environmental education (NAAEE, 2010).

*Structuring teacher identity*: In view of the significant role of schools in developing pupils' identity and worldviews, developing teacher identity is one of the central goals and challenges of preparing teachers. With respect to this, we contend that environmental identity should be one component of the educator's self identity. Clayton (2004) proposes that "[E]nvironmental identity is a sense of connection to some part of the nonhuman natural environment . . . that affects the ways in which we perceive and act toward the world; a belief that the environment is important to us and an important part of who we are" (pp. 45–46). According to Clayton, environmental identity can be paralleled to other collective identities such as national or ethnic identities, which provide us a sense of connection to a larger whole. This is all the more crucial in a world characterized by urbanization and technology, which is creating a human-nature disconnect—a perception of humans and human systems as not being a component of nature (Payne, 1998; Robertson, 1998; Goldman, Pe'er, & Yavetz, 2010).

*Developing skills*: EEfS does not aim to advocate (indoctrinate) a particular viewpoint or a course of action with respect to the environment and ethical issues that arise from the complex man-environmental interrelationships. Rather it aims to create learning experiences that teach learners how to weigh various sides of an issue through critical thinking, and enhance their problem-solving and decision making skills. In other words EEfS aims at providing learning experiences, and developing and broadening the learners' repertoire of abilities that stimulate them to explore and develop their own value system in a sound and rational way.

## IMPLICATIONS FOR TEACHER EDUCATORS

This section addresses the adapting of teacher education to fulfill its role in promoting EEfS, through the perspectives provided in the previous sections and with emphasis on teacher educators.

Increasingly, countries, such as Australia, Canada, various European countries, and Israel, are supporting implementation of EEfS within the school system (Babiuk & Falkenberg, 2010; Ferreira, Ryan, Davis, Cavanagh, & Thomas, 2009; Ministry of Education, 2007; Sleurs, 2008). In spite of this, recent studies indicate a gap between these developments in the school system and preparation of teachers. Preservice teacher education lags behind the school system in developing programs that prepare new teachers equipped to initiate and conduct meaningful EEfS (Steele, 2010; Yavetz et al., 2009). The perspective of sustainability may be integrated, by "early adopters," within existing courses, or addressed in a number of courses focusing explicitly on sustainability issues, but to prepare effective educators toward sustainable lifestyles this needs to be addressed within the institution and curricula in a holistic and systemic approach (Babiuk & Falkenberg, 2010; United Nations Educational Scientific and Cultural Organization, 2005).

The following case study conducted in Queensland, Australia, describes one such approach ("Whole-School Approach") for integrating EEfS within teacher education. The assumptions underlying this approach are that sustainability will be mainstreamed within teacher education if there is engagement of all the stakeholders, defined as key agents of change across the wider teacher education system, and these key agents of change are "deeply" involved in the process of making the change. The agents of change identified included ministries of Education and of Environment, teacher education institutions, schools, teacher accreditation committees, professional teacher associations, and student teachers. The process involved ongoing cooperation between all the stakeholders through joint meetings, workshops, and networking to seek solutions through collaboration and to ensure that the outcomes are useful to all of them. The process was accompanied by action research, viewed as a collaborative, social, and reflexive component that contributes to recruiting partners' commitment to the process of change, to the ability to learn throughout the process from the experience of peers, and to implementing insights gained throughout the process (Ferreira et al., 2009; Steele, 2010). Reorienting teacher training programs to EEfS cannot be dependent on the interests or commitment of teacher educators as individuals; rather, it depends on the interests and commitment of the programs that mirror institutional policy (Babiuk & Falkenberg, 2010; Ferreira et al., 2009; Mckeown & Hopkins, 2002). By addressing, concomitantly, all stakeholders, the "Whole School Approach" model overcomes various obstacles that often exist at the institutional level to integrating EEfS in teacher training. Furthermore, it provides a strategy that can overcome the general resistance to major change that characterizes institutions of higher education (Scott & Gough, 2007).

The complexities that accompany change can be exemplified by the following example. At the time of writing this chapter, the Israeli Ministry of Education and Ministry of Environmental Protection initiated financing the Colleges of Education to develop and conduct a mandatory introductory course on Education for Sustainability. This initiative is an example of policy change at the national level toward providing a systemic response of the teacher education institutions to the increased implementation of sustainability education within the school system. It also illustrates the complexity of change within these institutions. For example, competing agendas in an already overloaded curricula (Van Petegem, Blieck, Imbrecht, & Van Hout, 2005; Mckeown & Hopkins, 2002) means that curricular change must occur within the existing framework of credits (hours, points, etc.) allocated to teacher training programs by national guidelines. This entails replacing existing courses with new ones or altering existing courses, and such decisions depend on the innovation and flexibility of the teacher education institutions.

Another issue relates to the framework most suitable for integrating the course—should it be placed within the disciplinary studies component or the educational and pedagogical studies component? The traditional disciplinary structure of higher education institutions and curriculum frameworks makes incorporating sustainability, which is inherently trans-disciplinary, difficult (Liu, 2009; Steele, 2010; Yavetz et al., 2009). This issue has direct implications for the academic staff—teacher educators—who are to conduct the course. Who should teach it—disciplinary or educational and pedagogical staff? If disciplinary lecturers, should they be from conventionally environment-related subjects or from other disciplines? What is required of the teacher educators with respect to their content knowledge, skills for teaching sustainability issues, and creating active learning experiences so that the course is meaningful for the students as future environmental educators? What is required regarding their personal environmental identity, which significantly influences their commitment to this subject?

Conventionally, the traditional "science" disciplines are considered the most suitable framework for inclusion of environmental education (Campbell, Medina-Jerez, Erdogan, & Zhang, 2010; Van Petegem, Blieck, & Van Ongevalle, 2007). This approach results from the fact that environmental subjects, from their biophysical and ecological aspects, are components of nature-related disciplines. Findings of a study conducted by Van Petegem et al. (2007) support this tendency. They compared views of the environment and of involvement in environmental education between Zimbabwean secondary teacher educators of traditional environment-related subjects (such as science, agriculture, and geography) and nonenvironment-related subjects. Science teacher educators were found to be more concerned and better informed about the environment, and were more active in environmental education as compared to their counterparts. Teacher educators from all the disciplines felt that the "science" subjects are most suited to include environmental education. Such a disciplinary-oriented approach is not congruent with the multidimensionality of sustainability and EEfS.

The above and following studies are the few that address perceptions of teacher education faculty regarding the many issues related to integrating sustainability in teacher preparation. From interviews with eighteen education lecturers in Queensland University, Australia, Hickey and Whitehouse (2010) elicited five levels of engagement with sustainability education practice: *explicit practice, opportunistic practice, cultural and social focus, integrated focus, and not included.* They found that the majority of lecturers do not include sustainability education in their courses. Gough (2009, pg. 1) emphasizes "almost universal lack of success in introducing coherent or consistent programs of environmental education/education for sustainable development into teacher education courses."

This reality indicates existence of numerous constraints to reorienting teacher education to sustainability. Ferriera et al. (2009) report time and funding constraints, and lack of priority and of opportunity for up-skilling academic staff as factors that lead to the sidelining of sustainability education as opposed to its coordinated implementation in teacher education.

Another prevalent problem is lack of awareness, at the administrative level and at the level of faculty members, of what sustainability means as well as its relevance to preparation of teachers (Babiuk & Falkenberg, 2010; Liu, 2009; McKeown & Hopkins, 2002). Surprisingly, very little research has investigated teacher educators' views and perceptions regarding sustainability and relevance of its education for them. Teacher educators may have different worldviews regarding sustainability (Ferreira et al., 2009). Babiuk, and Falkenberg (2010), in a study of nine Manitoban education faculty members, found that the focus on sustainability education is influenced by the area of the teacher educator's professional engagement. While most teacher educators acknowledged interdependence between the different aspects of sustainable lifestyles, the prominent focus was on the environmental dimension and none explicitly linked sustainability to cultural matters or poverty. The issue of lack of awareness is a fundamental barrier, which underlies other constraints, hence McKeown and Hopkins (2002) emphasize building awareness as an essential first step towards reorienting education to address sustainability.

Another obstacle, at faculty level, may be lack of adequately trained professionals knowledgeable about education for sustainable development (Liu, 2009). This has implications for teacher educators' self-efficacy, as they may feel inexperienced and incompetent to teach this field. Furthermore, they may feel they don't have the mandate to implement such change. In addition to these, overload of academic obligations may also limit availability of the time required to develop courses based on such a new approach.

Conventional academic autonomy is another issue: Universities and their academic staff place high value on professional autonomy and protect their independence (Scott & Gough, 2007), and are thus not willing to integrate top-down dictated changes into their teaching. It is clear that reorienting teacher education to EEfS requires a comprehensive, systemic and organizational change at the institutional level addressing all the institution's community—administration and academic staff (Fullan, 1991).

The following recommendations, based on insights gained from current projects (Babiuk & Falkenberg, 2010; Ferriera et al., 2009; Sleurs, 2008; Steele, 2010) and addressing the constraints and challenges reviewed above will focus on teacher educators. It is important to first emphasize that teacher educators do not function in isolation and the institutions play a significant role in creating a climate that supports transformative efforts on the teacher educators' side to incorporate sustainability into their teaching. Promoting an institutional culture of sustainability, such as accrediting "Green Campuses" is one such example (ULSF, 1990).

The fundamental assumption of the following recommendations is that sustainability education, especially as value education, is relevant to every discipline, and hence, every teacher and teacher educator can, and should, contribute to it.

*Professional development*: Professional development of teacher educators is one of the key components toward mainstreaming EEfS within teacher training programs. Sleurs (2008) identifies five domains of competencies that are required of teachers: knowledge, systems thinking, ethics and values, emotions, and action. Development of these in teacher educators can increase their competence to incorporate the sustainability perspective into their field of teaching. A relevant resource is the "Guidelines for the Preparation and Professional Development of Environmental Educators" (NAAEE, 2010), which overviews the abilities and knowledge that are required of teachers as environmental educators. These guidelines provide a mechanism that enables gauging the quality of preservice teacher programs, hence they also provide a framework for the professional development of teacher educators and teacher education programs.

*Creating learning communities through cooperation*: The significant challenges entailed in the processes of personal development render such transformative processes difficult to experience by oneself. Different projects emphasize the importance of collaboration within the teacher educator community in this process (Babiuk & Falkenberg, 2010; Ferriera et al., 2009; Sleurs, 2008; Steele, 2010). Collaborative frameworks can be established for faculty from different disciplines within the same institution and for teacher educators in similar disciplines from the same or different institutions. The focus of such collaborations can be to create learning communities, research communities, or a combination of these. Communication between community members can be face-to-face, by networking, or a combination. Conducting meetings, such as conferences, seminars, and workshops, is an effective way to bring together teacher educators and stimulate creation of learning communities. Professional meetings such as these also increase motivation, awareness, and exposure to the field of environment and sustainability, through exposure to current sustainability issues as well as recent developments and trends in the educational arena. Active participation of teacher education staff in the preparation of such professional meetings further enhances the processes of collaboration. Such learning and research communities also create the potential for preparing and disseminating EEfS teacher-learner resources.

*Institutional sustainability leadership*: Establishment of a cadre of sustainability leaders within the institution, based on faculty pre-oriented to this field, can promote transformative processes and support personal initiatives of teaching staff and provide consultation, supportive activities, planning, and conducting of professional development of the institutional community.

*Role of research*: Conducting reflective action research is reported as one of the factors that contribute to effective and successful processes of reorienting teacher education to sustainability (Babiuk & Falkenberg, 2010; Ferreira, Ryan, & Tilbury, 2007; Sleurs, 2008; Steele, 2010; Tilbury, 2004; UNESCO, 2005). Tilbury (2004) emphasizes critical thinking and values clarification as crucial steps in learning for change and suggests participatory action research as an opportunity to develop these and transform thinking into practice by also developing the action and management skills required to address sustainability at the practical level. Through the participatory action research process, all the participating agents of change engage in a continuous cyclic process of identifying challenges; designing action; implementing, reflecting, and learning about the action; and proceeding to new actions based on outcomes. The participatory action research approach is based on collaboration through cooperation, acquisition of knowledge, empowerment of participants, and social change. Hence, it has powerful potential to contribute to promoting the recommendations previously outlined. Babiuk and Falkenberg (2010, p. 224) contend that "self-study of teacher education practices has been so far the most developed approach to teacher educators' professional development with a focus on changing teaching practice."

Integrating research within the professional development process has additional advantages such as contributing to personal resumes, promoting a culture of research within institutions of education, and research-based teaching. It is noteworthy that a review of the research literature on teacher educators indicates a general paucity of studies that can provide information leading to recommendations to the many practical issues of incorporating sustainability into teacher education presented in this section. Implied from this, promoting research addressing aspects related to teacher educators may also supply the empirically based information that can contribute to both theoretical and practical aspects of reorienting teacher preparation to EEfS.

## CONCLUDING REMARKS

Being a teacher entails being a role model. This modeling aspect of educators places a particular responsibility on them with respect to their ways of living. Conduct of educators, in their professional functioning as well as in their personal behavior patterns within the campus, reflects their environmental identity. Through these patterns, they directly and indirectly are significant influential figures/factors for their students. The lessons students take from educators and educational institutions that do not "walk their talk" is twofold: one of hypocrisy and one of despair—an unsaid message of helplessness to bridge the gap between ideals and reality (Orr, 1992).

Orr (1995, p. 12) expressed his view of the educator's responsibility in his essay "What Is Education For?" as follows: *"All education is environmental education. By what is included or excluded students are taught that they are part of or apart from the natural world."* Every educational program embodies a hidden curriculum. By analogy, the choice educators make of what to teach and how to teach this resonates with a clear message.

The global environmental crisis of the twenty-first century, as a social-ethical crisis, presents education with one of the most complex challenges. Our choice to ignore this issue will not make it disappear. The current world situation is proof that the significant and important work that has and is being conducted in education, has yet to achieve the desired results. Hence, the challenge of educating a society oriented to sustainable values and lifestyles is relevant and cries out to each and every educator.

## NOTE

1. According to the definition of the Millennium Ecosystem Assessment, ecosystem services are the benefits people obtain from ecosystems. These include provisioning services such as food and water; regulating services such as flood and disease control; cultural services such as spiritual, recreational, and cultural benefits; and supporting services such as nutrient cycling that maintain the conditions for life on Earth.

## REFERENCES


Babiuk, G., & Falkenberg, T. (2010). *Sustainable development and living through changing teacher education and teaching in Manitoba. Research Report.* Retrieved from www.mern.ca/reports/Falkenberg-Babiuk.pdf.

Blackburn, S. (2001). *Being good.* Oxford: Oxford University Press.

Bright, C. (2003). A history of our future. In L. Starke (Ed.), *State of the world 2003: Progress towards a sustainable society* (pp. 3–14). New York: W. W. Norton.

Campbell, T., Medina-Jerez, W., Erdogan, I., & Zhang, D. (2010). Exploring science teachers' attitudes and knowledge about environmental education in three international teaching communities. *International Journal of Environment and Science Education, 5*(1), 3–29.

Clayton, S. (2004). Environmental identity: A conceptual and an operational definition. In S. Clayton and S. Optow (Eds.), *Identity and the natural environment: The psychological significance of nature* (pp. 45–66). London: MIT Press.

Ferreira, J., Ryan, L., & Tilbury, D. (2007). Mainstreaming education for sustainable development in initial teacher education in Australia: A review of existing professional development models. *Journal of Education for Teaching, 33*(2), 225–239.

Ferreira, J., Ryan, L., Davis, J., Cavanagh, M., & Thomas, J. (2009). *Mainstreaming sustainability into preservice teacher education in Australia.* Report prepared by the Australian Research Institute in Education for Sustainability. Canberra: Australian Government Department of the Environment, Water, Heritage and the Arts.

Fien, J., & Tilbury, D. (2002). The global challenge of sustainability. In D. Tilbury, R. B. Stevenson, & J. Fien (Eds.), *Education and sustainability: Responding to the global challenge* (pp. 1–12). Gland, Switzerland, and Cambridge, UK: Commission on Education and Communication, IUCN.

Fullan, M. (1991). *The new meaning of educational change.* London: Cassell.

Goldman, D., Pe'er, S., & Yavetz, B. (2010). What is environment in the eyes of student teachers? Implications for developing environmental literacy. *Ecology and Environment 1*, 50–56 [In Hebrew: Mahi sviva be'eyney studentim lehora'a? Hashlachot lepituach oryanut svivatit behachsharat morim. In: ecologia vesviva].

Gough, A. (December, 2006). *A rhetoric-practice gap: The DESD agenda and sustainable schools.* Presented at the 10th APEID (Asia-Pacific Program of Educational Innovation for Development) International Conference on "Learning Together for Tomorrow: Education for Sustainable Development," Bangkok, Thailand.

Gough, A. (2009). *Not for want of trying: Strategies for re-orienting teacher education for education for sustainable development.* 12th APEID (Asia-Pacific Program of Educational Innovation for Development) International Conference, UNESCO Bangkok.

Haney, J. J., Wang, J., Keil, C., & Zoffel, J. (2007). Enhancing teachers' beliefs and practices through problem-based learning focused on pertinent issues of Environmental Health Science. *The Journal of Environmental Education, 38*(4), 25–33.

Hickey, R. L., & Whitehouse, H. (July, 2010). *Building capacity in education for sustainability: A model of practice.* Proceedings of Australian Teacher Education Association Conference, Townsville, QLD, Australia.

Hines, J. M., Hungerford, H. R., & Tomera, A. N. (1986/1987). Analysis and synthesis of research on responsible environmental behavior: A meta-analysis. *The Journal of Environmental Education, 18*(2), 1–8.

Huckle, J. (2000). *Education for sustainability: Some guidelines for curriculum reform.* Retrieved January 10, 2012, from http://john.huckle.org.uk/publications.jsp.

International Union of Conservation of Nature (IUCN). (1970). *Resolution adopted at the IUCN international working meeting on environmental education in the school curriculum.* Gland, Switzerland: IUCN.

International Union of Conservation of Nature (IUCN), United Nations Environment Programme (UNEP), & World Wildlife Fund (WWF). (1980). *World conservation strategy: Living resource conservation for Sustainable Development.* Gland, Switzerland: IUCN.

International Union of Conservation of Nature (IUCN), United Nations Environment Programme (UNEP), & World Wildlife Fund (WWF). (1991). *Caring for the earth: A strategy for sustainable living.* Gland, Switzerland: IUCN, UNEP, WWF.

Kleinberger, A. F. (1961). The right to educate toward material values. *Megamot 11*(4), 332–337. [In Hebrew: Al hazchut lechanech le'arachim chayavim. In Megamot.]

Liu, J. (2009). Education for sustainability development in teacher education: Issues in the case of York University in Canada. *Asian Social Science, 5*(5), 46–49.

Maslovaty, N., & Iram, Y. (Eds.). (2002). *Values education in various teaching contexts.* Tel Aviv: Ramot, Tel Aviv University. [In Hebrew: Chinuch le'arachim beheksherim hora'ati'im meguvanim.]

McKeown, R., & Hopkins, C. (2002). Weaving sustainability into pre-service teacher education programs. In W. F. Filho (Ed.), *Teaching Sustainability at universities: Towards curriculum greening* (pp. 251–274). Frankfurt: Peter Lang.

McKeown-Ice, R., & Dendinger, R. (2000). Socio-political-cultural foundations of environmental education. *Journal of Environmental Education, 31*(4), 37–45.

Milbrath, L. (1984). A proposed value structure for a sustainable society. *Environmentalist, 4*, 113–124.

Millenium Ecosystem Assessment (2005). *Living beyond our means: Natural assets and human well-being.* Retrieved January 10, 2012, from www.millenniumassessment.org/en/BoardStatement.aspx.

Ministry of Education. (2007). *General director: Environmental education—a main challenge in the educational system in Israel, action program to promote environmental education.* Jerusalem: Ministry of Education. [In Hebrew: Igeret mankal misrad hachinuch (no. 14422139). Chinuch svivati—etgar merkazi bema'arechet hachinuch be'Israel: tochnit peula lekidum hachinuch hasvivati. 4.6.2007, Jerusalem.]

Morrone, M., Mancl, K., & Carr, K. (2001). Development of a metric to test group differences in ecological knowledge as one component of environmental literacy. *Journal of Environmental Education, 32*(4), 33–42.

Moseley, C., Reinke, K., & Bookout, V. (2002). The effect of teaching outdoor environmental education on preservice teachers' attitudes toward self-efficacy and outcome expectancy. *Journal of Environmental Education, 34*(1), 9–15.

National Council for Science and the Environment. (2008). *Environmental research and education needs: An agenda for a new administration.* Washington, DC: NCSE.

National Curriculum Council (NCC). (1990). *Curriculum guidance 3: The whole curriculum.* York, UK: National Curriculum Council.

North American Association for Environmental Education (NAAEE). (2010). *Guidelines for the preparation and professional development of environmental educators.* B. Simmons (Director of writing), Washington DC: NAAEE. Retrieved January 10, 2012, from http://eelinked.naaee.net/n/guidelines/posts/Guidelines-for-the-Preparation-amp-Professional-Development-of-Environmental-Educators.

Orr, D. W. (1992). *Ecological Literacy: Education and the Transition to a Postmodern World*, Albany: State University of New York Press.

Orr, D. W. (1994). *Earth in Mind: On Education, Environment, and the Human Prospect.* Washington, DC: Island Press.

Payne, P. (1998). Children's conception of nature. *Australian Journal of Environmental Education, 14*, 19–26.

Potter, G. (2010). Environmental education for the 21st century: Where do we go now? *Journal of Environmental Education, 41*(1), 22–33.

Richardson, V. (1997). *Constructivist teacher education: Building new understandings*. London: Falmer.

Robertson, A. (1998). Engaging students' eco-philosophies in research and teaching. *Canadian Journal Environmental Education 3*, 171–188.

Roth, C. E. (1992). *Environmental literacy: Its roots, evolution and directions in the 1990s*. Columbus, OH: ERIC Clearinghouse for Science, Mathematics and Environmental Education.

Schwartz, S. H. (1992). Universals in the content and structure of values: Theory and empirical tests in 20 countries. *Advances in Experimental Social Psychology 25*, 1–65.

Schwartz, S. H., & Bilsky, W. (1990). Toward a theory of the universal content and structure of values: Extensions and cross cultural replications. *Journal of Personality and Social Psychology, 58*, 878–891.

Science Advisory Board, Environmental Futures Committee. (1995). *Beyond the horizon: Using foresight to protect the environmental future*. Washington, DC: Author.

Scott, W., & Gough, S. (2007). Universities and sustainable development: The necessity for barriers to change. *Perspectives: Policy and Practice in Higher Education, 11*(4), 107–115.

Scott, W., & Oulton, C. (1998). Environmental values education: An exploration of its role in the school curriculum. *Journal of Moral Education, 27*(2), 209–225.

Sia, A. P., Hungerford, H. R., & Tomera, A. N. (1986). Selected predictors of responsible environmental behavior: An analysis. *Journal of Environmental Education, 17*(2), 31–40.

Simmons, B. (2001). Education reform, setting standards, and environmental education. In H. Hungerford, W. J. Bluhm, T. L. Volk, & J. M. Ramsey (Eds.), *Essential readings in environmental education* (2nd ed., pp. 65–72). Champaign, IL: Stipes.

Sleurs, W. (Ed.). (2008). *Competencies for ESD (Education for Sustainable Development) teachers: A framework to integrate ESD in the curriculum of teacher training institutes*. Retrieved January 10, 2012, from www.unece.org/fileadmin/DAM/env/esd/inf.meeting.docs/EGonInd/8mtg/CSCT%20Handbook_Extract.pdf.

Smith, P. B., & Schwartz, S. H. (1997). Values. In J. W. Berry, M. H. Segall, & Ç. Kağıtçıbaşı (Eds.), *Handbook of cross-cultural psychology* (2nd ed., vol. 3, pp. 77–108). Needham Heights, MA: Allyn & Bacon.

Steele, F. (2010). *Mainstreaming education for sustainability in pre-service teacher education in Australia: Enablers and constraints*. Report prepared by the Australian Research Institute in Education for Sustainability. Canberra: Australian Government Department of the Environment, Water, Heritage and the Arts.

Suavé, L. (2002). Environmental education: Possibilities and constraints. *Connect, 27*(1/2), 1–4.

Sustainable Development Education Panel. (1999). *First Annual Report 1998*. London: Department of Environment, Transport and Regions.

Tate, N. (1997). Values in the curriculum. *RSA Journal* (August/September), 9–12. London: Royal Society of Arts, Manufactures and Commerce.

Tilbury, D. (1995). Environmental education for sustainability: Defining the new focus of environmental education in the 1990s. *Environmental Education Research, 1*(2), 195–213.

Tilbury, D. (2004). Environmental education for sustainability: A force for change in higher education. In P. B. Corcoran & A. E. J. Wals (Eds.), *Higher education and the challenge of sustainability: Problematics, promise and practice* (pp. 97–112). Netherlands: Kluwer Academic Publishers.

United Nations Environment Programme (UNEP). (2011). *Keeping track of our changing environment: From Rio to Rio+20 (1992–2012)*. Nairobi: Division of Early Warning and Assessment (DEWA), United Nations Environment Programme (UNEP).

United Nations Educational, Scientific and Cultural Organization (UNESCO). (1992). United Nations Conference on Environment and Development: Agenda 21. Switzerland: UNESCO.

United Nations Educational, Scientific and Cultural Organization (UNESCO). (2005). *Guidelines and recommendations for reorienting teacher education to address sustainability*. Paris: UNESCO. Retrieved January 10, 2012, from http://unesdoc.unesco.org/images/0014/001433/143370e.pdf.

UNESCO-UNEP. (1978). The Tbilisi Declaration. *Connect, 3*(1), 1–8.

UNESCO-UNEP. (1996). Education for sustainable development. *Connect, 21*(2), 1–3.

University Leaders for a Sustainable Future (ULSF). (1990). *The Talloires declaration.* Washington, DC: ULSF.

Van Petegem, P. V., Blieck, A., Imbrecht, I., & Van Hout, T. (2005). Implementing environmental education in preservice teacher training. *Environmental Education Research, 11*(2), 161–171.

Van Petegem, P. V., Blieck, A., & Van Ongevalle, J. V. (2007). Conceptions and awareness concerning environmental education: A Zimbabwean case study in three secondary teacher education colleges. *Environmental Education Research, 13*(3), 287–306.

Wals, A. E. G., & Kieft, G. (2010). *Education for sustainable development.* Stockholm: Sida.

World Commission on Environment and Development (WCED). (1987). *Our common future.* New York: Oxford University Press.

Yavetz, B., Goldman, D., & Pe'er, S. (2009). Environmental literacy of preservice teachers in Israel: A comparison between students at the onset and end of their studies. *Environmental Education Research, 15*(4), 393–415.

## *Chapter Ten*

# Teacher Education for the Twenty-First Century

## *Are We Preparing Teachers for Obsolete Schools?*

Debbie Samuels-Peretz

The "twenty-first century" has become one of those buzz words in education that everyone is talking about. In order to prepare our children for life in the twenty-first century, we are told, they need twenty-first-century skills. Upon closer look, however, many of these skills are quite familiar to educators; in fact, Dewey and Vygotsky would recognize and long ago advocated for such so-called twenty-first-century skills as collaboration, critical thinking, and problem solving. What really characterizes the twenty-first century, and what skills and knowledge do our children need to have in order to be contributing members of this new society? What does this mean for education in general and for teacher education in particular? This chapter will explore social issues unique to the twenty-first century that are leading to a paradigm shift in how we communicate and navigate our world. It will discuss how these changes affect education and suggest ways that teacher education can best prepare teachers to meet these challenges at each stage of their careers from initial teacher preparation and induction to professional development for experienced teachers.

### TWENTY-FIRST CENTURY SOCIETY: WHAT'S DIFFERENT?

Internet technology has come of age since the turn of the millennium. Social networking and mobile connectivity have changed not only the way we communicate, but also the way we interact with each other and with our environment. Sociologists are comparing the societal shift of digital networking with the industrial revolution or the invention of the printing press (Shirky, 2011; Levy & Murnane, 2004). Through computers, cell phones, and other wireless devices, people can be available twenty-four hours a day, seven days a week. Though parents may welcome the opportunity to check in with children at any time, employees may not. This "always-on" connectivity has resulted in blurred lines between an employee's professional and personal life. Along with the possibility of constant availability, an expectation has arisen that we are, therefore, always reachable. A manager may complain that an employee didn't respond to an urgent e-mail on a Sunday morning. Students in higher education may grumble when professors don't respond right away to their e-mails, even at 1:00 in the morning. In personal communication, too, constant availability has become an expectation and individuals may be upset when their friends don't respond immediately to a text.

Socially, the telephone is no longer the favored mode of communicating. Even e-mail, which characterized a major shift in professional and personal communication at the end of the twentieth century, is considered by many to be passé. Many national universities no longer provide e-mail accounts to their students. Text messages are often the preferred way of communicating among friends, whether to arrange plans for getting together or just to say "hello." "Blind" dates are a thing of the past as web-based dating enables two people to get to know each other quite well before ever meeting in real life. In fact, according to Rosenfeld and Reuben (2012), one in five heterosexual relationships begins via the Internet.

## Social Networking

Social networking sites such as Facebook and Twitter are changing the way we interact in our society. We are reconnecting and staying in touch with friends from long ago by searching for them in Facebook. Geographic distance is no longer an obstacle as we share our personal photo albums and watch our friends' children grow up from afar. Webcams enable us to see each other regardless of how many miles and time zones away we are. Thanks to wireless technology we can even give friends from overseas a tour of our new homes or offices.

People broadcast their locations and activities to their friends in an instant via status updates. Instead of trying to guess which café or pub is where the action is, anyone can know instantly where the crowd is, using Foursquare, an app that integrates geographic location tagging with social activities such as dining and entertainment. In the professional world we can now navigate conferences and business trips more efficiently. Meeting venues can be easily selected or changed. We can share recommendations, notes, questions, and even complaints during conference sessions and presentations via the back-channel.

One of the most compelling uses of this new ability to instantly broadcast personal news can be seen in politics and journalism. The way we get our news has changed forever, as individuals can now videotape newsworthy events as they happen and instantly upload them to the Web. The terrorist attack in Mumbai, India, in 2008 was first reported by Twitter and Flickr users. Likewise, news of the attack leading to Osama bin Laden's death in May 2011 was first "leaked" when an IT professional living nearby tweeted about unusual helicopter activity.

Social media has done more than disrupt how we receive our breaking news, however; it is also an active player in political activities. Social media has been credited with the downfall of Philippine president Joseph Estrada in 2001 (Shirky, 2011). In the 2008 U.S. presidential elections, Barack Obama successfully leveraged social media to support his campaign. Kosuke Tsuneoka, a Japanese journalist held hostage in Afghanistan for five months in 2010, was released two days after he tricked his captors into letting him access Twitter. Protesters in Egypt used social media to organize and publicize the uprising in 2011. In June 2011, a Facebook campaign successfully pressured Israeli dairy companies to limit prices on cottage cheese. This past summer, the Israeli social justice movement used Facebook to organize protests. Occupy Wall Street followed suit a few months later using social media, especially Twitter, to organize protests around the United States.

The role social media is playing in world news and events has led to a revival of grassroots democratic values. The ability of everyone to be a producer of information and media, where before we were just consumers, has given rise to the notion of renewed power to the people. Social scientists are busily engaged in studying this phenomenon. Clay Shirky (2010) explores the phenomenon of sharing via digital technology in his book, *Cognitive Surplus*. He argues that the "low cost and low hassle" of the Internet have enabled us to pursue basic human needs such as creating, sharing, and connectedness. However, participation does not necessarily involve civic value. Some participation centers on communal value, focusing on the group of participants. Other participation in digital social networks centers on civic value, something for the benefit of all in society, not just participants.

## Information Overload

Now that every individual has the power to instantly publish his/her message to a potential audience of millions, we are faced with an information explosion with several important implications. If anyone can publish his/her analysis of a situation or evaluation of a product, how do we know how reliable the information we are accessing is? This has emphasized the importance of evaluating information sources. Researchers at the New Media Literacies project identified judgment as a key skill for twenty-first century. They define judgment as the act of evaluating the trustworthiness of information sources. In spite of the proliferation of amateur pundits, much of the knowledge base on the Web is quite accurate. A special investigation carried out by Jim Giles (2005) for *Nature* magazine found that Wikipedia was nearly as accurate as the *Encyclopedia Britannica.*

Although quality of Web-accessible information remains a concern, quantity is by far the more daunting challenge. The English Wikipedia has more than 3,813,702 articles, totaling more than two billion words. It would take an average reader nearly thirteen years to read it all, by which time, much of the information would be outdated. WordPress, the number one blog-hosting service, claims that their bloggers publish about a half million new posts per day. Each day's worth of new information would take nearly 580 days to read. Overall, Lyman, and Varian (2003) estimate that approximately five exabytes of information was produced in 2002. To help illustrate how much five exabytes of information is, they compare it to the information contained in thirty-seven thousand new libraries the size of the Library of Congress. Another analogy shows five exabytes to be equivalent to every word ever spoken. Eli Pariser (2011) quotes Eric Schmidt, CEO of Google, as saying that all human communication from the beginning of civilization through to 2003 would take up about the same amount of storage that we now create every two days.

We are still grappling with how best to navigate the information explosion. Knowledge "curation" is a new term being bandied about. Where once news editors sifted through pieces of information from a wire service or other professional source choosing the best content for an audience, now sophisticated computer algorithms determine which information and media to stream to individuals. This is called personalization, and it ensures that one will be given information based on one's interests and preferences. Human curation is still available when someone handpicks information for a particular audience and consolidates it in a way that is easily accessible. Sometime the curator will be an expert in the field, but more often than not, it is a hobbyist.

## Negative Implications of the Social Media Revolution

There is a shadow side to the amazing advances enabled by mobile technology and social media. The idea of personalization sounds appealing at first glance. We save precious time reading only news that interests us. Google searches are more successful since personalization ensures we get matches most likely to meet our needs and interests. But what happens when a computer algorithm determines our news diet by dint of our personal preferences and interests? Eli Pariser explores the dark side of personalization in his book, *The Filter Bubble*. According to Pariser, 36 percent of Americans under thirty get their news from social media. Since social media is personalized to stream information according to our likes and interests, what does it mean when we are only given information that is skewed to our tastes and preferences? Pariser describes it as a "kind of invisible auto-propaganda, indoctrinating us with our own ideas, amplifying our desire for things that are familiar" (p. 15). He argues that chance encounters with divergent opinions can spur understanding and learning: "Creativity is often sparked by the collision of ideas from different disciplines and cultures . . . a world constructed from the familiar is a world in which there is nothing to learn" (p. 15).

Aside from affecting our ability to grow and evolve through diversity of opinions and experiences, social media can also negatively impact our relationships with friends and loved ones. Sherry Turkle (2011) has studied computer and then Internet use for thirty years and has discovered several disturbing trends. Participants in her research paint a picture of the new "always-on" family: There is the family dinner table where members are texting rather than conversing about their days; there is the playground scenario where a parent pushes a child in a swing with one hand while checking e-mail with the other; there is also the teen who feels that his avatar-driven identities are often more satisfying than his real-world identity. Turkle suggests that new technology is especially seductive because it plays up to our very human vulnerabilities. She writes, "These days, insecure in our relationships and anxious about intimacy, we look to technology for ways to be in relationships and protect ourselves from them at the same time" (p. xii). She concludes that technology provides us with "the illusion of friendship without the burden of companionship" (p. 1).

Our multitasking, social-networked lifestyle affects more than just our personal growth and relationships. There are indications that it may even affect our brains and how we think. Nicholas Carr (2011), in his book *The Shallows: What the Internet Is Doing to Our Brains*, concludes that there is abundant research showing that the online environment is characterized by cursory reading and hurried and distracted thinking that leads to superficial learning. He quotes Jordan Grafman, a leading neuropsychologist, who has said, "the more you multitask, the less deliberative you become; the less able to think and reason out a problem" (p. 140). Carr quotes another neuroscientist, David Meyer, who argues that training the brain to be better at multitasking is also training the brain to be better at shallow thinking. It is perhaps too early to really know the long-term effects of our new always-connected behaviors, but clearly the time to think about it is now.

As in most time periods, equity and social justice remain important issues in twenty-first-century society. Automation has led to the elimination of many jobs—from supermarket cashier to administrative assistant. The shift in employment has serious economic repercussions and is resulting in a new division of labor between those who are employable in a digital society and those who are not (Levy & Murnane, 2004). Studies of economic trends have found both a large decrease in median wealth and a sharp rise in wealth inequality over the past decade (Wolff, 2010). There is also a racial and ethnic component to wealth inequality. CNN cited a recent (2009) report published by the Urban League that concludes "Blacks remain twice as likely to be unemployed, three times more likely to live in poverty." According to the National Poverty Center (2012), in 2010, 15 percent of Americans lived in poverty. The numbers are much higher for black Americans (27.4 percent) and Latino Americans (26.6 percent). Regardless of the technological gains, twenty-first-century society still must deal with inequity.

## EDUCATION FOR THE TWENTY-FIRST CENTURY

The foregoing discussion depicts the radical shift happening in our society as a result of digital technology and social media. Educators, busy preparing the next generation of cyber citizens, cannot afford to ignore it. We must strive to better understand the implications of the digital revolution on society.

### Preparing Students to Enter the Workforce

One important goal of education is to prepare the next generation to successfully enter the workforce. This can be challenging for educators at the elementary and middle school levels of schooling, since the workforce is changing rapidly because of technology. In 2004, former U.S. secretary of education Richard Riley predicted that soon we would be preparing children for jobs that don't exist yet (Gunderson, Jones, & Scanland, 2005). Eight years later, *US News and World Reports*' 2012 edition of *Best Colleges* includes an article on nine new college majors that reflect developments in the workforce (Gearon, 2012). They include brand-new fields such as health informatics, cyber security, and nanotechnology. Levy and Murnane (2004) have argued that technology is altering the workforce. Jobs that are capable of being done by machine will be. That means that in order to be employable, humans need to have skills that computers can't imitate. Levy and Murnane caution against a new division of labor that could threaten the United States or any democratic society.

Will business as usual prepare future generations to succeed in the rapidly changing workforce? A recent report on employers' views on employee readiness when entering the workforce concludes that high school graduates are deficient in both basic skills such as writing, reading comprehension, and mathematics, as well as skills such as critical thinking, problem solving, and collaboration (Conference Board, Partnership for 21st Century Skills, Corporate Voices for Working Families, & Society for Human Resource Management, 2006). Tony Wagner, in his book, *The Global Achievement Gap* (2008), argues that there is a gap between what even the best schools teach and test and what students need to succeed in today's global knowledge economy.

There seems to be wide agreement that public education is not effectively preparing future U.S. citizens ever since the report *A Nation at Risk* was published in 1983. Calls for teacher accountability and the use of quantitative data have created an obsession with standardized testing and a culture of "blame the teacher." At the beginning of the twenty-first century there were signs of growing public awareness of the flaws behind the culture of testing. John Edwards, during the 2008 presidential campaign, was quoted in the *New York Times* as criticizing the overemphasis on testing in school reform. Edwards commented, "You don't make a hog fatter by weighing it" (Dillon, 2007). Rejecting obsessive testing that leaves no room for creativity, scholars and researchers have been turning their attention to reenvisioning education for the twenty-first century. The next section of this chapter will explore new approaches such as the twenty-first-century skills movement, educational neuroscience, and leveraging participatory culture.

## Keeping Curriculum Up-to-Date

Heidi Hayes Jacobs (2010) argues that school curricula are woefully out of date and do not prepare students for the world they will live in after graduation. She calls on educators to be aggressive in their search for ways to assess student learning with products and performances appropriate for the twenty-first century. The Curriculum 21 Project, developed by Jacobs and colleagues, includes a Web-based resource to help educators update their curriculum and instruction. According to Jacobs, teachers need to be active participants in reviewing and updating curriculum.

Figuring out what kinds of goals and performances are appropriate for our new, "always-on" society can be challenging. Do we focus on basic skills such as reading and math, or on more complex skills such as problem solving and critical thinking? Do we teach specific content in history and science or do we teach skills such as inquiry and synthesis? Given the information explosion, is it even possible to be a master of the content available on a topic? If general mastery is not possible, given the sheer volume of information, there will likely be a growing emphasis on specialization within professions. The information explosion also has serious implications for the longevity of knowledge and professional training. With the exponential growth of technical knowledge from year to year, we must also expect a faster rate of knowledge obsolescence. Cetron and Davies (2008) predict that "knowledge turnover" will soon be a high-priority issue. They claim that an engineer's knowledge has a half-life of only five years. For electronics students, they argue, half the curriculum they learn their freshman year will be obsolete by the time they are seniors. This will lead to growing emphasis on life-long learning and retraining in the professions.

If we can no longer expect to master all of the content in our fields, what does this mean in terms of what to teach our students at all levels of education—from "basic skills" to professional expertise? Daniel Willingham (2009) cautions against a misplaced focus on skills over content. Both are essential for comprehension and learning.

## Habits of Mind for the Twenty-First Century

Howard Gardner (2009), famous for his theory of multiple intelligences, argues that there are five kinds of minds educators should strive to develop to ensure that we will thrive in the new age. Leaving his comfort zone of describing minds at work, in *Five Minds for the Future*, Gardner unabashedly offers a value-laden recommendation of what we *should* cultivate in our children. Gardner recognizes that our new digitally enabled society will require "capacities that until now have been mere options" (p. 2). He warns us that human values have a role to play beyond a description of minds. Focusing on "policy rather than psychology," the five minds he describes are "broad uses of the mind" that can be nurtured in schools or the workplace; these kinds of minds make use of our multiple intelligences (p. 4).

According to Gardner, the following five kinds of minds are essential to our success in the rapidly changing twenty-first century. The *disciplined mind* represents mastery of at least one scholarly discipline or way of thinking. The *synthesizing mind* reflects on information from a variety of sources and recombines in new ways to represent an author's understanding and perspective. The *creating mind* asks challenging questions and generates new and innovative ideas. The *respectful mind* is successful working in groups with others as it celebrates human diversity and difference. The *ethical mind* goes beyond self-interest to focus on the good of society.

## New Developments in Educational Neuroscience

Both Gardner and Willingham are cognitive scientists. The field of cognitive science has been very active grappling with the burgeoning of interest in brain research over the past couple of decades. Functional MRIs (fMRI) are being used to study how the brain works, resulting in exciting new findings. Although this research is still quite young, early findings have important implications for how we educate our children. This has led to the development of the new, somewhat controversial, interdisciplinary field of educational neuroscience. Proponents of educational neuroscience recognize the potential benefits of integrating brain research with the science of learning. Those against the new field cite examples of misuse of the findings.

Judy Willis (2010), a neurologist who left medicine to become a classroom teacher, agrees that we need caution when applying findings from brain research to education. However, while she recognizes that links from brain research to education are more suggestive than empirical, Willis believes that neuroscience findings can guide teaching practice. An example of this is our new understanding of how stress and pleasure affect the filtering of sensory input in the brain. Willis cites research that shows stress as filtering sensory input to the lower, reactive brain rather than the prefrontal cortex, the brain's thinking center. This research suggests that classroom practice aimed at reducing stress among students will lead to more sensory input (via learning activities) reaching the prefrontal cortex. Research exploring which sensory input is routed to the prefrontal cortex has similar classroom applications. Willis also cites research indicating that novelty and change are more likely to get through the brain's reticular activating system (RAS), causing us to pay better attention. Classroom implications of this finding are clear: students will benefit from change and novelty to keep their attention in the classroom.

Mary Helen Immordino-Yang also recognizes the relevance of brain research to classroom practice from her research on social and emotional aspects of brain activity. Immordino-Yang and Faeth (2010) claim that neuroscience has clearly established that learning cannot be considered independent of emotion. Likewise, as Vygotsky pointed out many years ago, the role of social interaction is essential to learning. Although it is premature to assume direct links from the findings of brain research to educational strategies, Immordino-Yang and Faeth propose that the findings are important in regard to the functionality of emotions in learning. Specifically, Immordino-Yang and Damasio (2007) argue that "emotions comprise cognitive as well as sensory processes. Furthermore, the aspects of cognition that are recruited most heavily in education, including learning, attention, memory, decision making, motivation, and social functioning, are both profoundly affected by emotion and in fact subsumed within the processes of emotion" (p. 7).

Like other scholars in educational neuroscience, both Willis and Immordino-Yang are very cautious regarding the relationship between brain research findings and classroom practice. This is the result of several misapplications of neuroscience findings to education. Commonly referred to as "neuromyths," educational neuroscientists are careful to disassociate themselves from those who misuse research to promote particular professional development programs or commercially marketed curricula. According to Ansari (2008), a background in basic neuroscience can help educators be informed consumers who use their judgment to evaluate knowledge claims.

## The Purpose of Schooling

Education reform has been a contentious topic primarily because, as a society, there is little agreement about the purposes of schooling. Much of the previous discussion emphasized one purpose of schooling, that of making our students employable in a digitally connected, twenty-first century workforce. According to Nel Noddings (2004, 2005), our schools need to nurture and teach our children to care. Rather than focusing on economic success, Noddings argues that school should include happiness among its goals. She believes that including parenting, personal growth, and character building in the curriculum can help foster more caring adults. Another, equally important, purpose of schooling is to educate future citizens of a thriving democracy. Michael Apple (2011) reminds us that education is by nature a political act. Both what and how we teach involves decisions and choices that include and exclude. Whose knowledge counts? Who decides what students need to know? According to Apple and critical theorists, it is important that schools teach children to understand power relations and that curricula take a critical approach to what is taught. Noddings also views education as political. Caring and happy adult citizens will contribute more meaningfully to a democratic society. These purposes go hand in hand with twenty-first-century needs. Shirky (2011) and others have demonstrated that the social media revolution has led to a renewal of people-driven participatory democracy. While not all digitally mediated participation is politically motivated, and social uses still dominate, education can take advantage of the new participatory culture to nurture future citizens.

## "New Media Literacies"

Recent research exploring how youth engage in social media and how they use the Internet has shown that today's youth are actively creating and sharing media. Lenhart and Madden (2005) found that 57 percent of online teens are content creators. Jenkins, Clinton, Purushotma, Robison, and Weigel (2006) cite several advantages to youth online participation including "peer-to-peer learning . . . diversification of cultural expression, the development of skills valued in the modern workplace, and a more empowered conception of citizenship" (p. 3). Jenkins and colleagues identified three issues related to youth involvement in a participatory online culture that should concern educators: The Participation Gap relates to equity of access and opportunities that prepare youth for participation in our twenty-first century's digital society. They do not refer so much to technical access as to opportunities to develop the cultural competencies and social skills necessary for full participation. The Transparency Problem suggests that youth need a better understanding of the role media plays in society. The Ethics Challenge concerns alternative forms of professional training and socialization that youth receive as a part of this culture. Teens learn to produce and share media out of school, often via mentor-type relationships. Intellectual property rights are often ignored as teens remix and mash up using clips from various artists. By integrating what Jenkins calls the participatory media culture into education, we can nurture youth development according to ethical principles that will help teens contribute positively to society.

Together with colleagues at the New Media Literacies project (New Media Literacies, n.d.), Jenkins has identified twelve cultural competencies and social skills that youth need in order to fully participate in the new digital culture. They call them the New Media Literacies. Jenkins calls for a more systematic approach to media education in order to ensure that our students will be ready to be full participants in a democratic online culture. Mastering the New Media Literacies supports schooling goals that focus on future employability, as well as those advocating for critical thinkers to participate in making our democracy stronger. Most of the literacies represent still another purpose of schooling by emphasizing social skills and collaboration, which will help with character building and the nurturing of individuals.

## TEACHER EDUCATION FOR THE TWENTY-FIRST CENTURY

Given the many promising approaches to revitalizing education for the twenty-first century, what are the implications for teacher education across a teacher's professional life span? What might teacher education for the twenty-first century look like when preparing teachers for initial licensure or for induction as new teachers enter the profession? What might professional development for experienced teachers look like? Rather than provide answers, the following discussion seeks to identify trends and issues in teacher education for the twenty-first century and identify questions that can help guide us on the road to teacher education for the schools our society needs, rather than for the schools we already have.

While, clearly, society has changed and is continuing to do so at breakneck speed, our schools have not. School reforms of the past few decades have gone backward rather than forward, focusing on disciplinary content coverage guided by fixed, uniform standards and assessed through compulsory and obsessive standardized testing. Teacher education is caught in a difficult situation: If we prepare teachers for the schools our society needs, they are unprepared to teach in the schools we have. If we prepare teachers for the schools we have, we will have no one prepared to teach in the schools we need.

## Teaching as a Lifelong Learning Profession

Sharon Feiman-Nemser (2001) reminds us that teaching is a lifelong learning profession. We continue to learn to teach for as long as we stay in the classroom. Feiman-Nemser positions teacher education along a continuum that encompasses all stages of a teacher's career from initial preparation, through new teacher induction, to the years of classroom experience until retirement. As teachers advance along the continuum, their learning needs change. Feiman-Nemser argues that effective teacher education is driven by the requirements of good teaching within the context of where teachers are along the continuum.

## Teacher Preparation for Initial Licensure

If the lack of consensus regarding the purpose of schooling has complicated school reform efforts, there is a similar lack of agreement regarding the role of the teacher and what effective teaching practice looks like. Mary Kennedy (2008) describes several tensions within teacher education that makes it challenging to identify a single program of teacher education that would lead to effective teachers and improved practice. One of these tensions relates to the knowledge teachers require. Some scholars, such as Weiland (2008), argue for a strong liberal arts background. Others, such as Ball and Forzani (2009), see the necessary knowledge in vocational terms as they focus on the specific application of content knowledge in classroom situations. Many policy makers advocate for more content courses in teacher preparation while others call for a more intensive clinical model. Still others, such as former secretary of education, Rod Paige (2002), advocate for eliminating current models of teacher preparation altogether in favor of recruiting teachers with deep content knowledge who can pass rigorous standardized tests.

### *Teaching as a Profession Focused on Clinical Practice*

Linda Darling-Hammond and Gary Sykes (1999) have argued that teaching is a profession much like other professions and needs to be developed as such. The profession of teaching needs a clinical practice model to ensure that teachers get appropriate preparation and support to be effective in an uncertain context with growing diversity among multiple human dimensions. Darling-Hammond (2006) recognizes the importance of core knowledge, but emphasizes that teachers need intensive, guided experiences to develop skillful practice. According to Darling-Hammond, three characteristics of successful teacher education programs are (1) coherence among courses and practice opportunities, (2) extensive practice via a clinical model that connects theory to practice, and (3) close relationships with placements sites that exemplify effective teaching for diverse student populations. A longtime proponent of professional development schools, Darling-Hammond sees closer relationships between teacher education and schools as of key importance. Ball and Forzani (2009) also call for a practice-focused curriculum in teacher education. They argue that a program needs to focus not only on knowledge demands, but also on the tasks and activities that teachers need to be able to perform effectively.

### *Transformative Teacher Education*

Carroll, Featherstone, Featherstone, Feiman-Nemser, and Roosevelt (2007) identified five themes that are essential to transformative teacher education at the initial preparation level. The first theme relates to the central tasks of learning to teach as identified by Feiman-Nemser (2001) as well as to the need for preservice teachers to see themselves as beginning a lifelong professional learning commitment. They argue that teacher candidates need "subject-matter and foundational knowledge and skills as well as the commitments and tools to continue developing their practice" (p. 3). According to Feiman-Nemser, preservice teaching tasks involve critical self-reflection relating to a vision of good teaching, development of pedagogical content knowledge, and understanding of diverse needs and characteristics of learners. The second theme focuses on the development of the preservice teacher's professional identity, one that is "committed to the growth of children and to knowing and teaching subject matter in intellectually engaging ways" (p. 3). The third theme recognizes the conflicting views of good teaching and calls for teacher education to "help prospective teachers develop intellectual habits and a capacity for judgment that will allow them to embrace and negotiate the tensions and dilemmas in their work" (p. 3). The fourth theme emphasizes the culture and structures needed to support the ongoing learning of all participants in teacher education, including supervising practitioners in the schools. The final theme argues for the critical role that experience in the schools plays in preservice teacher learning. Like Darling-Hammond (2006) and Ball and Forzani (2009), Carroll and colleagues see the need to cultivate close relationships between teacher education programs and the schools where preservice teachers are placed. This relationship must include attention to the learning needs of all.

The themes described here are central to teacher education in any time period. However, how do the themes relate to the particular challenges of our twenty-first-century society? One central task for preservice teachers is to reflect on a vision of good teaching. To be relevant to the twenty-first century, such a vision should recognize the shifts in how society communicates and gets information. It should reflect competencies such as the New Media Literacies. How likely are preservice teachers to engage such a digitally influenced vision? Lortie (2002) and Britzman (2003) found that teachers tend to teach the way they themselves were taught as students, in what Lortie calls an apprenticeship of observation. Given the lack of thoughtfully integrated, digitally mediated learning in schools, it is unlikely that new teachers will conceive of a vision of teaching that reflects the digital shift in society.

### *The Role of Content Knowledge in Teacher Preparation*

An important component of initial teacher preparation is a solid grounding in subject matter and foundational knowledge. While there is wide agreement that core content knowledge is essential to good teaching, how do we define that knowledge in a way that is compatible with twenty-first-century society? Current school reforms emphasize a fixed set of content standards to be covered by all teachers in all schools. Teacher candidates are tested on content knowledge in fixed, standardized tests. There have been calls for a focus on disciplinary teaching in schools; students should be taught to approach history like historians, science like scientists, and literature like literary critics. Gardner's (2009) disciplined mind emphasizes understanding major modes of thinking from the disciplines, including each discipline's distinct methods of studying the content area. What does this mean in the twenty-first century?

In the age of the Internet, anyone can publish his/her ideas to a potential audience of billions. An article we access online could be written by a recognized expert or by a seventh-grade student doing a homework assignment. This is one reason that judgment is one of the New Media Literacies. It is essential that we all be able to critically evaluate knowledge claims or the trustworthiness of our sources. However, even recognized experts in their fields must be subject to critical review. As Apple (2011) and other critical theorists have demonstrated, what is considered important or desirable knowledge is heavily influenced by power structures in society. Given the achievement gap prevalent among dominant and nondominant groups in society, teaching for equity is imperative. Should teachers' foundational knowledge reflect established disciplinary thinking or that of critical theorists?

Popkewitz (2010) offers an alternative to teaching both disciplinary thinking and critical theory. He claims that teachers cannot teach students disciplinary thinking; a child, after all, is not a scientist or historian. Instead, "translation tools" are always necessary when teaching the disciplines to students. It would follow, then, that the teacher's job is to employ the most effective translation tools in the content areas. In this sense, pedagogical content knowledge might be considered a type of translation tool that teachers employ when teaching content. However, this is not what Popkewitz advocates. It is the disciplinary approach itself that he wishes to unpack, for it determines what is recognized, thought about, and acted on within the content area. This, Popkewitz argues, is the true political component of schooling.

He writes, "Learning more 'content' knowledge, then, is never just that. It embodies learning how to see, think, act, and feel" (p. 416). Popkewitz believes that a sociohistorical view of disciplinary thinking can expose cultural frames of reference and their relation to knowledge production in a discipline. This should be part of the foundational content knowledge that teacher education provides teacher candidates.

### *The Learning Sciences in Teacher Preparation*

Given that the ultimate goal of teacher education is to prepare teachers who have an impact on student learning, teacher education programs should provide teacher candidates with deep understanding of the learning sciences. As discussed previously, Ansari (2008) calls for teachers to be literate in basic neuroscience. He believes such a background would help teachers better understand the "physical organ" that underlies teaching, as well as protect teachers from fraudulent claims of misleadingly marketed brain-based curricula. Willis (2010) also suggests that a familiarity with neuroscience research related to education can help teachers feel more invested in teaching strategies that are truly supported by brain research.

### *Preparing Teachers Who Will Model Effective Use of Technology*

Since technology has revolutionized twenty-first-century society, it stands to reason that teacher education should ensure both a familiarity with salient digital applications, and an understanding of how to use them to support student learning. According to Gray, Thomas, and Lewis (2009), only 40 percent of teachers used computers often during instructional time. Of that 40 percent it is unclear how computers were being used. Ertmer (2005) found that teacher beliefs about the value of technology influenced its use in practice. In addition to teacher beliefs about value and their experiences using technology, Miranda and Russell (2011) found that the greatest predictors of teachers' intended use of computers in their practice were principals' use of computers and perceived pressure to integrate technology into teaching. Teacher education programs can support teacher use of technology in their practice by helping teacher candidates become familiar with the benefits of technology-infused instruction, as well as by providing them with opportunities to explore the use of technology to support student learning in their field experiences.

The International Society for Technology in Education (ISTE) developed comprehensive technology standards (NETS) for students and teachers that can help ensure meaningful integration of technology in teaching and learning. There are five broad standards for teachers: Facilitate and inspire student learning and creativity; design and develop digital-age learning experiences and assessments; model digital-age work and learning; promote and model digital citizenship and responsibility; and engage in professional growth and leadership. Meaningful integration of technology in teaching can help prepare students to be successful contributors to twenty-first-century society. Taking advantage of technology's ability to support diverse student needs and abilities can make learning more equitable by providing multiple means of engagement with and assessment of learning goals.

## Induction: What's Important for the First Three Years?

Many of the themes and issues mentioned in the previous section are relevant to new teachers as well. Many new teachers graduated from initial preparation programs that did not explore a vision of teaching specific to twenty-first-century needs and that did not provide a good grounding in educational neuroscience or a sociohistorical view of disciplinary thinking. As the Center for Educational Statistics survey shows, most teachers don't yet have the skills or desire to meaningfully integrate technology into their practice.

### *The Unique Needs of New Teachers*

In addition to integrating technology meaningfully into their practice, new teachers have their own set learning tasks for the induction stage of their professional lives. According to Feiman-Nemser (2001), these teachers are busy learning the student, school, and curricular cultures they are immersed in, figuring out how to plan responsive curriculum, creating a classroom learning community, and implementing their repertoire of teaching strategies. They are doing all this at the same time as developing their professional identities. Professional development for new teacher induction must support teachers in all these activities.

Due in large part to state education policies, most first-year teachers receive some form of induction support; however there is great variability in the types and quality of support offered (Smith & Ingersoll, 2004). A key figure in new teacher induction programs is the mentor (Strong, 2009); however as with induction programs in general, there is wide variability along many dimensions, including who is chosen as a mentor and how, whether or not mentors receive professional development or guidance, how often mentors meet with new teachers, and the content and nature of the mentor-mentee relationship (Ingersoll & Strong, 2011). There is, likewise, a lack of empirical research that explores explicitly what type (content and duration) of induction activities are most effective in which contexts. Haggarty, Postlethwaite, Diment, and Ellins (2011) argue that induction mentors need professional development to change their beliefs and practices while developing their skills for engaging in meaningful discussion of teaching practices. Given the radical changes in twenty-first-century society described in the first part of this chapter, mentors need to be skilled teachers themselves for twenty-first-century learning.

## Professional Development for the Experienced Teacher

Since teaching is a lifelong learning profession, continual professional development of teachers is important. Given the great variation in teacher preparation and induction programs, the professional development of experienced teachers will need to meet a wide variety of teacher needs. As William Marinell (2010) writes, "Tomorrow's leaders will have to recruit and support teachers who have pursued different preparation programs, possess a range of skills and experiences, and come from a variety of professional and academic backgrounds. This is in addition to the well-documented challenges of teachers' demanding schedules" (p. 65).

### *The Needs of Experienced Teachers*

Garet, Porter, Desimone, Birman, and Yoon (2001) found three characteristics of effective professional development: a focus on content knowledge, opportunities for active learning, and coherence with other learning activities. According to Feiman-Nemser (2001), experienced teachers should: "Extend and deepen subject matter knowledge for teaching; Extend and refine repertoire in curriculum, instruction and assessment; Strengthen skills and dispositions to study and improve teaching; Expand responsibilities and develop leadership skills" (p. 1050). Given the digital media and social networking revolution, in order to meet the needs of our twenty-first-century society, professional development for experienced teachers needs to do more than this. It must also help instructors prepare students to succeed in a radically altered twenty-first-century society.

Some professional development alternatives that could help teachers meet the above needs can be found among twenty-first-century skill advocates. Jacobs (2010), who criticizes the obsolescence of much of our curricula and teaching approaches, suggests that teachers have protected time in their schedules for the specific purpose of reviewing and updating the curricula. Ansari (2008) calls on teachers to engage in practitioner research and be an active part of knowledge generation rather than just knowledge consumption and application. Fischer and Heikkinen (2010) combine these ideas into an argument for a new model of schooling that he calls research schools. Reminiscent of professional development schools, in research schools, practitioner researchers work together with cognitive scientists each informing the other's work. Judy Willis writes that "collaboration will propel the education advancements of this century. The one-way street of scientists telling teachers what to do . . . has been modernized to a bridge between classroom and laboratory" (p. 66).

## WHERE DO WE GO FROM HERE?

Tony Wagner (2008) advises us that "[s]chools haven't changed; the world has. And so our schools are not failing. Rather, they are obsolete—even the ones that score the best on standardized tests." (p. xxv). If we need new schools, we also need to prepare teachers in new ways to teach in them. Can teacher educators rise to the challenge? Will they find ways to be leaders in a brave, new, socially connected world, or will they remain followers, reacting to the latest policy edict or crisis? Will teachers continue to emphasize coverage of material in an age of information overload? Will they set their goals at passing high-stakes tests or at preparing children for the society they will eventually join as adults?

In their analysis of research on teacher education, Cochran-Smith and Fries (2008) conclude that how the "problem" of teacher education is conceptualized influences how it is studied and what policy contexts ensue. They have identified four distinct constructions of the teacher education "problem" covering the last century: the curriculum problem (1920s–1950s), the training problem (1960s–1980s), the learning problem (1980s–2000s) and the policy problem (1990s–present). Each of these constructions has led to different recommendations for best practices in teacher education. None of these constructions speak to the unique needs of our always-on, socially networked society. In fact the current "policy problem" is responsible for the culture of testing that has resulted in the impoverished curricula and scripted learning experiences in our schools. The field of teacher education is at a critical crossroads. Is there a new way of viewing the teacher education problem that will speak to the educational needs of a society that generates exabytes of information and is threatened by a narrow-minded and self-indulgent filter bubble while losing its ability to deeply focus on a single task? Teacher educators need to make a conscious choice to either continue preparing new teachers for obsolete schools or to find the courage to break the mold and enter into uncharted territory to meet the new challenges of the twenty-first century. Ray Kurzweil (2006), well-known inventor and futurist, believes that "No matter what quandaries we face . . . there is an idea that can enable us to prevail. Furthermore, we can find that idea. And when we find it, we need to implement it" (p. 2). Perhaps teacher educators need to think like inventors and reconceptualize teacher education for the twenty-first century.

## REFERENCES

Ansari, D. (2008). The brain goes to school: Strengthening the education-neuroscience connection. *Education Canada, 48*(4), 6–10.

Apple, M. W. (2011). Global crises, social justice, and teacher education. *Journal of Teacher Education, 62*(2), 222–234.

Ball, D. L., & Forzani, F. M. (2009). The work of teaching and the challenge for teacher education. *Journal of Teacher Education, 60*(5), 497–511.

Britzman, D. P. (2003). *Practice makes practice: A critical study of learning to teach.* Albany: State University of New York Press.

Carr, N. (2011). *The shallows: What the Internet is doing to our brains.* New York: W. W. Norton.

Carroll, D., Featherstone, H., Featherstone, J., Feiman-Nemser, S., & Roosevelt, D. (2007). *Transforming teacher education: Reflections from the field.* Cambridge, MA: Harvard Education Press.

Cetron, M. J., & Davies, O. (2008, May–June). Trends shaping tomorrow's world. *Futurist, 42*(3), 35–50.

CNN. (2009). Report sees "sobering statistics" on racial inequality. March 25, 2009. Retrieved from http://articles.cnn.com/2009-03-25/us/black.america.report_1_whites-blacks-urban-league?_s=PM:US.

Cochran-Smith, M., & Fries, M. K. (2008). Research on teacher education: Changing times, changing paradigms. In M. Cochran-Smith, S. Feiman-Nemser, J. McIntyre, & K. Demers (Eds.), *Handbook of research on teacher education: Enduring questions in changing contexts* (3rd ed., pp. 1199–1203). New York: Routledge, Taylor & Francis Group and the Association of Teacher Educators.

Conference Board, Partnership for 21st Century Skills, Corporate Voices for Working Families, & Society for Human Resource Management. (2006). *Are they really ready for work? Employers' perspectives on the basic knowledge and applied skills of new entrants to the 21st century US workforce.* Retrieved from www.p21.org/storage/documents/FINAL_REPORT_PDF09-29-06.pdf.

Darling-Hammond, L. (2006). Constructing 21st-century teacher education. *Journal of Teacher Education, 57*(3), 300–314.

Darling-Hammond, L., & Sykes, G. (1999). *Teaching as the learning profession: Handbook of policy and practice.* San Francisco: Jossey-Bass.

Dillon, S. (2007, December 23). Democrats make Bush School Act an election issue. *New York Times.* Retrieved from www.nytimes.com/2007/12/23/us/politics/23child.html?pagewanted=all.

Ertmer, P. A. (2005). Teacher pedagogical beliefs: The final frontier in our quest for technology integration? *Educational Technology Research and Development, 53*(4), 25–39.

Feiman Nemser, S. (2001). From preparation to practice: Designing a continuum to strengthen and sustain teaching. *Teachers College Record, 103*(6), 1013–1055.

Fischer, K. W., & Heikkinen, K. (2010). The future of educational neuroscience. In D. Sousa (Ed.), *Mind, brain, and education: Neuroscience implications for the classroom* (pp. 248–269). Bloomington, IN: Solution Tree Press.

Gardner, H. (2009). *Five minds for the future.* Cambridge, MA: Harvard Business School Press.

Garet, M. S., Porter, A. C., Desimone, L., Birman, B. F., & Yoon, K. S. (2001). What makes professional development effective? Results from a national sample of teachers. *American Educational Research Journal, 38(4),* 915–945.

Gearon, C. J. (2012). Nine hot new majors. In *Best Colleges.* Washington, DC: US News and World Report.

Giles, J. (2005). Internet encyclopedias go head to head. *Nature, 438,* 900–901.

Gray, L., Thomas, N., & Lewis, L. (2009). *Teachers' use of educational technology in U.S. public schools: 2009 first look* (NCES 2010-040). Washington, DC: National Center for Education Statistics, Institute of Education Sciences, U.S. Department of Education.

Gunderson, S., Jones, R., & Scanland, K. (2005). *The jobs revolution: Changing how America works.* Chicago, IL: Copywriters Incorporated.

Haggarty, L., Postlethwaite, K., Diment, K., & Ellins, J. (2011). Improving the learning of newly qualified teachers in the induction year. *British Educational Research Journal, 37*(6), 935–954.

Immordino-Yang, M. H., & Damasio, A. (2007). We feel, therefore we learn: The relevance of affective and social neuroscience to education. *Mind, Brain, and Education, 1*(1), 3–10.

Immordino-Yang, M. H., & Faeth, M. (2010). The role of emotion and skilled intuition in learning. In D. Sousa (Ed.), *Mind, brain, and education: Neuroscience implications for the classroom* (pp. 69–84). Bloomington, IN: Solution Tree Press.

Ingersoll, R., & Strong, M. (2011). The impact of induction and mentoring programs from beginning teachers: A critical review of the research. *Review of Education Research, 81*(2), 201–233.

Jacobs, H. H. (2010). *Curriculum 21: Essential education for a changing world.* Alexandria, VA: ASCD.

Jenkins, H., Clinton, K., Purushotma, R., Robison, A. J., & Weigel, M. (2006). Confronting the challenges of participatory culture: Media education for the 21st century. Chicago: The MacArthur Foundation. Retrieved from www.newmedialiteracies.org/files/working/NMLWhitePaper.pdf.

Kennedy, M. M. (2008). The place of teacher education in teachers' education. In M. Cochran-Smith, S. Feiman-Nemser, J. McIntyre, & K. Demers (Eds.), *Handbook of research on teacher education: Enduring questions in changing contexts* (3rd ed., pp. 1199–1203). New York: Routledge, Taylor & Francis Group and the Association of Teacher Educators.

Kurzweil, R. (2006). *The singularity is near: When humans transcend biology*. New York: Viking.

Lenhart, A., & Madden, M. (2005). *Teen content creators and consumers*. Washington, DC: Pew Internet & American Life Project. Retrieved from www.pewinternet.org/~/media//Files/Reports/2005/PIP_Teens_Content_Creation.pdf.pdf.

Levy, F., & Murnane, R. (2004). *The new division of labor*: *How computers are creating the next job market*. Princeton, NJ: Princeton University Press.

Lortie, D. (2002). *Schoolteacher: A sociological study* (revised 2nd edition). Chicago: University of Chicago Press.

Lyman, P., & Varian, H. R. (2003). *How much information*. Retrieved from www.sims.berkeley.edu/how-much-info-2003.

Marinell, W. H. (2010). Midcareer teachers and principals. In S. Conley & B. S. Cooper (Eds.), *Finding, preparing and supporting school leaders: Critical issues, useful solutions* (pp. 65–77). Lanham, MD: Rowman & Littlefield Education.

Miranda, H. P., & Russell, M. (2011), Understanding factors associated with teacher-directed student use of technology in elementary classrooms: A structural equation modeling approach. *British Journal of Educational Technology, 43*, 652–666. doi: 10.1111/j.1467-8535.2011.01228.x.

National Poverty Center. (2012). Poverty facts. Retrieved from www.npc.umich.edu/poverty/#2.

New Media Literacies Project. Retrieved from www.newmedialiteracies.org/about-us/.

Noddings, N. (2004). *Happiness and education*. New York: Cambridge University Press.

Noddings, N. (2005). *The challenge to care in schools: An alternative approach to education* (2nd ed.). New York: Teachers College Press.

Paige, R. (2002). *Meeting the highly qualified teachers challenge: The secretary's annual report on teacher quality*. Washington, DC: U.S. Department of Education, Office of Postsecondary Education.

Pariser, E. (2011). *The filter bubble: What the Internet is hiding from you*. New York: Penguin.

Popkewitz, T. (2010). The limits of teacher education reforms: School subjects, alchemies, and an alternative possibility. *Journal of Teacher Education, 61*(5), 413–421.

Rosenfeld, M. J., and Reuben J. T. (2012) Searching for a mate: The rise of the Internet as a social intermediary. *American Sociological Review, 77*(4), 523–547.

Shirky, C. (2010). *Cognitive surplus: Creativity and generosity in a connected age*. New York: Penguin.

Shirky, C. (2011, January–February). The political power of social media. *Foreign Affairs*. Retrieved from www.gpia.info/files/u1392/Shirky_Political_Poewr_of_Social_Media.pdf.

Smith, T., & Ingersoll, R. (2004). What are the effects of induction and mentoring on beginning teacher turnover? *American Educational Research Journal, 41*(3), 681–714.

Strong, M. (2009). *Effective teacher induction and mentoring: Assessing the evidence.* New York: Teachers College Press.

Turkle, S. (2011). *Alone together: Why we expect more from technology and less from each other*. New York: Basic Books.

Wagner, T. (2008). *The global achievement gap: Why even our best schools don't teach the new survival skills our children need, and what we can do about it*. New York: Basic Books.

Weiland, S. (2008). Teacher education toward liberal education. In M. Cochran-Smith, S. Feiman-Nemser, J. McIntyre, & K. Demers (Eds.), *Handbook of research on teacher education: Enduring questions in changing contexts* (3rd ed., pp 1204–1227). New York: Routledge, Taylor & Francis Group and the Association of Teacher Educators.

Willingham, D. T. (2009). *Why don't students like school? A cognitive scientist answers questions about how the mind works and what it means for your classroom*. San Francisco: Jossey-Bass.

Willis, J. (2010). The current impact of neuroscience on teaching and learning. In D. Sousa (Ed.), *Mind, brain, and education: Neuroscience implications for the classroom* (pp. 45–68). Bloomington, IN: Solution Tree Press.

Wolff, E. N. (2010). *Recent trends in household wealth in the United States: Rising debt and the middle-class squeeze—an update to 2007*. Levy Economics Institute Paper. Retrieved from www.levyinstitute.org/pubs/wp_589.pdf.

# Index

# About the Editors and Contributors

## EDITORS

**Miriam Ben-Peretz**, PhD, is professor emerita in the Faculty of Education, University of Haifa in Israel. She has served as the head of the Department of Teacher Education and as dean of the School of Education, University of Haifa, as well as the president of Tel Hai College. Her research interests are curriculum studies, teacher education, professional development, and policy-making in education. Ben-Peretz has been published widely in books, chapters in books, and articles in journals. She served as visiting professor abroad in universities in various countries including the United States, Canada, and Germany. In 1997 she received the Lifetime Achievement Award in recognition of outstanding contribution to curriculum studies over an extended period of time, Division B, Curriculum Studies, of the American Educational Research Association. In 2002 she received the Award of Merit from the University of Haifa. In 2006 she received the Israel prize for research in education. Ben-Peretz was the 2012 recipient of both the American Educational Research Association, Division K, Legacy Award and an Honorary Fellowship of the Open University of Israel. She is a member of the National Academy of Education in the United States. Her latest book is *Policy-Making in Education: A Holistic Approach in Response to Global Changes* (2009).

**Sara Kleeman** completed her PhD in the Institute of Education, University of London (1999) and became the head of the elementary teachers department at ORANIM. She serves as the head of the Center of Resource, Consultation and Training at ORANIM Academic College and as a coordinator of the pedagogical instruction specialization at the MOFET Institute. She currently focuses on the issue of professional development of teacher educators at Oranim and the MOFET Institute, as a researcher and lecturer.

**Rivka Reichenberg** completed her PhD at the School of Education, Bar-Ilan University in Israel (1996). She has served as head of the special education department at the Beit-Berl Academic College of Education and as a senior lecturer and researcher. Her research interests are teaching and teacher education, induction, and professional development. She serves as the head of the Pedagogical Instruction and Mentoring Specialization Program in the MOFET Institute, and as a lecturer and researcher, focusing on the issue of professional development of teacher educators in the colleges.

**Sarah Shimoni** completed her PhD in the School of Education at the Hebrew University (Jerusalem, 2001) and became head of the research and development department at the Levinsky College of Education. She serves as a senior lecturer in the MEd department at th Levinsky College of Education, lecturing and mentoring students in the areas of curriculum development and research design. She currently focuses on studying the issue of professional development of teacher educators at the MOFET Institute.

## CONTRIBUTORS

**Sally Brown** studied physics at University College London and Smith College, Massachusetts. She lectured in London colleges and Nigerian universities before teaching in Scotland. She moved to Stirling University (1971) for research on children's attitudes to science, teaching, and assessment; spent four years in the Scottish Office (Edinburgh) as research and assessment advisor; and became director of the Scottish Council for Research in Education and president of the British Educational Research Association. After chairing national committees on child protection, disability, Gaelic research, arts education, and adult education, she returned to teacher education at Stirling and became deputy principal. She has published widely on educational research, served on Economic and Social Research Council Boards, chaired the Education panel for the UK Research Assessment Exercise (2001), is a fellow of the Royal Society of Edinburgh and was awarded an OBE for educational research. Edinburgh, Queen Margaret, Stirling, and the Open Universities have awarded her honorary degrees.

**John Chi-Kin Lee** is currently and since 2010 the vice president (academic) and chair professor of curriculum and instruction of the Hong Kong Institute of Education. He is also the director of School Partnership and Field Experience Office and co-director of Centre for Development and Research in Small Class Teaching. He was dean of education and a professor in the Department of Curriculum and Instruction at the Chinese University of Hong Kong (CUHK). He is active in leading and securing education research and development projects, and one of his projects, The "Accelerated Schools for Quality Education Project," won the Quality Education Fund Outstanding

Project Award in 2008. He has served as the regional editor (Asia) of Educational Research and Evaluation and associate editor of Teachers and Teaching as well as editorial board members or advisory editors of many local, regional, and international journals. He has edited and written more than twenty-five books, and published over one hundred journal articles and book chapters. He has served as a board member of Geography Teaching Research Society of China and the Chinese Association of Higher Education. He has also held many visiting/guest/adjunct professorships at universities overseas and in Mainland China.

**David Crook** is Reader in Education at Brunel University, London and co-editor of the journal History of Education. Previously he worked for 16 years at the Institute of Education, University of London, where he remains a Visiting Fellow, and, before that, he was a comprehensive school teacher. He has published widely in the field of history of education and is presently co-authoring a book about the teaching of English in post-war London schools, based on a project funded by the Leverhulme Trust.

**Yuval Dror** is a professor in the School of Education, Tel-Aviv University and the incumbent of the Joan and Jaime Constantiner Chair for Jewish Education. He was the head of the Tel Aviv University School of Education (2006–2010) and earlier the head of Oranim, The Teachers College of the Kibbutz Movement, and Haifa University (1990–1997). His areas of specialization are the history of Zionist and Israeli education (including policy making) in the pre-State and the State of Israel, and all types of new/progressive and social-moral education (mainly kibbutz education).

**Daphne Goldman** is a senior lecturer in the Department of Environmental Science and Agriculture, Beit Berl Academic College, where she served as chair for seven years. She spearheaded the Environmental Literacy Center at Beit Berl and the National Annual Conference on Environmental Education. She was invited by the National Council for Environmental Quality to lead the preparation of the first position paper on environmental education in Israel and has since participated in preparation of other position papers. She sits on the Ministry of Education Committee for the High School Environmental Science Curriculum and on the National Committee for Accrediting Green Campuses. Dr. Goldman received her PhD in environmental biochemical toxicology. Her current fields of research include environmental education (focus on teacher and higher education) and interdisciplinary research on the oasis effect in arid environments.

**Esther Hertzog**, PhD, is a social anthropologist and teaches at Beit Berl and Levinsky Colleges in Israel. Among her academic interests are: bureaucracy; the welfare state; the educational system; immigration policies; gender issues in education, welfare, and politics, and the Holocaust. Among her published books are *Immigrants and Bureaucrats: Ethiopians in an Israeli*

*Absorption Center* (1999, Berghahn); *Patrons of Women: Literacy Projects and Gender Development in Rural Nepal* (2011, Berghahn).

**Lilian G. Katz** is professor emerita of early childhood education at the University of Illinois (Urbana-Champaign), where she serves on the staff of the Clearinghouse on Early Education and Parenting (CEEP). Dr. Katz is a past president of the National Association for the Education of Young Children, and the first president of the Illinois Association for the Education of Young Children. Dr. Katz is editor of the first online peer reviewed *trilingual* early childhood journal, *Early Childhood Research & Practice (English, Spanish &Chinese).* Dr. Katz received her PhD at Stanford University in 1968 after being a nursery school teacher. She has lectured in all U.S. states and fifty-five other countries and held visiting posts in Australia, Canada, England, Germany, India, Israel, the West Indies, and many parts of the United States. Dr. Katz is the recipient of many honors, including two Fulbright Awards (India and New Zealand), an honorary Doctor of Letters degree (DLitt.) from Whittier College, and an honorary PhD from the University of Goteborg, Sweden.

**Chun Kwok Lau**, PhD, has worked as a secondary school teacher, research associate, and assessment consultant in addition to his teaching in the teacher education field for over fifteen years. He is currently a senior teaching fellow of the Department of Curriculum and Instruction at the Hong Kong Institute of Education. His major research areas include assessment, human diversity, school reform, and narrative inquiry.

**Gary McCulloch** is the Brian Simon Professor of the History of Education at the Institute of Education, London, and head of the Department of Humanities and Social Science. He is a former president of the History of Education Society (UK) and a previous editor of the journal *History of Education*. His recent publications include *Cyril Norwood and the Ideal of Secondary Education* (2007) and *The Struggle for the History of Education* (2011). He is currently working on a book on the raising of the school leaving age and is leading a research project on the social organization of educational studies.

**Sara Pe'er** is head of the Department of Science and Environment Teaching at Oranim Academic College. Her PhD is in plant pathology. Sara is head of the Green Council at Oranim Academic College and head of the Think Tank on Sustainability Education in Teacher Training at the MOFET Institute. Her field of research is in environmental education.

**Colette Rabin** is an assistant professor in elementary education and director of the Critical Research Academy in Elementary Education at San Jose State University in California. Her areas of interest are in care ethics, aesthetics, and education.

**Anna E. Richert** is a professor of education in the School of Education at Mills College in Oakland, California. She is director of the Master of Arts in

Education Program with an Emphasis on Teaching (MEET) program at Mills and faculty director of the Mills Teacher Scholars, a professional development program that supports the inquiry practice of teachers in local urban schools. Her latest book is: *What Should I Do? Confronting Dilemmas of Teaching in Urban Schools* (2012).

**Debbie Samuels-Peretz** is an assistant professor in the Elementary Education Department at Wheelock College in Boston, Massachusetts. Her research interests include the integration of technology in teacher preparation and the effective use of technology in higher education pedagogy to meet the needs of diverse learners in the twenty-first century. Dr. Samuels-Peretz has presented nationally in the United States on these topics.

**Efrat Toov Ward** is a graduate student of curriculum design and development at the School of Education in Tel Aviv University. She has a B.Design in visual communication design from the Holon Institute of Technology (HIT). Efrat is currently writing her master's thesis on "Teachers' Perceptions of Holistic Education." She is working with Professor Ben-Peretz on several research projects.

**Teresa Tsui-san Ng** is the chair of the Hong Kong Creative Education Practitioners Organization (HKCEO). She is currently an assistant professor at the Department of Curriculum and Instruction at the Hong Kong Institute of Education (HKIED) where she served as the coordinator of the Master of Education (MEd) program with a specialization on "Curriculum and Innovative Teaching." Her teaching specialization focuses on creativity studies. She also participates in the course development for various undergraduate and postgraduate programs. Dr. Ng has extensive experience in conducting academic research with both quantitative and qualitative analysis. Her research interest focuses on creativity enhancement and assessment, creativity in teacher education, creative teaching strategies in diversified classrooms, and implementation of drama education in local schools. Her publications include newspaper articles, journal articles, international conference papers, and book chapters. She has close contacts with local principals and teachers through workshops, seminars, and projects. She endeavors to make valuable contributions in conducting scientific research on creativity and in cultivating innovative teaching practices within local, regional, and international areas.

**Bela Yavetz** is a lecturer in the departments of Biology and Environmental Education at the Kibbutzim College for Education, Technology and the Arts. Her PhD is in endocrinology. She currently is head of the Committee for the Science and Technology Curriculum for Junior High Schools, Ministry of Education. Her research interest is in environmental education and computer integration in teaching.

**Michal Zellermayer** is a professor of Teacher Education at Levinsky College of Education in Tel Aviv. She currently heads the Graduate School at the college. Professor Zellermayer served as a co-coordinator of the

Teaching and Teacher Education Special Interest Group at the European Association for Research on Learning and Instruction. She was a member of the editorial board of the *Educational Research Review* as well as *Teachers and Teaching, Theory and Practice*. She has published numerous papers on writing instruction, on developing rich communicative environments, on teacher learning, and on action research. Among her books *Women Teachers in Israel: A Feminist Perspective* (2002, with Pnina Peri) opened the conversation in Israel on teaching as a feminized profession.